Library of
Davidson College

Also by William M. Johnston

Vienna, Vienna
The Austrian Mind: An Intellectual and Social History, 1848–1938
The Formative Years of R. G. Collingwood

IN SEARCH OF ITALY
Foreign Writers in Northern Italy Since 1800

IN SEARCH OF ITALY
Foreign Writers in Northern Italy Since 1800

William M. Johnston

THE PENNSYLVANIA STATE UNIVERSITY PRESS
University Park and London

Library of Congress Cataloging-in-Publication Data

Johnston, William M., 1936–
In search of Italy.

Bibliography: p.
Includes index.
1. Italy, Northern—Description and travel.
2. Travelers—Italy, Northern—History—
19th century. 3. Travelers—Italy, Northern—
History—20th century. I. Title.
DG601.J64   1987   914.5′04   86-43029
ISBN 0-271-00496-7

Copyright © 1987 The Pennsylvania State University
All rights reserved
Printed in the United States of America

For Andrew the Self-Renewer

"What I like about the landscape of Italy," Gianni informed me, "is that there's none of this nonsense about the great outdoors. That sort of thing's all right elsewhere. Here you could practically say it's an indoor landscape. It's Nature with beautiful manners—no, that's too tame. Rather, it is as if Nature were capable of thought, of joy."

Shirley Hazzard, *The Bay of Noon* (1970)

Contents

Glossary of Italian Terms	xi
Map of Northern Italy	xiv
1 Introduction: Essayists of Historical Landscape	1
Uses of Travel Literature	1
Varieties of Travel Essay	3

PART ONE   PIEDMONT AND LIGURIA

2 Turin, Threshold of Italy	9
First Taste of the Baroque	9
Outlandish Churches	12
Nietzsche and De Chirico	14
3 Many-Tiered Genoa and Its Ambivalent Admirers	18
Images of Slope and Slum	18
Michelet's Misgivings	21
Bubbling Invective	24

PART TWO   LOMBARDY

4 Glamor Amid Clamor: The Shock of Milan	29
A European Capital	29
Spleen	30
The Cathedral	31
Vicissitudes of *The Last Supper*	34
Assorted Churches	36

5 Brescia the Bellicose	38
City of Stage Sets	38
Word Painting and the Painters of Brescia	40
The Founding of the Red Cross	44
6 Magnificence Moldering in Mantua	48
Dithyrambs on Disrepair	48
Giulio Romano	51
The Palazzo del Tè	52
Shakespeare's Italy	54

PART THREE VENICE AND VENETIA

7 Venice, or Describing the Indescribable	59
Color Tonalities	59
The Church of Saint Mark's	62
Other Churches: Zanipolo and the Frari	67
Adrian Stokes on Ensembles of Buildings	71
Tintoretto: The Shakespeare of Venice	74
Misgivings	78
8 Tuscan Art on the Venetian Plain: Padua	83
City of the Bull	83
Suarès on Donatello	84
Frescoes	87
9 Verona, Epitome of Italy	91
Contradictions	91
Verona Marble	96
Roman Architecture	98
The Scaliger Tombs	100
Ecstasy Among the Cypresses	103

PART FOUR EMILIA-ROMAGNA

10 Literary Ghosts in Parma	107
Stendhal in the City of Correggio	107
The Ecstasies of Maurice Barrès	110
Osbert Sitwell on the Toy Court	112
Appraisals of Correggio	115
11 A City with Sunset in Its Walls: Bologna	122
Arcades	122
Painters	125
Churches	129

12 Ravenna, Tomb of Tombs	133
An Island in Time	133
French Elegists	135
Churches Without Facades	137
Aladdin's Cave in San Vitale	141
13 Reminiscences of Rome in Rimini	145
An Inhuman Humanist	145
The Malatesta Temple	147
A Turning Point on the Journey Toward Self-Renewal	151
Notes	155
Bio-Bibliography	169
Index	195

Glossary of Italian Terms

Broletto	Town hall (in Lombardy), also known as Palazzo della Ragione (i.e., Palace of Reason)
Campo Santo	Cemetery (i.e., Holy Field)
Castello	Fortress
Certosa	Charterhouse (a monastery for Carthusian monks)
Chiaroscuro	"Light-dark," a technique of contrasting light and shade in painting
Chiesa	Church
Duomo	Cathedral
Lago	Lake
Monte	Mountain
Palazzo	Palace
Piazza	Public square
Prato della Valle	Meadow in the Valley (a monument in Padua)
Quattrocento	The fifteenth century
Reggia	Royal Palace (in Parma)
Risorgimento	"Resurgence": the movement of national recovery (from about 1780 to 1880) that accomplished the unification of Italy
Rocca	Fortress
il Santo	The Saint (a church in Padua)
Tempio	Temple

Note: The names of most cities yield an adjective by adding -ese in the singular and -esi in the plural (for example, Bolognese, Milanese, Veronese).

IN SEARCH OF ITALY
Foreign Writers in Northern Italy Since 1800

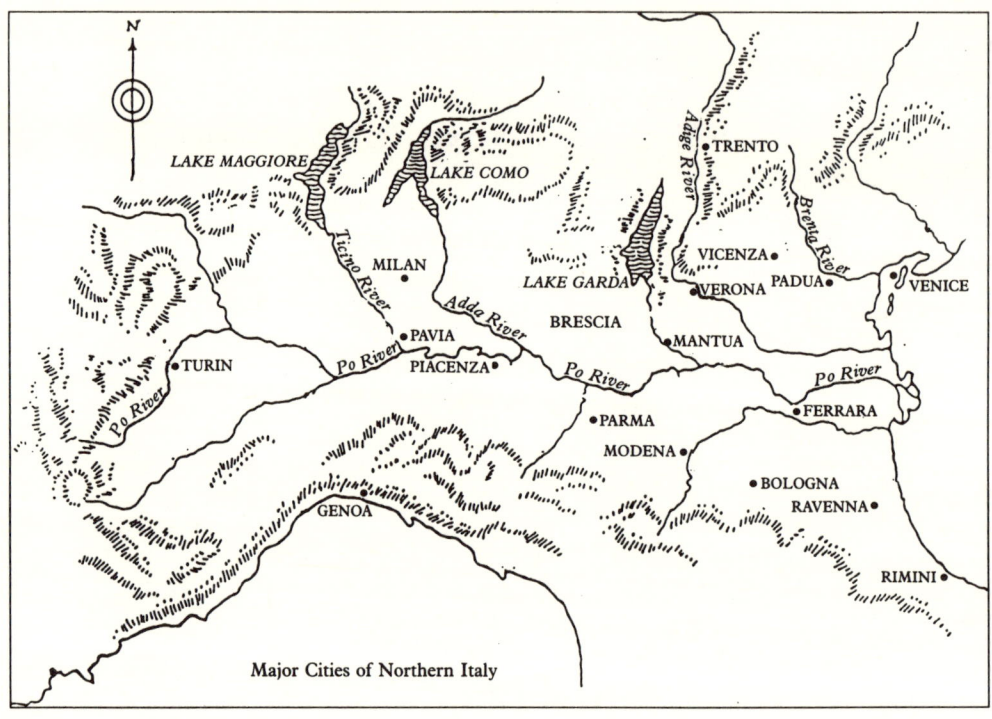

Major Cities of Northern Italy

1
Introduction: Essayists of Historical Landscape

USES OF TRAVEL LITERATURE

Almost everyone who knows Italy feels that too much has been written about it. Travelers feel so daunted by books about Italy that many never discover the best of them. That is why a book about foreign writers in northern Italy needs to begin by stating what can be learned from travel writing. If one begins by being awed at the quantity of writing about Italy, one ought to end by being dazzled at the quality of the best of it.

By definition, travel writing needs a specific target. This book presents not generalized impressions of Italy or even of individual cities, but rather encounters with specific spots, some of them world renowned like Saint Mark's in Venice or *The Last Supper* in Milan, others as obscure as the gallery of Brescia or the Roman bridge of Rimini. By digesting what great writers have said about significant places, this book treats not Italy in general but certain of Italy's special places. The first use of travel literature, then, is to alert travelers to spots that they might overlook.

Although this book assesses many writers, its intended audience is first and foremost travelers. Its chapters are arranged to be read in almost any order, and it aims to illuminate each city separately as well as in relation to the others. Whether read before or after a trip, the book points out wonders that no other single volume assembles and tells how particular writers reacted to them.

A second use of travel writing is to illuminate literary tradition.

Certain trips to Italy changed the direction of a country's literature. Goethe's sojourn of the late 1780s redirected his career and with it the course of German letters. Thirty years later the poets Shelley and Byron sojourned in Italy, where they produced their finest work. During the 1840s Robert Browning devised the dramatic monologue in order to express his rapture at the vigor of the Renaissance, while John Ruskin revolutionized art writing in order to convey his wonder at Venice and Verona. Although these episodes are treated, this book also emphasizes less famous individuals, some of whom invented or perfected new forms in which to express travel experiences. Between 1830 and 1860 two French savants, Antoine Valery and Charles de Rémusat, invented a form of essay known as "historical landscape," a genre that is usually attributed to a younger German, Ferdinand Gregorovius. Around 1900 an English woman, Vernon Lee, composed travel miniatures with such delicacy that even today she has more subtle things to say about enjoying places than almost anyone else. At the same time, the French novelist Maurice Barrès perfected the art of the self-centered travel piece.

While innumerable men and women expounded on Italy, a more awesome kind of importance attaches to certain other travelers. While on holiday in 1859, a Genevan named Henry Dunant blundered onto the battlefield of Solferino near Brescia. The horrors that he witnessed there impelled him to found the International Red Cross a few years later. Although few trips have benefited mankind so tangibly as Dunant's, this book will explore every sort of stimulus that foreigners have derived in northern Italy, not just literary or artistic, but historical and philanthropic as well.

Certain cultural historians excel at juxtaposing a city with the artists who lived there. This book abounds in comments about how a creator's work may be said to mirror the places that fostered it. The "inventor" of opera, Claudio Monteverdi, illustrates such correspondences between locale and creativity. For twenty years he lived in the Ducal Palace at Mantua, whose empty rooms today echo the sadness of the arias that he wrote there. The melancholy of his opera *Orfeo* seems to anticipate the sack of the palace a generation later. To take another example, painters from Bologna around 1600 may be said to have practiced on canvas a kind of synthesis that the city's professors had applied for centuries to law. In Bologna both painters and professors recombined the advance of predecessors into a form held to be superior to them, making artists such as the Carracci and Guido Reni something like lawyers in paint. The analogy helps to explain why Bolognese painting has appealed to lovers of rhetoric but has repelled lovers of spontaneity. Since travel writers excelled at showing how a site gets echoed in a creator's work, this may be their greatest service to scholarship.

Adepts of German literature may be surprised to find that French and English writers predominate in this book. That is because the classic German works on Italy begin in Tuscany rather than in the North. Hardly any Germans wrote "Journeys Through Northern Italy" to compare with those of the French. Of the cities discussed here, Goethe wrote only about Verona, Padua, Venice, and Bologna; Heine only about Genoa; and Gregorovius only about Ravenna. Even Goethe did not hit his stride until he reached Rome.

VARIETIES OF TRAVEL ESSAY

Before we begin in Turin, it is necessary to attempt some classification of travel writing. The most trenchant recent study of travel writers is Paul Fussell's *Abroad* (1980). His essays on British travel writers between the wars single out five figures, Graham Greene, Robert Byron, Evelyn Waugh, Norman Douglas, and D. H. Lawrence, of whom only the last wrote about northern Italy. Since writing about Italy reached its apogee not between the wars, but rather in the two decades before 1914, not all of Fussell's comments apply here, but his typology of travel writing does. As a point of departure, Fussell distinguished a travel book from a guidebook: A travel book, on the one hand, is "a sub-species of memoir in which the autobiographical narrative arises from the speaker's encounter with distant or unfamiliar data, and in which the narrative—unlike that in a novel or a romance—claims literal validity by constant reference to actuality";[1] a guidebook, on the other hand, is not autobiographical and is "not sustained by a narrative exploiting the devices of fiction."[2] In characterizing the travel book, Fussell placed it in a hitherto unrecognized genre, that of the "displaced quest or pastoral narrative," in which a traveler recounts adventures from a more or less exotic milieu.

Few books on northern Italy fulfill the definition of a "travel book," although Norman Douglas's *Old Calabria* (1915) exemplifies the genre to perfection in evoking southern Italy, and so does a forgotten masterpiece about central Italy, Maurice Hewlett's *The Road in Tuscany* (1904). The chief example to concern northern Italy is Hilaire Belloc's *The Path to Rome* (1902), a chatty work that illuminates Italy less well than do those of either Douglas or Hewlett. Another candidate is Sean O'Faolain's *A Summer in Italy* (1950), a quest for the exotic in cities of northern and central Italy narrated by a novelist. Almost none of the French or German books about Italy fit Fussell's category of the "travel book," unless it be Goethe's seminal *Italienische Reise [Italian Journey]* (1816). The travel book as Fussell conceived it was mainly English.

In order to classify writing about Italy, Fussell's categories need to be enlarged. He acknowledged that certain "travel books," such as those by Aldous Huxley or Osbert Sitwell, comprised collections of essays masquerading as travel books. During the 1920s the popularity of travel books made the genre a useful disguise in which to publish a collection of old-fashioned essays. In this spirit, Osbert Sitwell coined a term, "discursion," to denote a "discursive excursion" to foreign places. Most writing about northern Italy takes the form of what I call the travel essay—in other words, a short prose piece recounting a personal response to specific places, the commonest type being the travel essay about a city. Such essays may get strung together to constitute a longer account, as in Rémusat's articles of 1857 and 1861, or dozens of them may accumulate, as in the fifteen hundred pages of Valery's *Voyages en Italie* (1831–33). Although they contain essays on more than a hundred localities, Valery's volumes can be read in any sequence, for they follow no fixed pattern and abound in personal judgments. German equivalents include three volumes by Alfred Steinitzer on out-of-the-way places, and, of course, Ferdinand Gregorovius's five volumes of *Wanderungen* (1853–81).

As every historian of literature knows, England was the homeland par excellence of the familiar essay. William Hazlitt and Charles

Lamb pioneered a way of expressing idiosyncratic views in a style at once refreshing and pointed. This tradition bore rich fruit when Englishmen went to Italy. Among the less flamboyant essays are Edward Hutton's twelve volumes covering every region of Italy except Piedmont and Friuli. Briefer in compass is Cecil Headlam's *Venetia and Northern Italy* (1908), which narrates visits to major cities of the North. Rather more arresting are travel essays by novelists like Henry James, historians like Edward Freeman, and painters like Edwin Blashfield. Although none of them outdoes William Hazlitt in the finer passages of his *Notes of a Journey Through France and Italy* (1826), a crucial lesson emerges: Skill in travel writing cannot be predicted from excellence in other genres. Two distinguished women novelists, George Eliot and George Sand, wrote mediocre travel pieces, and even Charles Dickens often faltered in *Pictures from Italy* (1846). Among the French, Stendhal does not rank among the finest travel writers, while Flaubert was too terse and Zola too verbose to hold interest for long.

The finest travel essays come from those who dedicated themselves to the genre in hope of imprinting their enthusiasms on others. Looming over any city that he chose to describe is John Ruskin, whose *Modern Painters* (1843–60) and *The Stones of Venice* (1851–53) furnish what Northrop Frye would call an anatomy of their subject, that is, a discursive compendium on all its aspects. Ruskin's lectures, letters, and diaries supply additional passages that teach one to heed details better than anyone else's.

Fussell rightly emphasized the pastoral tone of much writing about foreign places. Because travelers usually possess more money and mobility than those whom they visit, they easily fall into patronizing the natives. Most writers shared with Fussell's questers a preference for the past, often fleeing from industrialism into a pastoral vision. Many of them, like John Ruskin and Evelyn Underhill, discerned in the Italian countryside what William Empson called "a beautiful relation between rich and poor."[3]

Travel essays about northern Italy, then, are elegiac in tone, learned in substance, and personal in judgment. Although essayists sometimes quoted others, most preferred to erect a vision of their own.

What above all separates travel writers from scholars is a refusal to cite sources. To treat travel writers as though they were scholars violates a taboo that required these writers to ignore all others wherever possible. To have assembled these writers, as is done in the Bio-Bibliography of this book, would have seemed unthinkable to most of them. Each one wanted to portray an Italy of his or her own.

Part One
PIEDMONT AND LIGURIA

2
Turin, Threshold of Italy

FIRST TASTE OF THE BAROQUE

Since 1500 northern Italy has boasted five major cultural centers. Two of them, Milan and Venice, are universally acclaimed. Another, Bologna, is well known for schools of painting and law, while a fourth, Genoa, became renowned for its palaces and its seamanship. The fifth, Turin, lacks such a clear profile, partly because it became the capital of Piedmont only in 1559. Although it occupies the site of an ancient Roman camp, whose grid plan it enlarged, Turin began to flourish rather late for an Italian city. A city that preserves the ideals of its baroque planners, Turin lacks the winding streets, diverse architecture, and Renaissance aura of places as different as Brescia, Padua, and Bologna. And yet, between 1859 and 1866, this straitlaced capital consummated the unification of Italy, imposing Piedmontese administrators on regions that had known no such efficiency for nearly two thousand years.

"Deep in Italy towns are poor in their economies, but rich in architecture and art. Here in Piedmont they are economically rich and architecturally poor."[1] So the English cultural critic Bernard Wall stated the paradox of Turin. Henry Bordeaux, a Frenchman who grew up in a region of Savoy just after it had been ceded to France in 1860, captured the starchy atmosphere when he called Turin a "drill-ground" for administrators.[2] The dukes of Savoy believed in discipline, and they subjected their city to dressage, as though it were a military camp. Who were these Piedmont dukes, that they aspired after 1840 to unite Italy? How had they learned to rule such a diverse country as the peninsula of Italy? The monotony of Turin can lull one into forgetting what a disparate realm the Duchy of Savoy once embraced. French-speaking mountaineers eked out a living in the Alps, while farmers prospered on the plain and wine growers flourished in the hills just east of Turin. Not for nothing did the word Piedmont enter geographers' terminology to denote uplands that join plain to mountains, for Savoy straddled both kinds of landscape. In 1720 Savoy acquired half-wild Sardinia, which resembled Africa more than it did northern Italy. Because Sardinia was a kingdom, it brought the dukes a royal title. In 1796 Piedmont belonged to the first regions conquered by Napoleon. In 1815 the Congress of Vienna disregarded promises of independence made to the Genoese by an English governor, Lord Bentinck, and ceded Genoa, together with its strip along the Rivieras, to the Kingdom of Sardinia, so that for the first time Savoy acquired an outlet to the sea. Thereafter the royal family of Piedmont ruled not only mountain and plain but seacoast and semi-African wastes, making their realm more diverse than a visit to Turin suggests. French remained the language of court into the 1850s, as economic ties with Geneva flourished. Under a new king, Victor Emmanuel II, and his prime minister, Count Cavour, Piedmont was preparing to accomplish the unification of Italy.

A city of discipline and bigotry might hardly seem a promising start for a tour of Italy. Yet what impressed visitors was the contrast between the stiffness of the city and the flowering of nature in its environs. Palaces set among hills evoked an air of majesty that thrilled William Hazlitt,* an English essayist who entered Savoy from France in 1824: "My arrival at Turin was the first and only moment of intoxication I have found in Italy. It is a city of palaces . . . I walked out, and traversing several clean, spacious streets, came to a promenade outside the town, from which I saw the chain of the Alps we had left behind us, rising like a range of marble pillars in the evening

---

*For biographical details on the major figures discussed, see the Bio-Bibliography.

sky. Monte Viso and Mont Cenis resembled two points of cones of ice, shooting up above all the rest."[3]

When Hazlitt glimpsed the countryside outside Turin, he could as well have been describing a painting, for the real thing reminded him of art, not nature.[4] To someone like Hazlitt, who had wanted to be a painter, the effect was all the more exhilarating: "I could distinguish the broad and rapid Po, winding along at the other extremity of the walk, through vineyards and meadow grounds. The trees had on that deep, sad foliage, which takes a mellower tinge from being prolonged into the midst of winter, and which I had only seen in pictures. A monk was walking in a solitary grove at a little distance from the common path. The air was soft and balmy, and I felt transported to another clime—another earth—another sky. The winter was suddenly changed to spring. It was as if I had to begin my life anew."[5]

Another traveler who fell under the spell of Turin arrived more than thirty years later. This was a French philosopher and politician, Charles de Rémusat, who in 1857 undertook a first journey to Italy at age sixty, when he already knew France and England thoroughly. Rémusat commended the location of Turin on the left bank of the northward-flowing Po, exclaiming how much lovelier it is to gaze into countryside than to have a river look out onto more city, as happens in Paris or London.[6] The appeal of the hills seen from the quays was captured by Friedrich Nietzsche, whose fuller reactions to Turin we shall explore later. Unable to contain his enthusiasm, he spoke of Turin as affording glimpses of "Claude Lorrain on permanent view."[7] Even after two decades of traveling in Italy, Nietzsche, like Hazlitt, instinctively compared landscape to painting.

Almost a century after Rémusat, another French writer started in Turin while making a first trip to Italy at the age of nearly sixty. In 1953 Jean Giono, too, relished the view across the Po toward "those depths of dark foliage, across those rococo convents, those villas in the style of 1900 emergent from groves which seemed always to have played a role in his heart."[8] Even more striking is Giono's description of the equestrian statues of kings of Sardinia that dot the piazzas. The statues show "a man, always the same, dressed like a cashier of the Bank of France or a member of the French Academy. He is on horseback; sometimes he gallops, once he has stopped and brandishes his small sword [Ferdinand of Savoy at the Battle of Novara]. Where he is most astonishing, is when he is portrayed in the act of riding pell-mell; his horse runs with four hooves in the air. It takes a certain philosophy to make a statue of a king in this posture."[9] With wry humor the old peasant noted a fitting symbol of the House of Savoy: Its kings rode hell-for-leather.

Instead of haunting the river or ogling the statues, Henry James concentrated his first impression on the piazza outside his hotel room. Having arrived by train from France on this his second visit to Italy, James saw in the view pleasant reminders of what Italy meant to him: "Half an hour after my arrival, as I stood at my window, which overhung the great square [Piazza Castello], I found the scene, within and without, a rough epitome of every pleasure and every impression I had formerly gathered from Italy: the balcony and the Venetian-blind, the cool floor of speckled concrete, the lavish delusions of frescoed wall and ceiling, the broad divan framed for the noonday siesta, the massive medieval Castello [Palazzo Madama] in mid-piazza, with its shabby rear and its pompous Palladian front, the brick campaniles beyond, the milder, yellower light, the range of colour, the suggestion of sound."[10] As usual, James invoked each of the five senses (only odors and taste being omitted here). The view onto the Piazza Castello condensed evidence that he had indeed reached Italy.

OUTLANDISH CHURCHES

It fell to James's friend and colleague, Edith Wharton, to explain how Piedmont's Catholics owed their zeal to contact with Protestants along and even inside their borders. The heresy of Peter Waldo, who died in 1217, spread through his Poor Men of Lyons into the mountain valleys southwest of Turin. No amount of persecution could root out the primitive Christianity of mountaineers who cherished poverty and purity of life. With the coming of the Reformation, the so-called Waldensians, or Vaudois, began to see themselves as precursors of Luther and Calvin, and after a brief respite suffered even more savage persecution. John Milton wrote one of his best-known sonnets, "On the Late Massacre in Piedmont," following a slaughter of Waldensians in 1655. Milton's cry, "Avenge, O Lord, thy slaughtered saints," carried no weight in Turin, especially after Louis XIV took the lead in expelling Calvinists from France in 1685. As Edith Wharton explained in her novel *The Valley of Decision* (1902), Catholics in Piedmont could not relent even a century later. She doubted whether by the 1760s any of the nobility of Turin remembered "a Swiss vagrant called Rousseau," who had converted in one of their monasteries and then "hastened to signalize his conversion by robbing his employers and slandering an innocent maid-servant."[11] As Rousseau recounts in Book Two of his *Confessions* (1765), at age sixteen he took refuge in Annecy with Madame de Warens, a Swiss Calvinist who had recently converted to Roman Catholicism and had received a royal pension for inducing others to do so. In 1728 she sent Rousseau to the Convent of the Holy Spirit in Turin, in whose church near the Roman Palatine Gate he abjured his Calvinist "heresy."

Wharton explained how the religion taught by the Jesuits in the 1760s suited the aristocracy of Turin: "For the use of their noble supporters, the Jesuits had devised a religion as elaborate and ceremonious as the social usages of the aristocracy: a religion which decked its chapels in imitation of great ladies' boudoirs and prescribed observances in keeping with the vapid and gossiping existence of their inmates."[12] Chapels decorated like boudoirs still adorn the churches of Turin, whose rococo interiors resemble "aristocratic drawing-rooms, of which some Madonna wreathed in artificial flowers seemed the amiable and indulgent hostess, and where the florid passionate music of the mass was rendered by the King's opera singers before a throng of chattering cavaliers and ladies."[13] The notion of the Madonna presiding at a salon redeems churches, whose clutter might seem unbearable in the absence of a hostess.

The architect who set the tone for the prettified interiors of Turin was a priest from Modena, Guarino Guarini, who worked in Turin from the 1660s until his death in 1683. The most extravagant geometer perhaps among all Italian architects, Guarini articulated intersecting arches in the cupolas of two churches next to the royal palace. The cupola of San Lorenzo has eight arches interlaced above eight cockleshell windows to define an octagonal lantern. Soaring above one of the most ornately sculpted interiors in all of Italy,

Guarini's geometry stuns the observer. It is as though the analytical geometry that Descartes had invented two decades earlier has shaped a house of God.

The effect of harnessing geometry to glorify God is even more staggering in the chapel that Guarini designed to house the Shroud of Turin. Although Antoine Valery objected that these cupolas look like "demonstrations of geometrical problems," even he admired how dozens of superimposed triangles interconnect in the Chapel of the Holy Shroud to dazzle and even bewilder the beholder.[14] The fact that the shroud, which Duke Emmanuel Philibert purchased from Burgundy in 1578, is rarely on view is soon forgotten, for the cupola's infinite regress deters one from thinking about anything else.

NIETZSCHE AND DE CHIRICO

In April 1888 Turin received a visitor who could lay some claim to being Europe's foremost essayist. The Piedmontese capital so captivated ailing Friedrich Nietzsche that he chose it as his home during six of his last nine months of activity. Having dwelt there during April and May 1888, he returned from September 1888 until he went out of his mind in January 1889. In several letters he described Turin in glowing terms. Himself a master, like Henry James, of generalized description, he offered composite images of the Alpine capital, exclaiming, for example, to Peter Gast, "What a worthy and serious city! Not at all a metropolis, not at all modern, as I had feared, but a princely residence of the seventeenth century, which has only *one* taste giving commands to everything, the court and its *nobility*. Aristocratic *calm* is preserved in everything: there are no nasty suburbs: a unity of taste which extends even to color (the whole city is yellow or reddish brown)."[15]

The core of Turin impressed Nietzsche as comprising an aristocratic, nay, a regal city, where a will to power had excluded discordant elements. The very uniformity that had disappointed Valery and James delighted Nietzsche during his final year of productivity. Here was a city where the will to power had shaped a way of life. He repeated the same themes to Carl Fuchs: "Do you know Turin? It is a city after my own heart. Indeed the only one. Calm, almost solemn. A classical land for foot and eye (through a superb pavement and a shade of yellow and brown-red in which everything becomes one). A breath of genuine eighteenth century. Palaces, such as speak to *our* senses; *not* Renaissance castles."[16] This manly utterance, with its overstatement and broken syntax, is typical of Nietzsche's last year, when the ravages of syphilis made every mental act a torture. At a time when he had to assert his will to perform the simplest function, the drill ground of Turin met his needs.

His room across from the Palazzo Carignano thrilled him with its view of the Piazza Carlo Alberto. Whereas French and English writers called Turin regal, Nietzsche rightly compared it to a German *Residenzstadt,* meant to house not kings but lesser princes. Yet, when one beholds a genuine Italian *Residenzstadt,* such as Piacenza, Parma, or Modena, one sees that compared to Turin they lack the regal touch. Indeed, among European capitals Turin resembles none so much as Madrid, the center of which was built at the same era to mirror a similar ethos, both Catholic and royal. Turin is the Madrid of Italy.

At the same time that he was saluting the will to command of the dukes of Savoy, Nietzsche was celebrating the Will to Power in his final books. The dukes who planned rectilinear Turin could scarcely have imagined that one day a German philosopher would find stimulus there for works entitled *The Anti-Christ* (1888), *Ecce Homo,* and *The Twilight of the Idols* (1889). While, of course, the seeds of such iconoclasm lay in Nietzsche's earlier career, it is piquant to think of him completing them in a city of martinet kings, who would have been as annoyed as they were baffled by such un-Piedmontese effrontery.

Yet, at a deeper level, a city built to please single-minded rulers seems a fitting birthplace for Nietzsche's last writing. The feminine curves of the hills to the east contrast sharply with the masculine grid of the city itself. To walk from the heart of old Turin into the hills is to experience two opposite modes of accommodating nature: masculine imposition of will and feminine acceptance of nature, that same nature that, as Italo Svevo once said, does not produce a single ninety-degree angle.[17] Turin, the city of ninety-degree angles, nestles in a sinuous setting that mocks all right angles. This most Euclidean of European cities rests among rounded hills, bounded to the north and east by winding rivers.

Such a setting suited Nietzsche as he penned his last outbursts in a desperate struggle to reconcile similar opposites within himself. Nietzsche combined both the iron will of the dukes of Savoy and the feminine sensibility of those welcoming hills, uniting them in a balance that threatened always to veer into one extreme or the other. Unfortunately, not even Turin could save him from the ravages of his disease, contracted in a heedless moment almost twenty years before. In the first days of 1889 he collapsed in his room overlooking the Palazzo Carignano, a building which in all its years had never witnessed a sadder scene. The palace in which Italian unification had been proclaimed twenty-eight years before stood helpless and mute while across the street Europe's liveliest mind fell silent.

Only one kindred soul chose to celebrate Turin as a seat of Nietzsche's burst of creativity. The Italian painter Giorgio De Chirico (1888–1978) spent just a few days in Turin in the summer of 1911. But that was enough to imprint images that lasted throughout several years that followed in Paris. De Chirico prized Turin both as a city in which Nietzsche had spent his final months and as one in which his Sicilian father had studied engineering. Having frequented Nietzsche's favorite spots, the neurotic twenty-three-year-old conceived his "metaphysical" paintings as an attempt to paint ideas that had poured from Nietzsche in that final volley. Certain of De Chirico's "metaphysical" images, notably lofty arcades with narrow arches, equestrian statues, and soft hills, have entered the twentieth-century imagination. Images that many people associate with Florence or Rome derive not from these quintessentially "Italian" cities but from regal Turin.

One of De Chirico's metaphysical paintings, *Nostalgia of the Infinite* (1911), shows a square tower modeled on Turin's truncated skyscraper, the Mole Antonelliana. A work of three years later, *Melancholy and Mystery of a Street*, features an arcade without moldings, very like that of the Piazza Vittorio Veneto, formerly known as Piazza Vittorio Emanuele. The equestrian statue that casts its shadow into the picture derives from one on Nietzsche's Piazza Carlo Alberto. De Chirico wants us to believe that this is how Nietzsche might have conceived these monuments, and that is what makes their depiction "metaphysical." Nietzsche's euphoria made him see in Turin whatever he needed to see. His would-be disciple De Chirico used its motifs to create images of the "twilight of the idols," in which all vigor has drained out of the stage-properties of a bourgeoisie, dozing amid relics. The same ensembles that stirred Nietzsche and De Chirico had moved Henry James to extol Italian palaces. As a native who had to dwell among them, the Italian emphasized the emptiness of such buildings, whereas the German let them confirm fantasies of an all-regulating intelligence, while the American saw in them forebodings of other cities.

All of these artists, like Hazlitt and Wharton before and after, projected fantasies onto Turin, a city that sets no barrier to fantasizing. In Florence one dithers about how much demands to be seen, in Venice the water lulls one into a blissful torpor, while in Milan one vibrates to the sound of money being earned. In Turin a dearth of obligatory sights seems to encourage deeper musings.

3

Many-Tiered Genoa and Its Ambivalent Admirers

IMAGES OF SLOPE AND SLUM

A different kind of overture awaits travelers in Genoa. Most writers emphasized how this seaport differs from the rest of Italy and indeed from the rest of Europe. To many it seemed beautiful in an un-Italian, or at least an un-Tuscan, way. As Valery facetiously remarked, "Genoa has only three streets and yet is one of the most beautiful cities in the world."[1] Although since 1945 no traveler would pronounce Genoa one of Europe's lovelier cities, earlier its harbor had vied with those of Naples and Palermo for the title of most spectacular. Even more breathtaking than from the sea were views from seventeenth-century forts above the city. Before airplanes made such vistas routine, Genoa was one of the few cities that could be perused from above, whence to east and west stretched the Rivieras and far out to sea glimmered the former Genoese possession of Corsica.

Within the old city stood some of Europe's best preserved slums, dwellings from the fourteenth and fifteenth centuries that ascended seven stories, having enjoyed running water supplied by aqueduct since the thirteenth century. Lanes no wider than an arm span admitted mules but no sunshine, shutting out a grandeur that patricians had installed on the heights above. Henry James hailed this labyrinth as "the tightest topographical tangle in the world, which even a second visit helps you little to straighten out. In the wonderful crooked, twisting, climbing, soaring, burrowing Genoese alley the traveller is really up to his neck in the old Italian sketchability."[2]

One of the last writers to evoke the tiers of the city devised a striking image for them. Adrian Stokes, a young English critic, who wrote brilliantly about Venice, Verona, and Rimini as well, described Genoa in 1932 as being shaped like a ship, which invites one to ascend from a hold in the old city to a promenade deck among palaces to a superstructure of apartment houses on the bluffs. Although Genoa prompted others to coin metaphors about how its tiers reflect class differences, no one put the matter so graphically as Stokes: "Proud Genoa, historic emblem as much as Venice of sea-power in Italy, herself is the pattern of a vessel. I do not intend anything so far-fetched as the shape of the town seen from an aeroplane. I am thinking of the old city by the harbor, gloomy, narrow, loaded and guttered like the hold of a ship; then the emergence into space about the main thoroughfares, and then above, reduplications of levels like poops and superstructure over the deck, and above, the long line of tall tenements which catch all the staccato noises like the wireless upon the masts, washing and telegraph wires making the strands."[3] Other writers only elaborated one or another aspect of this image, showing how Genoa's zones separated the classes as tidily as any ocean liner.

The two faces of Genoa, comprising a seat of resplendent wealth and a hellhole of poverty, were captured best by the Irish novelist Sean O'Faolain, who came there in 1947 to meditate on an Irish patriot, Daniel O'Connell, who had died in a Genoese boardinghouse exactly one hundred years before. From the sea, O'Faolain rhapsodized, "Genoa will rise before the eye and the memory as a city of matchless beauty, all cream and pink and yellow as a tea-rose, or like old worn pearls, or bleached bones on a sun-baked shore, one great shimmering mass of pastel colour circled in an amphitheatre of sunlight about the cup of the throbbing port."[4] In defiance of his romantic prelude, O'Faolain devoted himself to describing the lowlife of Genoa, no one else enjoying its clatter as he did: "But if you are not so favoured you walk the panting streets of a barbaric stews, raucous, sweating, stinking, villainous, jammed with the crews of ships from every nation of the world. There is no sleep. The trams

scream as if they were being tortured. The trains rattle and shunt. . . .
It is a devil-town; a seaman's whore. It is the best port in the Mediterranean for the sailor's money from Gib to Port Said. If you want to see life pullulating like an ant-heap go to Genoa."[5]

Most of all, O'Faolain bridled at the slums. Like Michelet nearly a hundred years before, he flayed wealthy shippers who for eight centuries had done nothing to alleviate distress in the narrow lanes. "We explored them at random. We found that each entry opens into a warren of others, all alike, all dark, twisting, turning, climbing over rubble, leaning and tottering, diving down steps and up steps, a maze of what must be the worst slummery of all the slummeries of the world, a rookery of palpitating poverty smelling like its own corruption, an insidious, low, throaty smell . . . a goat-smell clinging to the nostrils all day long. . . ."[6]

An earlier English novelist, equally known for depicting lowlife, found even less to delight him in Genoa. In 1844 Charles Dickens spent three months in what he called the "pink jail" of Albaro, growing to love the town only after he had moved to the Palazzo Peschiere overlooking it. Everything about the port disgusted him, from offal in the fish market to the "repulsive countenances" of priests and stucco that had turned black.[7]

Forty years after Dickens, the juxtaposition of poverty and the sea inspired Thomas Hardy to record his first impression of the Mediterranean, stolen from a train window down a lane that happened to be hung with laundry. The shock of first glimpsing the sea of Homer and Virgil through a rainbow of underwear prompted Hardy to declare:

> O epic-famed, god-haunted Central Sea,
> Heave careless of the deep wrong done to thee
> When from Torino's track I saw thy face first flash on me.
>
> And multimarbled Genova the Proud,
> Gleam all unconscious how, wide-lipped, up-browed,
> I first beheld thee clad—not as the Beauty but the Dowd.
>
> Out from a deep-delved way my vision lit
> On housebacks pink, green, ochreous—where a slit

Shoreward 'twixt row and row revealed the classic blue
    through it.

And there across waved fishwives' high-hung smocks,
Chrome kerchiefs, scarlet hose, darned underfrocks;
Often since my dreams of thee, O Queen, that
    frippery mocks.[8]

The contrast of hyphenated epithets like "god-haunted," "multi-marbled," and "deep-delved" with monosyllables like "slit," "smocks," and "hose" evokes the gulf between high and low in Genoa.

That gulf stunned another poet, the German Heinrich Heine, into lambasting the Genoese: "There lies Genoa on the sea like the blanched skeleton of a huge beached animal; dark ants, called Genoese, crawl around inside; the blue waves wash ashore rippling like a lullaby; the moon, the blue eye of night, looks down upon it in melancholy."[9] The image of ants picking over the skeleton of a beached whale while waves sing a lullaby suggests a city where nature ignores humans and humans ignore one another.

MICHELET'S MISGIVINGS

A city like Genoa, which evoked ambivalence and even hostility, impelled writers to dwell on people rather than monuments. Genoa ranks with Naples as a city where writers noticed street life more than architecture. Edith Wharton, with her talent for summary, captured the conjunction of magnificence and meanness when she had her protagonist in *The Valley of Decision* (1902) react to Genoa as it looked in 1778: "Seated by this halcyon shore, Genoa, in its carved and frescoed splendor, just then celebrating with the customary gorgeous ritual the accession of a new Doge, seemed to Odo like the richly-inlaid frame of some Renaissance 'triumph.' But the splendid houses with their marble peristyles, and the painted villas in their orange-groves along the shore, housed a dull and narrow-minded society, content to amass wealth and play biribi under the eyes of their ancestral Vandykes, without any concern as to the questions agitating the world. A kind of fat commercial dulness, a lack of that personal distinction which justifies magnificence, seemed to Odo the prevailing note of the place. . . ."[10] One would never guess that Wharton was very fond of Genoese gardens, for like their builders she did not let moral objections impede aesthetic delight.

The "fat commercial dulness" that disturbed Wharton found its most eloquent accuser in the French historian Jules Michelet, who spent the winter of 1853–54 convalescing with his young wife in nearby Nervi. There he got over the shock of having been fired by Napoleon III from a professorship at the Collège de France. Having come to the Riviera for his health, the great psychologist of peoples could not refrain from recording his reactions to the rabbit warren of Genoa, ten kilometers to the west. Partly because he was ill, Michelet was one of very few to decry the climate, which most others have extolled for providing the warmest winter north of Tuscany. With typical ingenuity he cited the blast of the mistral as having honed the ruthlessness of the Genoese: "It is true that such a climate, fearsome for a sick person, is admirable for hardening the strong. Genoa is the land of harsh rude geniuses born to conquer the ocean and master storms. . . . A race strong, small, and tough, rudely gifted with a genius of steel, I don't know what sort of tip to pierce iron. It doesn't matter if they are ignorant; they discover, they invent, expedients at least."[11]

Having disposed of the climate, Michelet went on to deride the splendor: "Without a care for the land which she did not know and scorned, she [Genoa] piled up, on the narrow shore between sea and mountain, from level to level, as it were, a titanic ladder of marble palaces, which from a distance appear one on top of the other. These magnificent sites, divided by orange trees and terraces, arrest and surprise the beholder more than they charm him."[12] Wondering why Genoa does not charm, Michelet responded that it is because ". . . one shares in the fatigue of such a great effort; one feels all too well that such a people, little enamored of nature, did not do all this simply to amuse themselves."[13] Only pirates, the Frenchman affirmed, would have settled such a narrow shore.

Most foreigners admired the spaciousness of Italian palaces, but Michelet struck a harsher note: The vaunted palaces of Genoa were nothing but fortified banks: "These palaces are fortresses, barred on the bottom, shut in by massive iron gates as imposing as those of a city, which serve to defend the strongbox."[14] Scolding shippers, each of whom had built higher than the next, Michelet mocked their palaces as "observatories from which the capitalist gazes at his ships at sea, from which the ship-owner follows his corsairs with his eye."[15] Even readers familiar with similar overemphasis in Ruskin must feel that this insult exhausted the topic of Genoa as a bankers' paradise. But no, the banklike palaces piqued Michelet to sketch their history with yet another telescoping of effects: "Genoa was a bank before it was a city; early on it was a company of lenders of *bottomry bonds* [loans on shipping], an association of armed sailors. Love of the lottery is wild here; and for a very long time the city loved the big lottery, war."[16]

Michelet portrayed Genoa's maritime exploits with similar abandon. He narrated the orphaning of Pisa in 1282 and the siege of the Venetian port of Chioggia, which would have subdued Venice in 1379, he argued, if the besiegers had not reverted to being merchants and opened their ships to sell salt, whereupon the Venetians rallied, capturing the besiegers and reducing Genoa to the haplessness of Pisa, at least in the eastern Mediterranean. However overstated, this vignette introduced a compelling conclusion: "Petty interests, pursued too strenuously, made Genoa fail at large ones. While it hammered away at its *Kingdom of Corsica*, it refused America which the Genoese Columbus offered it."[17] In reality, Columbus, who was cast ashore in Portugal in 1476 when a Genoese fleet sank in battle against the French, did not "offer" America to Genoa, but he did make provision in his Spanish will of 1498 for a fund in the Bank of Saint George to maintain a house in Genoa for the Columbus family. Michelet must have meant that the Genoese did not grasp the significance of what their compatriot had discovered. In fact, neither did Columbus himself, since he died in the conviction that his "Indies" could only be those of the East. Genoese pertinacity, which enabled him to complete his voyages, also kept him from changing his mind in order to identify what he had discovered. Michelet was right that a Genoese in service to Spain sealed the decline of Genoa, for the New World lay beyond the city's capacity to imagine.

To sum up the exploits of Genoa, Michelet reverted to an image drawn from landscape. No one else could have formulated the matter so aptly: "The history of Genoa is singular, full of great things performed abruptly; it is uneven and exhausting, like the countryside. All the time one climbs in order to descend. Individual heroism is everywhere, and beside it, narrow-mindedness."[18] Whereas most travel writers enjoyed good health and good spirits while abroad, Michelet showed that there is a place for disgruntled travel writing. A tendency to manic-depressive swings predisposed him to discern a similar rhythm in Genoese history.

BUBBLING INVECTIVE

A French essayist of equal penetration, André Suarès, is one of the major writers on northern Italy. Having written a scintillating volume on Lombardy, Venetia, and Romagna in *Vers Venise* (1910), he waited almost twenty years to do a sequel, *Fiorenza* (1929), which opens with a sparkling chapter on Genoa. The cascade of images that Suarès used to evoke the view from the sea makes Adrian Stokes's trope seem staid.

Suarès construed Genoa first as a bird, then as a ladder, then as a series of animal faces, and finally as an amphitheater. Such chains of images constitute one of his trademarks: "Fairly close, finally distinct, when Genoa appears at dawn, it rises, spreads out like a huge concave bird, a strange and magnificent ladder of countless facades, faces of variegated stones, perforated with shining eyes and windows. Eyes of glass, carbuncles, reflections the color of molten metal, all the houses are painted in red, yellow, pink, green, and even black. The huge solid flag expands into an amphitheater. . . ."[19] No sooner is it sketched than this picture of Genoa as a concave bird, as a ladder of facades, and as a flag gives way to other images. From the sea Genoa now looks like a beehive split in twain, its two halves spread out to form a crescent. Then again it looks like two pincers of a crab, with the mole to the west and Sisagno to the east enclosing a conch.

Once he came ashore, Suarès felt the beehive turn into a nest of termites—shades of Heine!—the lanes becoming runs of ants. Even the slums smacked of nature. For Suarès as for O'Faolain, to encounter poverty ingrained over seven centuries evoked primal urges: "It seems to me suddenly that I am populace and hunger, thirst and whore. I violate and am violated. I smell of the belly, the vulva, and coarse wine. I stink and enjoy life tremendously, like an animal in heat."[20] For a moment the haughty sixty-year-old felt what it must be like to be a woman of the people, ravished, stinking, pulsing with life. He deplored the hellish existence of the consumptives and the blind, who he imagined must inhabit these dim rooms. Newer sections of Genoa, where the well-to-do had fled, contained "houses of cardboard and frangipane," while the workers all seemed like sailors, for "the sea has given everyone a second blood in their veins."[21]

The banking soured Suarès less than it did Michelet, because making loans to foreign powers had enabled Genoa to keep its independence. Having begun as pirates, the Genoese had turned to banking when piracy became too dangerous, and now, instead of hiding their wealth, they flaunted it in massive objects that offended less than one might expect: "They love solid gold, heavy silverware, lavish marble, thick velvets, bulky furniture with inlaid woods, stately paintings: all their palaces are full of Rubens and Van Dyck. There is neither grace nor lightness; a will that is often peevish, a joviality that is a little sly."[22] What the Genoese lacked was good taste, the Tuscan gift of knowing when to say "Enough."

This city of excess nurtured the popular leaders of the Risorgimento, just as Turin supplied its diplomats and manipulators. Mazzini, Garibaldi (though born in Nice), and the Ruffini brothers were all Genoese, as was their feisty predecessor, the lad Balilla, who incited the people against the Austrians during a siege of 1746.

Not content to characterize the Genoese as sailors, or pirates turned bankers, or as rebels, Suarès added one of his most provocative insights. Meditating on the word "Ligurian," which harks back to pre-Roman mountain tribes, Suarès declared the term to be misleading because he had seen the people's like in Corsica and especially Sardinia. The Genoese are not Ligurians, he decided, but Phoenicians, Carthaginians refined by Christianity.[23] Their pertinacity, bellicosity, and pomposity recall Carthage and its settlements in Sardinia, just as their harsh dialect recalls Arabic. In a stroke of genius, Suarès propounded a connection that everyone else missed: Even if the Genoese have scant Punic blood, they carry on traditions of Phoenicia and its North African colony, Carthage. Although as Christians the Genoese practiced no human sacrifice, to match that of Carthage, neither did they value human life. They ran their city like a ship, whose crew could always be replaced. Their leaders took the long view, like the Carthaginians at war with Rome. Thus Mazzini resembled Hannibal in tackling superior odds and refusing to settle for half a victory, while Columbus became a Hannibal who commanded ships instead of elephants. No wonder Genoa seems un-Italian.

Part Two
LOMBARDY

4

Glamor Amid Clamor: The Shock of Milan

A EUROPEAN CAPITAL

The largest and most prosperous of North Italian cities, Milan is anything but the most beloved. Writers like Henry James and Edith Wharton, who liked the city, defended it only in apologetic tones. "The last of the prose capitals [rather] than the first of the poetic," as James put it,[1] Milan preserves only scant traces of some of its most memorable events. Following the razing of ancient Milan by Urias the Goth in 639 and again five hundred years later in 1162 by Frederick Barbarossa, almost nothing remains of the leading city of Christendom as it was in the fourth century, when Saint Ambrose overcame the heresy of Arianism and Saint Augustine was baptized. Readers of Augustine's *Confessions* have no hope of retracing his footsteps in today's Milan. A similar disappointment awaits readers of Stendhal who may wish to relive his enthusiasm for the capital of Lombardy. Little remains of the city as he knew it, except the opera house of La Scala, where he spent much of his time. For the awful truth about Milan is that it is a city in a permanent state of urban renewal.

The habit of rebuilding Milan in every generation has encouraged foreign writers to compare it to foreign cities. It reminded Montaigne and Valery of Paris, Rémusat of Madrid, and Suarès of Munich. Since World War II it has become the New York of Italy, and someday soon it may be compared to Tokyo. Although Milan suffered more damage during World War II than any other Italian city, damage was repaired more quickly than anywhere else. Jean-Louis Vaudoyer could hardly restrain his grief in 1947 when he saw the ruins of the old Poldi-Pezzoli Museum, which he did not expect ever to see reopen. In fact, it reopened in 1951. Santa Maria delle Grazie lay in ruins except for Bramante's cupola, and the Ambrosian Library had already been restored thanks to proceeds from an exhibition of its treasures held in Lucerne.[2]

The ability of the Milanese to make good the holocaust of August 1943 continued a thousand-year-old tradition of rebuilding. Vaudoyer summed this up unwittingly when he remarked that Leonardo's *Last Supper* deteriorated so rapidly that it needed retouching five years after it was painted. His aphorism on the fresco might serve as a motto for the city of Milan: "The most famous painting in the world is also the one that has been most frequently repainted."[3] The most prosperous city in Italy is also the one that has been most often rebuilt.

SPLEEN

As a rule, we do not read travel writers for invective, for we want them to teach us to enjoy rather than to hate. The French critic André Suarès reverses this expectation, and never more so than in treating Milan. The opening chapters of *Vers Venise* (1910) contain some of the harshest abuse that any traveler showered upon an Italian city.

Suarès opened with a tirade on Milan's resemblance to a railroad station. It is hard to believe that he conceived this passage before automobiles had clogged the streets or before the gigantic railroad station was built: "The entire city is nothing but a railroad station. The hubbub, the sharp movement of the platforms fills the streets; and this famous cathedral is a marble railroad station. Who could ever pray in this warehouse of statues and ornament who has prayed in Chartres or merely in the shadow of Kreiz-Ker [in Brittany]? In Milan, even the street of pleasure and of books, where one goes to drink or to seek his own nourishment, is just a glassed-in-gallery, a railroad station within a station. And the crowd rushes, carrying packages, head down, eyes glued to the hands, with rapid steps the way one runs to the buffet between two stops, the way one catches a train."⁴ A more prophetic description could scarcely be imagined.

In his pique Suarès indulged a fault of his own, one which he imputed to the Milanese: He too did not know when to stop. Trenchancy gave way to disparagement, as when he dredged up stereotypes about the Chinese: "I believe that I can discern in Milan, the round ant heap, the most Chinese city of Europe, such as China will be when science has made it the most swarming scene of robots on the planet."⁵ The clangor of streetcars prompted this outburst, which he matched with one even more savage: "Milan rotates, absorbs, and invents nothing; Milan hardly digests; everything is artificial, like the lobby of an inn. It has the luxury, uproar, and wealth of a hotel."⁶

Suarès liked one or two buildings, above all the Ospedale Maggiore, whose terra-cotta pleased him as much as it did Symonds. In contrast to marble, which he called the "skin of kings,"⁷ brick recalled a young person showing off his or her skin. But such praise was only an interlude between tirades: "The belly of modern Italy is here and perhaps the heart drowns in it. Under a sky without lights and shades, life is violent and burdensome, hot and shrill, dumpy and frenetic. There is more wealth, more strength, more brutality than elsewhere. Houses are taller and darker or else whiter and wealthier than elsewhere. Poverty and affluence are more separated than in the rest of Italy. Everything which remains of old stones, palaces, and churches is hidden in corners. The engineer consigns them, like poor relatives, to exile in shabby neighborhoods."⁸ Like others before and after, Suarès came to Italy to escape a commercial metropolis such as the kind Paris and London had become. He could not bear to encounter in his first major city a magnified version of what he detested at home.

THE CATHEDRAL

The only buildings in Milan that have elicited piquant comments are churches. Of them, by far the most stimulating to writers has been the cathedral, which offers three highly diverse experiences. Its exterior, its interior, and the view from its roof appealed to different visitors in different ways. In his autobiography, *Praeterita*

(1885–89), John Ruskin recalled seeing it in perfect weather during a visit to Italy with his parents in 1840. The "frost-crystalline" marble of the "lace-like tracery" on the roof rhymed with the pinnacles of the Alps seen across the plain.[9] Later, when he examined the building in detail in 1849, he deplored finding "barbarous" flamboyant Gothic grafted onto impure early Gothic. Like many others, he despised the thousands of statues, which he said "are of the worst possible common stonemason's yard species, and look pinned on just for show; the only redeeming character about the whole being the frequent use of the sharp gable . . . , which gives lightness, and the crowding of the spiry pinnacles into the sky."[10] The same "crowding of the spiry pinnacles" prompted D. H. Lawrence to write slightingly of this "imitation hedgehog of a cathedral."[11] Whereas D. H. Lawrence liked only villages, Herman Melville adored Milan, especially the cathedral. In 1857 he boasted that one might place the host of heaven upon its top, from which vantage people below seen through "the turrets of open tracery look like flies caught in cobweb."[12]

In his measured way, Charles de Rémusat weighed the merits of the exterior and the interior of the cathedral, greatly preferring the latter. Although he conceded that the shape of the facade makes the exterior seem too small, Rémusat nonetheless admired the interior as one of the loveliest in Italy. Surprisingly, he even praised Napoleon for having undertaken to add 560 statues to the more than nineteen hundred already in place. Jean Giono, on the other hand, objected to this flaunting of wealth, which had placed the statues too far overhead to be enjoyed by anyone.[13]

Enhancing the contrast between the whited sepulchre of the exterior and the mystery of the vast interior is a crypt containing the corpse of Saint Carlo Borromeo. This tireless prelate, whose leadership in the sixteenth century personified the diligence of the Milanese, suffered the indignity of having his corpse exposed for a fee. Henry James waxed apoplectic at finding this saint turned into a mummy wreathed in jewels: "The black mummified corpse of the saint is stretched out in a glass coffin, clad in his mouldering canonicals, mitred, crosiered and gloved, glittering with votive jewels. It is an extraordinary mixture of death and life; the desiccated clay, the ashen rags, the hideous little black mask and skull, and the living, glowing, twinkling splendour of diamonds, emeralds and sapphires."[14]

Suarès dismissed the cathedral as a sugar castle designed to beguile German scholars, "those blind giants."[15] On the outside he noticed that the spires cut across the straight lines in a way that makes the mass seem to tremble: "That is why it is never so beautiful as in mist or rain: the detail disappears and the apparition becomes magical, like a castle of fog in the mountains."[16] The interior stung Suarès into one of those cascades of metaphor at which no other traveler could match him: "Inside, the marble has the hue of bone. The side naves double the great nave like plans for ribs. One walks in the hollow of a colossal beast, at the centre of the skeleton, amid a forest of vertebrae. A forest of dreams, a basilica of frost."[17]

Although English writers could scarcely hope to sound so sprightly, the poet Percy Bysshe Shelley came close. A letter of April 1818 to Thomas Love Peacock compared the interior beneath the cupola to "some gorgeous sepulchre." In a spot behind the altar, "where the light of day is dim and yellow under the storied window," he chose to sit and read Dante.[18] To picture Shelley reading Dante not far from the moldering body of Charles Borromeo is piquant in the extreme. It was one of the most unlikely spots for a poet to favor in all of Italy.

The English writer Cecil Headlam introduced an entirely different note by recounting the misdeeds of the cathedral's founder. In 1385 Gian Galeazzo Visconti, the "Viper of Milan," sallied forth from his abode in Pavia, ostensibly to go on a pilgrimage but in reality to murder his cousin Bernabò, whereupon he seized the Duchy of Milan. Both the cathedral of Milan and the even more ornate Charterhouse of Pavia were founded by this "cold, false, pitiless" adventurer, who also schemed to subdue Mantua by diverting the River Mincio so as to dry up the protecting lakes.[19] His career ended when he died of fever in 1402 without having attained his goal of conquering Florence and thereby uniting Italy. With ruthless system, he established a workshop to build the cathedral, endowing it with its own revenues and artists, just as he did at the Charterhouse of Pavia.

Unlike Gothic cathedrals in France, this one was willed into existence by one man, and he was a fiend. It expresses not the outpouring of a community's soul but rather subservience to a tyrant.

The most original of twentieth-century English writers on Italy, Adrian Stokes, did not care for Lombard architecture or sculpture. In his view, foreign artists, mainly French, had introduced a taste for detail, which conflicted with Italian preference for mass. The conflict abated only long enough to produce the outsized wedding cake of the Milan cathedral, in which "friction between the original foreign architects, French, German, Swedish, Belgian, and their Italian masons, resulted in the reinforcement of an Italian idea."[20] To proclaim the victory of Italian mass over northern delicacy, Stokes unfurled a string of metaphors worthy of Suarès: "Over and over again foreign designs for the cathedral structure were modified to the ends of unity, of something 'classical,' and away from the swept flying laceworks of the North, away from the confusion of ropes and buttresses that were ship-shape enough in northern skies, but which would have been grotesque if anchored over fair Lombardy flats."[21] Whereas Suarès saw Milan cathedral as a result of northern ideas botched by southern workers, Stokes rejoiced that the workers had won out.

He was less pleased, however, at how French taste had corrupted the terra-cotta work. Churches built of brick and terra-cotta adopted too readily a foreign fussiness that had been successfully banished from the cathedral. He discerned in Bramante's church of Santa Maria delle Grazie, as well as in the Charterhouse of Pavia, what he called "stumpy little arcades or roofed-in loggias that twist and turn and give a pagoda effect to many a Milanese edifice, including the Sforza castle."[22] Although no one else seems to have noticed, the umbrella roof of Bramante's church does indeed resemble a Chinese pagoda.

VICISSITUDES OF *THE LAST SUPPER*

The Cathedral of Milan challenged travel writers because it disappointed expectations of what Gothic should look like. One might expect that Leonardo's *Last Supper* would have posed a different challenge, that of describing one of the most familiar of paintings, but it did not. Leonardo's masterpiece taxed writers not in order to capture his conception, but simply to evoke the state of disrepair. Ruskin put the matter bluntly in 1846 when he reflected, "perhaps the beauty of the fragment left at Milan (for in spite of all that is said of repainting and destruction, that Cenacolo is still the finest in existence) is as much dependent on the very untraceableness resulting from injury as on its original perfection."[23] The "fragment of Milan," melting into "untraceableness," has fascinated visitors partly because of the neglect and vandalism that it has suffered. A French royalist, Louis Simond, who was ever eager to ascribe mischief to Napoleon's troops, in 1817 interviewed a woman who had heard soldiers firing at *The Last Supper* while living next door to it. A French hussar told her that he had shot it while guarding prisoners, some of whom had thrown stones at it. Only after Napoleon had toured the site did he order a balustrade installed, but even he could not drain the water that sometimes welled up out of the floor.[24]

Sixty years later, Rémusat expected to find *The Last Supper* more ravaged than it was. Paintings in churches, he noticed, had blackened from soot, but this one had only faded. Although at first disappointed, Rémusat lingered to garner one of his most vivid impressions, for he deemed the head of Christ one of the worthiest ever painted, and this for the reason that it has faded: "The Jesus Christ of *The Last Supper* is like an erased pastel, and despite that, or who knows, perhaps even because of that, this head, feebly indicated, half destroyed, only expresses all the better the barely material existence of an incomparable person and his divine humanity."[25]

It would be difficult to imagine anyone more different from the Parisian *philosophe* Rémusat than the Oxford don, Walter Pater, who wrote about Leonardo twelve years later. Yet, in his serpentine way, Pater interpreted *The Last Supper* in very similar terms.

On the damp wall of this gloomy spot, Pater recalled, Leonardo chose to apply newly developed oils, which he could not know would not cling to that surface. Loving the freedom that oils alone permitted, a freedom to indulge in afterthoughts, Leonardo not infrequently returned to the wall to add but a single stroke. Having remarked how unusual it was for an artist to interpret the Eucharist not as "the pale Host of the altar, but as one taking leave of his friends," Pater summed up the impression of transience that had enthralled Ruskin and Rémusat as well: "But finished or unfinished, or owing part of its effect to a mellowing decay, the head of Jesus does but consummate the sentiment of the whole company—ghosts through which you see the wall, faint as the shadows of the leaves upon the wall of autumn afternoons. This figure is but the faintest, the most spectral of them all."[26]

Pater went so far as to impute his philosophy of transience to Leonardo's patron, Duke Lodovico, known as the Mulberry, "il Moro." Pater's explanation of why the duke chose the mulberry for his emblem reflects an obsession with flowering that must wither. Pater explained that a mulberry tree is a "symbol, in its long delay and sudden yielding of flowers and fruit together, of a wisdom which economises all forces for an opportunity of sudden and sure effect."[27] In his essays, Pater, too, saved his strength for one outpouring of "flowers and fruit together." Like the mulberry tree, Pater put everything into one burst.

In an early essay written three years after Pater's, Henry James touched many of the same chords, but in jocular fashion. Comparing *The Last Supper* to an "illustrious invalid" whom people visit with "leave-taking sighs and almost death-bed or tiptoe precautions," James declared that "the picture needs not another scar or stain, now, to be the saddest work of art in the world; and battered, defaced, ruined as it is, it remains one of the greatest."[28] Whereas Ruskin, Rémusat, and Pater interpreted the decay as enhancing the religious impact of the image, James construed the ruin as an incentive to fellow artists. The fact that Leonardo worked for fifteen years on this wall should reassure every creator that such effort builds something that not even slow death can efface. Leonardo did not labor in vain, James insisted, because he created an image that is holding out to the last, resisting its own demise.

ASSORTED CHURCHES

One of the few sites in Milan to evoke ecstasy besides *The Last Supper* is the Portinari Chapel attached to the Romanesque church of

Sant'Eustorgio. Admiration for it stirred Edith Wharton to cries of praise unusual for her: ". . . for pure light, for a clear shadowless scale of iridescent tints, what can approach the Portinari Chapel? Its most striking feature is the harmony of form and colour which makes the decorative design of Michelozzo flow into and seem a part of the exquisite frescoes of Vincenzo Foppa."[29] This excerpt is nearly unique in literature on Italy in drawing imagery from the plumage of a bird: "From the cupola, with its scales of pale red and blue, overlapping each other like the breast-plumage of a pigeon, . . . the eye is led by insensible gradations of tint to Foppa's frescoes in the spandrils—iridescent saints and angels in a setting of pale classical architecture—and thence to another frieze of terra-cotta seraphs with rosy-red wings against a background of turquoise-green. . . ."[30]

During the very same years when Edith Wharton was touring Italy, a younger English woman destined for literary fame kept a diary of annual visits to many of the same places. No one thinks of Evelyn Underhill, the Anglican mystic, as a travel writer, but her diary of 1901 to 1907, published as *Shrines and Cities of France and Italy* (1949), offers many choice passages. No less enamored of Sant'Eustorgio than Wharton was, she deemed the nave with its round pillars alternating with thirteenth-century columns the archetypal Dominican church. She alone noticed that the Portinari Chapel, "renaissancy and fanciful but really delicious all the same," ill accords with the reputation of the saint buried within it.[31] The Dominican Saint Peter Martyr, patron of inquisitors, was murdered between Como and Milan in 1252 and received this exquisite resting place two centuries later. This *quattrocento* gem shows how readily in the 1460s innocence could be enlisted to embellish brutality.

One other church in Milan elicited comment from a writer who had little else to say about the city. Maurice Barrès opened his book about Venice, *Amori et dolori sacrum* (1903), by remarking that the title came from an inscription on a little church in Milan, Santa Maria della Passione, a rococo building located next to what is now the Music Conservatory. Milan is one of the last places one would have expected the phrase "Sacred to Love and Pain" to have originated.

5

Brescia the Bellicose

CITY OF STAGE SETS

Blessed by a magnificent site, Brescia has suffered even more than Milan from being a city that invaders must conquer. Lying at the cusp of the Alps, where the mountains reach furthest south into the Lombard Plain, Brescia, "the Armed One," has withstood sieges from time immemorial. The city was sacked by Attila in 452 and resisted Frederick II in 1238, only to succumb a few years later to the monster Ezzelino. Yet, as Edward Hutton wrote, "Brescia avenged herself. It was a Brescian sword in the hands of a Brescian that in 1259, at the bridge of Cassano, ended that life which had turned all this country into a hell."[1] In 1311 Emperor Henry VII exhausted his resources by reducing Brescia at the start of his expedition to Italy. In 1426 the city fell to Venice, from which the French wrested it in a disastrous siege of 1512. The French commander, Gaston de Foix, hastened in winter to rescue the garrison that a surprise Venetian attack had bottled up in the fortress. Gaston's descent down icy slopes resulted in the sacking of the city and inspired one legend. The knight Bayard, taken wounded to a house, spared the virtue of the two daughters, confirming his reputation as being "sans peur ni reproche." Yet, neither Brescia nor the French army ever quite recovered from this attack. Brescia was nearly depopulated, and many French soldiers who went home would be needed soon thereafter at the battle of Ravenna in which Gaston de Foix was killed.[2] Thereupon Brescia reverted to Venice until 1797.

Under Austrian rule from 1814 to 1859, Brescia rebelled in 1848 and again in 1849. In March of that year the Austrian general Haynau earned the sobriquet the "Hyena of Brescia" when he bombarded the city and killed hundreds in pointless street fighting, having refused to tell his opponents that their side had already suffered a defeat at Novara that made further resistance pointless.

In contrast to those like Hutton who recited a history of insurrection, the Goncourt brothers struck a note that better captures the mood of post-1859 Brescia. After a stop in Milan, they stayed in Brescia as only the second city of their first trip to Italy. Eager as they were to reach Venice, they took time to pen a paragraph that proclaims Brescia to be a stage set with no people in it: "There are nothing but massive buildings, with gates shaped out of heavy bosses, and overwhelmed in their misshapen pediments by enormous muzzles of animals; massive buildings with pot-bellied balconies swelling like the bellies of sirens and with huge roofs that raise into the sky statues whose draperies are whipped as it were by the wind.—A black city with pink slashes of brick in the old stone, which seems made to supply the decor of old-fashioned dramas of our boulevard."[3]

The Goncourt brothers' purely aesthetic stance disclosed how many of Brescia's sites seemed to invite dramatic performance. Naturally they thought first of the melodramas then popular in Paris. Two years later Charles de Rémusat noticed how *trompe l'oeil* paintings in Brescia's courtyards resembled stage drops for opera.[4] Other suggestions come to mind: The ruins of the Temple of Vespasian cry out to house a play by Alfieri or a reading of poems by Leopardi. The Loggia of Palladio would make an ideal backdrop for one of Shakespeare's Italian plays, combining as it does grandeur and clarity with a dash of pomposity. As if to show that the residents appreciated the stagelike character of their streets, after 1860 they converted the entrenchments of their fortress into a terraced garden, which resembles an eighteenth-century stage drop by a member of the Bibbiena family. In the 1920s Brescia erected a set piece of fascist architecture, the Piazza della Vittoria, whose massive rectangular forms express the mindless masculinity dear to Mussolini's followers.

The theatricality of Brescia made an indelible imprint on Jean Giono when he drove through the suburbs in the spring of 1953.

High walls, illuminated streets, and vistas devoid of people prompted him to exclaim, "I have never seen anything more romantic than the outer boulevards of Brescia at night."[5] Later he particularly enjoyed the houses on the slope below the Fortress, where the Via Contini seemed to belong in a village, not in a city of one hundred and fifty thousand. Artisans at work reminded him of an older rhythm of life, and plaques paying homage to skirmishes against the Austrians enchanted him. In truth, Brescia boasts more memorials to street fighting than perhaps any other city in northern Italy. Moss-covered walls bear an inscription about Haynau's horrors that Giono could not resist quoting: "On April 1, 1849, in this street covered with corpses, amid the despair which had been unleashed, Father Maurizio Malverti carried sweet words to an enemy mad for vengence. He hoped to calm those monstrous souls."[6]

WORD PAINTING AND THE PAINTERS OF BRESCIA

To pass from the ruminations of the kindly peasant Jean Giono to the reflections of the Oxford don Walter Pater is to enter a different world. Although neither Giono nor Pater is remembered as a travel writer, both possessed ideal gifts for the genre. Pater's potential as a travel writer came to the fore in Brescia, where the painters Moretto and Romanino elicited from him one of the most limpid of travel essays.

Having noted that Vercelli and Novara lie too distant from Monte Rosa and its range for "those awful stairways to tracts of airy sunlight" to seem quite real, Pater extolled Bergamo and Brescia for having hill and plain meet in their streets.[7] The following sentence tops all efforts to evoke Brescia as a city of stage sets, the clauses meandering like the path they describe: "Brescia, immediately below the 'Falcon of Lombardy' (so they called its masterful fortress on the last ledge of the Piè di Monte), to which you may now ascend by gentle turfed paths, to watch the purple mystery of evening mount gradually from the great plain up the mountain-walls close at hand, is as level as a church pavement, home-like, with a kind of easy walking from point to point about it, rare in Italian towns—a town full of walled gardens, giving even to its smaller habitations the retirement of their more sumptuous neighbors, and a certain English air."[8]

These lacquered phrases state a pair of homely thoughts: that in Brescia it is easier to find one's way about than in most Italian towns, and that its walled gardens impart a certain English atmosphere. No one else noticed this, least of all the Goncourt brothers, for whom Brescia recalled a boulevard theater. Yet, as he paused to savor the English-seeming gardens, Pater was merely making his way toward the painters Romanino and Moretto. From a stroller's diversions, seized in passing, he made a masterful transition to his real subject: "You may peep into them [the walled gardens] pacing its broad streets, from the blaze of which you are glad to escape into the dim and sometimes gloomy churches, the twilight sacristies, rich with carved and coloured woodwork. The art of Romanino still lights up one of the darkest of those churches. . . ."[9] No one except the Goncourt brothers, Ruskin, and Henry James could squeeze so many impressions into a few lines as Pater did here.

Until the 1890s Roman and medieval antiquities counted as the chief drawing cards of Brescia, but with the publication in 1890 of Walter Pater's essay, the focus for English people shifted abruptly to the two painters whom he singled out. His panegyric stimulated his disciple Arthur Symons to visit Brescia in quest of Moretto, only to find that painter of silvery gray sadly wanting. As Symons rightly said, Moretto is no one's favorite painter, and yet Pater exalted him as though he deserved to be.[10] The Oxford don saluted Moretto and Romanino as religious painters who had suffused technique from sixteenth-century Venice with the piety of Fra Angelico. What fascinated Pater in Moretto was a palette of white, black, and gray, out of which he fashioned a "very complex tone" peculiar to himself. He was "a lord of colour who, while he knows the colour resources that may lie even in black and white, has really included every delicate hue whatever in that faded 'silver grey,' which yet lingers in one's memory as their final effect."[11] Moretto's gradations of silvery gray appealed to the impressionist in Pater, whose eyes lingered on subtle distinctions. No doubt the same gradations would have appealed to the Goncourt brothers, and to Henry James as well, but these men of the world would have had the wit not to mistake a winsome technique for a world-shaking vision.

In his rapture Pater made a point that smacks of Ruskin, for he admired in Moretto above all a certain religiosity. In contrast to Titian, who either farmed out execution to assistants or else lost himself in overly large designs, "Moretto, in his work, is always all *there*—thorough, steady, even, in his workmanship. That, again, was a result of his late-surviving religious conscience."[12] Pater deployed a battery of comparisons in order to extol Moretto as a master of both color and composition. The light approximates the "pale effulgence of Correggio,"[13] the long folds of drapery suggest early Tuscan sculpture, while the "hieratic distinction" smacks of Perugino.[14] Above all, Moretto "attained full intelligence of all the pictorial powers of *white*."[15] It is touching to see the neo-pagan Pater fawning over Moretto because the painter clung to religion after others had abandoned it.

Moretto's older rival, Romanino, suggested to Pater "something between Titian and Rubens. Certainly, Romanino's bold, contrasted colouring anticipates something of the northern freshness of Rubens."[16] Even more surprising, Romanino's clarity of design was deemed "congruous with, a markedly religious sentiment, like that of Angelico or Perugino."[17] Pater delighted in a painter who fused "the steady glory of broad Italian noonday" with the religious fervor of an earlier century.[18]

Yet, however brilliantly Pater had sketched a stroll through Brescia, he failed to win plaudits for the city's painters. Arthur Symons, who arrived predisposed to admire, could not bring himself to do so, protesting that he had "never felt so forbidding an aspect in any picture gallery as in that picture gallery at Brescia, where Moretto and Romanino surround one with their hard, capable, and unlovely work."[19] Headlam, too, held the painters to have been overpraised by Pater, and Edith Wharton mentioned of Moretto's works only his frescoes in the Martinengo Palace.[20] She did like Romanino's altarpiece in San Francesco, which she saw bathed in August sunshine: "Perhaps he [the sacristan] vaguely felt, as we did, that Romanino, to be appreciated, must be seen in just that light, a projection of the suave and radiant atmosphere in which his own creations move. Certainly no Romanino of the great public galleries arrests the imagination like the Madonna of San Francesco; and in its presence one thinks with a pang of all the beautiful objects uprooted from their native soil to adorn the herbarium of the art-collector."[21]

Pater's essay of 1890 never reached a French audience. Instead, the two admirers of Brescian painters to come from France could not have differed more sharply from Walter Pater, for ebullient Gabriel Faure and inventive André Maurel abounded in the kind of discipline that Pater lacked. As might be expected, Faure discerned in Moretto no theological baggage, attaching him rather to a Venetian tradition that lacked the theological bent of Florence or Rome. The serenity of Moretto's women is, Faure insisted, purely pictorial and carries no trace of melancholy, so that Moretto's pictures light up the altars where they hang: "The colors oppose and balance one another with the most knowing art. Grays, yellows, and pale blues give all his compositions freshness and lustre."[22]

More ingeniously than anyone else, André Maurel contrasted the frescoes of Romanino with the canvases of Moretto. In Romanino he saw an echo of martial Brescia that had resisted the French in 1512, while in Moretto he saw the new Brescia that had accepted Venetian hegemony for good. Maurel explained Moretto's wistfulness as the "melting memory of those who, in accepting subjection, content themselves to dream of past days which they do not at all regret, since they recall them with peaceful pride. They do not repudiate their glory even in refusing to renew it."[23] The silvered blues, browns, and grays of Moretto blend into a farewell to a city's centuries of self-defense. Once citizens had accepted rule by Venice, it was only fitting that Brescia's subtlest painter should adapt Venice's art of color to solemnize the loss of freedom. In all likelihood, Moretto was not so much the religious painter venerated by Pater as he was the civic painter esteemed by Maurel. He represented less a rebirth of Christian ardor than a goodbye to municipal independence, adding a silvery note to the chorus of sixteenth-century masters who, like Bernardino Luini, Giulio Romano, and the Campi of Cremona, painted elegies to fading greatness.

The most haunting of these elegists was a pupil of Moretto, Giovanni Battista Moroni of Bergamo, who painted some of the choicest portraits of the mid-sixteenth century. His backgrounds employed a darker version of Moretto's palette to set off haunted faces of men whose careers have been stunted by the Counter-Reformation. Broken statues imply that men's lives will remain mere fragments of what they might have been. Although Moroni worked mostly in Bergamo, he owed much to Moretto, whose color schemes render heavy-heartedness so achingly. Radiating a woe they could not shed, these painters cried out to a fellow sufferer like Walter Pater. For having evoked nostalgia in silvery prose, Pater might be dubbed the Moretto of the late nineteenth century, since, like his predecessor, the Englishman offered "pensive, tarnished, silver side-lights, like mere reflexions of natural sunshine."[24]

THE FOUNDING OF THE RED CROSS

We get a refreshing taste of pre-Paterian prose from Edward Freeman's account of the citadel of Brescia, the "Falcon of Lombardy." What Pater called the "masterful fortress on the last edge of the Piè di Monte" became for Freeman an eyrie from which to survey the history of the Lombard Plain. In his unadorned way, Freeman lamented the vicissitudes that had visited the towns he could glimpse: "But to the south the eye ranges over the boundless plain of Lombardy, spreading like a sea, with a tall tower here and there, like the mast of a solitary vessel. Each of these towers marks a city, a city which once ranked alongside of princes, cities which made war and peace, and which contained within their walls the full life of a nation."[25] In a vein that mirrors J. A. Symonds's mountaintop passages, written during the same years, Freeman regretted how feebly the Alps had protected Lombardy. In a rare outburst of indignation, he singled out Gaston de Foix's assault in 1512 for having eviscerated the city "in a warfare as unprovoked and inexcusable as any in which French conquerors ever engaged."[26]

Considering how many times French conquerors from Charles VIII and Francis I to Napoleon engaged in "unprovoked and inexcusable" warfare in Italy, this is a heady statement. When he wrote it in 1876, Freeman could not have been thinking about events that had unfolded in Brescia seventeen years before. For unprovoked warfare in and around Brescia reached new ferocity in June 1859 during and after the battle of Solferino, where more than three hundred thousand men clashed. In this climax to Cavour's joint campaign with the French against the Austrians, French troops watched by their emperor, Napoleon III, defeated Austrian troops watched by their emperor, Franz-Joseph. Not only did the battle seal the fate of Austria in Lombardy and signal the unification of most of Italy, but the response to it by one eyewitness changed the way in which war has been conducted ever since. A thirty-one-year-old Swiss tourist, Henry Dunant, happened to be visiting the neighborhood at the time. His *Un Souvenir de Solférino*, published at his own expense in 1862, is one of the most influential accounts ever written by a traveler in Italy, for the outrage that it aroused against neglect of prisoners and the wounded led directly to the founding of the International Red Cross two years later.

The battle of Solferino was fought on June 24, 1859, largely between foreign armies, French and Austrian, across fields farmed by Italian peasants. This was the first large battle to involve modern artillery, which left at least twenty thousand wounded on each side. Many more thousands died of wounds and of thirst before they could be tended. Dunant exposed one scandal after another. Since both armies went into battle on a torrid day without having eaten or drunk adequately, a shortage of water during the next four days caused thousands of deaths. Dunant did not even try to describe the groans that filled the night after the battle, as the walking wounded lapped water from muddy pools full of blood. Notwithstanding claims that the task took only a day, in actuality it required four or five days to locate the dead, who lay across ten miles of rolling countryside. Corpses lay everywhere: on roads, in ditches, in thickets, in meadows, and among wheatfields. Artillery shells had devastated the landscape to create the kind of no-man's-land that would become familiar during World War I. Dunant was one of the first civilians to witness what artillery can do to farmland. Wounds from shell fragments were made worse when artillery caissons trundled over their victims, rubbing earth into broken limbs.[27] Having reported that most of the dead showed every sign of having expired in agony, with faces distorted and fingernails filled with their own flesh, he wondered what wives and mothers would think if they could have seen how their loved ones had died.[28]

Even while praising the energy with which Italians aided the survivors, Dunant lambasted the lack of planning for the wounded. As a matter of course, officers received medical care before any of the enlisted men did. Up to twenty thousand French wounded had to wait three days at Castiglione, a village of five thousand, before traveling by open oxcart beneath a blazing sun to Brescia. In particular, Dunant denounced the Austrian practice of telling soldiers before battle that the other side would take no prisoners. He reported seeing Austrians tremble for fear that they would be hanged by the dreaded *zouaves*, and he noted that several wounded Austrians had shot French soldiers who were trying to succor them.[29]

After describing the hunger and thirst that the wounded endured while waiting for removal to Brescia, Dunant painted the following scene in that city, one of the most moving ever recorded by a traveler to Italy: "This city, so charming and picturesque, has been transformed not into a huge first aid station like Castiglione, but rather into an immense hospital; its two cathedrals, its churches, its palaces, its convents, its schools, its barracks, in a word all of its buildings are choked with the victims of Solferino; fifteen thousand beds have been set up, as it were, from one day to the next; the generous inhabitants have done more than anyone has ever done anywhere else amid such events. In the heart of the city, the old basilica known as the Duomo vecchio or la Rotonda, with its two chapels holds a thousand wounded; the people crowd around them . . . the same scenes take place in the new cathedral, a magnificent temple in white marble with a vast cupola, where hundreds of wounded are packed, and those scenes are repeated in forty other buildings, churches or hospitals, which among them contain almost twenty thousand wounded and sick."[30]

Anyone who visits the cathedrals side by side on the Piazza del Duomo can imagine what these buildings must have looked like when more than a thousand wounded jammed them in late June 1859. These scenes helped to assure that Solferino would be the last European battle in which care of the wounded was left to a local population. Thereafter humanitarian concern became a task of armies as well as of bystanders. Thanks to Henry Dunant, Brescia taught general staffs to do what they should have undertaken long before, so that care of the wounded and of prisoners became as solemn an obligation as drill itself.

Henry Dunant found his vocation during the days after Solferino. Like the organization he inspired, he sympathized impartially with all combatants while advocating measures to help all victims of disaster. By dispelling the mist of sentiment that had shrouded battlefields, his account galvanized people to take action. Coming in the midst of the American Civil War, the congress that Dunant convened at Geneva in 1864 founded the International Red Cross and drafted the Geneva Convention, which has protected prisoners of war ever since.

By showing what can be done to aid survivors of a modern battle, Brescia's citizens pioneered a mode of conduct that the Red Cross has spread worldwide. The generosity of Brescia's volunteers bordered on the superhuman, considering that the city had ousted Austrian rule only seven days before the battle and that ten years earlier General Haynau had killed hundreds of people, whose fellow citizens would soon save thousands of Austrians. There must have been more than one family that lost a son to General Haynau only to help save some of his veterans ten years later. Because of such gallantry, the Piazza del Duomo deserves to be a pilgrimage site of the modern world. To accompany the plaques about the horrors of 1849 that attracted Giono, there ought to be another that reads, "In this city where so many died in vain for Italian freedom, in 1859 the people of Brescia taught the world how to treat an enemy humanely."

6

Magnificence Moldering in Mantua

DITHYRAMBS ON DISREPAIR

Once a center of Roman power, Mantua emerged after 1400 as one of the stateliest cities of the Renaissance. Just as Ferrara owed its glory to the Este family, so Mantua owed its to the Gonzaga, who ruled from 1328 until defeated by the Austrians in 1630. A succession of five marquises and seven dukes built what was by 1600 the largest palace in Europe, which embraced five hundred rooms around fifteen courtyards. To decorate its walls, Marquis Ludovico hired Andrea Mantegna, who dwelt in Mantua from 1460 to 1506, just as three generations later Duke Federico hired Giulio Romano to further embellish the domain. Federico's widowed mother, Isabella d'Este of Ferrara, became synonymous with patronage of the arts, and it was partly to escape her influence that Federico built the Palazzo del Tè as a pleasure palace at the other end of town. Today Mantua stretches between these two palaces, a city of brick buildings lining narrow streets.

One might expect that writing about Mantua would exalt the Gonzaga as model princes. Unfortunately, damp from the lake and neglect by subsequent owners deflected comment away from the magnificence onto the decay. By 1850 the five hundred rooms had fallen into such ruin that writers stood mesmerized by the wreckage. How could the Austrians, who ruled here from 1707 to 1866, have allowed the largest and gaudiest palace in Europe to become a rotting hulk? Why did the Kingdom of Italy wait until the 1920s to begin to stem the blight? Finding no answers to these questions, around 1910 Hutton, Maurel, and Suarès stared in disbelief at empty rooms sapped by damp-rot, rats, and mosquitoes. Thanks to restoration begun by the Fascists, today Mantua is a flourishing textile center surrounded by a hinterland of Virgilian fecundity. With fascist buildings like those of Milan and Brescia anchoring its center, Mantua gives scant hint that during the nineteenth century the decay of this city evoked greater dismay than that of Rome.

A graphic description of the disrepair came from an English Jew, Israel Zangwill, who in 1910 evoked the crumbling palace in a prose whose blend of magniloquence and rot aped that of the building: "It was not till I had walked for many minutes through an endless series of dilapidated chambers and mutilated magnificences—propped-up ceilings, and walled-up windows and rotting floors . . . and mouldering tapestries and paintings, and musty grandeurs multiplied in specked mirrors, and faded hangings and forlorn frescoes, and chandeliers without candles, and fly-blown gilding and broken furniture and beautiful furniture and whitewash and blackened plaster and bare brick and a vast unpeopled void—that there began to grow upon my soul the sense of a colossal tragedy of ruin, a monstrous and melancholy desolation, an heroic grandeur of disarray, a veritable poem of decay and destruction."[1] By adding epithets as recklessly as the Gonzaga had added rooms, Zangwill allowed his syntax to collapse as limply as their decorations had. His shapeless sentence displayed a "heroic grandeur of disarray" quite in keeping with its subject.

A writer of far greater gifts and knowledge, Edward Hutton, also wrote at his best about Mantua, which he evoked with a languor worthy of Walter Pater: "Something of the stillness and silence of her lakes seems to have fallen upon this city of large and level spaces, of sunlight and shadow and all quietness. Gradually, imperceptibly, she is decaying in the damp of her lagoons, and is passing from us slowly, softly, little by little, bit by bit, as a dream passes."[2] The gentleness of Hutton breathes through these sentences, for the decay of Mantua, as of other Italian cities, stirred him not to anger but to melancholy: "How dreary is Palazzo del Tè now, and how forlorn, the most forlorn thing in forlorn Mantua, a palace of faëry that arose out of the mists of the lagoons and might seem already to be dissolving into mere damp and desolation."[3]

Visiting a few years before Hutton, André Maurel detected the same pall, but French candor led him to recount horrors from which Hutton recoiled: "The interior of the palace is desolation itself. It is a haunting nightmare. The very invasion of rats brings out some grandeur. . . . The mosquitoes, imponderable and imperceptible, methodically detach, day by day, a grain of each object, one of the thousand atoms of which everything is composed. . . . The wood, the stucco, the marble, even, one might say, diminishes, and soon flies away in the wind that whistles under the door, and in at the ill-fitting windows."[4] As if this catalog were not enough, Maurel invited the reader to imagine a Versailles left to rack and ruin beside a marsh. What a visitor might have seen there after centuries of decay waited in the Corte Reale at Mantua: "Yet at Versailles, the bronze and marbles would be victorious against wear and decay. Here there is neither bronze nor marble. Nothing but things ephemeral, made of wood, of stucco, of plaster, or frescoes, furnishing nests for mosquitoes, who add their incessant biting to neglected oozing grottoes, which the damp blackens, and the fog liquifies."[5] Walking through a palace larger than Fontainebleau, Maurel shivered as he stumbled over ceiling beams and broken statues hour after hour. The bedchamber of Isabella d'Este looked a wreck: "The door—there were two, there is only one now—trembles in the frame. The wainscoting is splitting, and coming away from the wall, from which scales of plaster have fallen, leaving the stones bare. The ceiling, in little squares, still holds, all discoloured. . . . Above the wainscoting, are great square holes, old frames, widowed of their canvasses."[6]

Already in 1857 Charles de Rémusat had noted the palace's disrepair; even though Austrian administrators were still using it, the rooms reminded him, as they would Maurel, of a neglected Fontainebleau. Some had been hastily restored, while others were abandoned, and still others contained furniture that might have adorned a French prefect's office around 1810. In a stroke of rare insight, he detected a resemblance to buildings being erected in Paris during the 1850s. Decayed or not, decorations two centuries old reminded Rémusat of a boulevard café: "What ought to be gilded is painted yellow.

Mouldings in plaster replace marble and bronze. Water-color, annealing, fresco, and stucco do not possess in Italy a feeling of care or solidity, and in this Ducal Palace of Mantua at certain moments one can believe that one is traversing the ruins of a café."[7]

GIULIO ROMANO

The sharpest rebuff to these would-be admirers came from André Suarès, who experienced Mantua as a hellhole of damp, decay, and decadence. Arriving after a succession of disappointments in Milan, Pavia, and Parma, relieved only by ecstasy in Cremona, Suarès lambasted Mantua more severely than any other city: "One arrives in the marshes. One is caught in the marsh, one smells the swamp. Even the dust is muddy. The pavement sweats. . . . Everything is false in this den; false like the foul water. The palaces are temples of false taste; and the churches are false palaces open to prayer. The marble is stucco; the stone is plaster; the bronze is mildewed brick. The disreputable Giulio Romano has corrupted this city: everything here seems to be by him."[8]

Suarès singled out Giulio Romano as the evil genius of Mantua. While Giulio's distorting hand does seem to affect much of the palace, this does not excuse a tasteless reference to Giulio's given name of Pippi, the "pisser." Yet, even if he sometimes exaggerated as much as Giulio did, the Frenchman generated worthwhile insights: "Giulio the Pisser, called Julius the Roman to make us laugh, bears to my mind all the faults of Mantua, its princes and its people. He never lived, he never thought except for effect. It is the kingdom of mockery, where an everlasting lie reigns. False grandeur, false materials, false workmanship, there is no form of falseness in which this Bandinelli of painting did not pass for a master."[9] The Bandinelli of painting! This Florentine sculptor, who aped Michelangelo's mightiest torsos, carved muscular figures that resemble those of Giulio's frescoes. He distorted Michelangelo's legacy in the same way that Giulio distorted that of Raphael, and Suarès could not bear betrayals of greatness.

The tirade against Giulio climaxed with a reference to another startling figure, who suggests all sorts of odd parallels: "The nudes which this disreputable painter tosses off would revolt even lechery; they are nothing but drunks the color of beet, bodies reddened with herpes, exantheme, and every skin disease: the poet who inspires this Pisser is Fracastoro, and could only be he."[10] At first glance, it sounds like a blow below the belt to call Giulio a painter of syphilitics who resembles Gerolamo Fracastoro, a physician who wrote three books of hexameters entitled *Syphilis sive de morbo gallico* (1530). Yet the monstrous disease, named for a lovely nymph, does suggest the sort of contradictions that Suarès saw in Giulio's art, an art contorted, misleading, and corrosive.

The association between Giulio and Fracastoro suggests a parallel that even Suarès did not spell out. How ironic it is that Fracastoro, the poet of syphilis, became fifteen years later physician to the first session of the Council of Trent. It was he who ordered the prelates to abandon that city for Bologna when plague struck in 1547. Had he thought about it, the mischievous Suarès might well have seen the decrees of the council as displaying the same love of deception as do Giulio's frescoes, for in a very real sense the Counter-Reformation introduced the deceits of mannerist art into Catholic doctrine. At least to Lutherans and Calvinists, the decrees of the Council of Trent resemble a gigantic Palazzo del Tè of theology, where appearance is glorified over reality and everything is sacrificed to effect. To paraphrase what Suarès said about Romano, "false grandeur, false materials, false workmanship" afflict the edicts of these Bandinellis of theology, who strove to enforce obedience the way Giulio strove to compel admiration. The prelates flexed their muscles and sought to encase the soul, which ends up writhing in bondage like the giants in Giulio's frescoes. The substitution of display for devoutness that prevailed at the Council of Trent may be said to have a precursor in the art of Giulio Romano.

THE PALAZZO DEL TÈ

As Suarès recognized, everything in Mantua comes down to praise or blame of Giulio Romano, who began his work there with the building and frescoing of the Palazzo del Tè, which he designed for the son of Isabella d'Este. Operagoers know the sinister renown of this palace because Verdi chose it as the home of the wicked duke in *Rigoletto* (1851). An exterior marked by heavy columns that have no function and a half-dozen rooms of bizarre frescoes, including portrayals of Duke Federico's favorite horses, have both fascinated and repelled visitors. Valery's classical taste led him to contrast the regularity of the architecture with the imagination and "fire" of some of the frescoes. He noted a two-headed Austrian eagle that Primaticcio placed among the squires of Emperor Sigismund, while Giulio's Room of the Giants appealed to the Frenchman's fondness for historical portents. With Jupiter hurling thunderbolts from the ceiling and a floor painted with debris from rocks tumbling off the walls, the scene seemed to foretell the downfall of the Gonzaga a hundred years later.

The ever-courteous Rémusat reiterated Valery's judgment when he called Giulio "a somewhat crude Raphael and a theatrical Michelangelo."[11] He praised the room of the six horses for perfect execution of a bizarre idea but deemed the Room of the Giants an overdone homage to Michelangelo. A Parisian *philosophe* could not bring himself to admire a world turned upside down.

Neither could the Goncourt brothers, who visited here in 1856 on their way from Venice to Bologna. Jules de Goncourt's penchant for heaping up phrases reached an apogee in his tirade against Giulio: "The Palazzo del Tè, an omelette of men and women, viewed from the soles of feet, the perineum, the underside of the belly, the underside of the breasts, the underside of the chin, the underside of the nostrils; an acute sickness of the technique of foreshortening which makes all these undersides land and weigh upon the eyes. Oh, the stupid and almost comical monstrosity of this 'Room of the Giants,' this swarm of antediluvian wrestlers, this salad of exaggerated muscles, this inept mass of super-human nudities, fabricated with *cupfuls* of vermilion, this crushing and mangling of legs, arms, heads, with which a wall is splattered. One might call it a museum of statues by Michelangelo, which had exploded and stuck to the walls, a world given over to Force, a world flattened, broken, smashed, and demolished."[12] Goncourt piled image upon image to convey the sense of disjointedness that swept over him. As he piled up metaphors to mimic the tumbling giants, his sentence toppled over from the weight of exotic words—words as weird as the vermilion and turquoise that startled him.

Whereas every French writer censured the Room of the Giants, Charles Dickens was the only Englishman to compose a purple passage about it. Giulio's vision so blatantly violated laws of both nature and art that Dickens could express only bewilderment at "that exhausted cistern of a palace, . . . [where] there are dozens of Giants (Titans warring with Jove) on the walls of another room, so inconceivably ugly and grotesque, that it is marvellous how any man can have imagined such creatures. In the chamber in which they abound, these monsters, with swollen faces and cracked cheeks, and every kind of distortion of look and limb, are depicted as staggering under the weight of falling buildings, and being overwhelmed in the ruins; upheaving masses of rock, and burying themselves beneath; vainly striving to sustain the pillars of heavy roofs that topple down upon their heads. . . . The figures are immensely large, and exaggerated to the utmost point of uncouthness; the colouring is harsh and disagreeable; and the whole effect more like (I should imagine) a violent rush of blood to the head of the spectator, than any real picture set before him by the hand of an artist."[13] Such outrage surged through Dickens that he could not discern a parallel to his own gifts. Even if he did not carry exaggeration to "the utmost point of uncouthness," not a few of his figures are "ugly and grotesque." Perhaps if the frescoes had been in grisaille instead of acidic colors, and if the bodies had been scrawny instead of muscular, then he might have noticed a similarity to the portrait of Fagin in *Oliver Twist* (1838) or of Scrooge in *A Christmas Carol* (1843). Of course, in Dickens's stories right and wrong are clearly defined, while Giulio painted a scene of irrevocable punishment without indicating whether it is deserved. The ambiguity of the scene, an ambiguity that lay at the heart of mannerism, troubled Dickens more than he knew.

SHAKESPEARE'S ITALY

It fell to Vernon Lee, that most poetic of travel writers, to sum up all these associations by construing Mantua as the city that best embodies what Italy meant to Shakespeare. For her the Ducal Palace, glowering across its waters, epitomized the world of intrigue and pomp that Shakespeare conjured up in northern Italy. Although Shakespeare, of course, never saw Italy, he situated a half-dozen plays in the North. *The Merchant of Venice* and *Othello* take Venice for granted the way *The Taming of the Shrew* does Padua, and *Romeo and Juliet* Verona. The latter play features as well Romeo's ill-fated flight to Mantua, while *Two Gentlemen of Verona* links Verona and Milan, and *Twelfth Night* unfolds on the Venetian coast of Illyria. Vernon Lee seemed to hear Shakespeare stalking the Ducal Palace.

This revelation dawned gradually, as she tramped through the palace one day in the late 1890s. The greens and blues of Mantegna's ceiling in the Camera degli Sposi enchanted her less than colors she glimpsed from the window: "The pale blue water, edged with green reeds, the poplars and willows of the green plain beyond; a blue vagueness of Alps, and, connecting it all, the long castle bridge with its towers of pale geranium-colored bricks."[14] Of course she could not help noticing the desolation: "Forlorn, forlorn! And everywhere, from the halls with mouldering zodiacs and Loves of the Gods and Dances of the Muses; and across hanging gardens choked with weeds and fallen in to a lower level, appear the blue waters of the lake, and its green distant banks, to make it all into Fairyland."[15] Inland Lee whiffed an odor that confirmed the rot, for silkworm cocoons filled the porticoes on market day, lacing the air with their "sickly smell."[16] The decay brought a flash of illumination: "For these endless rooms and cabinets—some . . . quite delicate and exquisite; or scantily modernized under Maria Theresa for a night's ball or assembly; or actually crumbling, defaced, filled with musty archives; or recently used as fodder stores and barracks—all this colossal labyrinth, oddly symbolized by the gold and blue labyrinth on one of the ceilings, is, on the whole, the most magnificent and fantastic thing left behind by the Italy of Shakespeare."[17]

Vernon Lee was the only writer to observe how the Ducal Palace mirrors Shakespeare's Italian plays. She specified, for example, how characters from *Twelfth Night* belonged there. She imagined "some chivalrous Gonzaga duke, perhaps that same Vincenzo who had the blue and gold ceiling made after the pattern of the labyrinth in which he had been kept by the Turks, not too unlike, let us hope, Orsino of Illyria, and by his side a not yet mournful Lady Olivia; and perhaps, directing the concert at the virginal, some singing page Cesario. . . ."[18]

Lee rounded out her evocation of Shakespeare by connecting the Dwarfs' Apartments to works of his pen. The creator of *Measure for Measure* could easily have imagined, as she asks us to do, "a whole piece of the building, set aside for their [the dwarfs'] dreadful living, a rabbit warren of tiny rooms, including a chapel against whose vault you knock your head, and a grand staircase quite sickeningly low to descend. Strange human or half-human kennels, one trusts never really put to use, and built as a mere brutal jest by a Duke of Mantua smarting under the sway of some saturnine little monster, like the ones who stand at the knee of Mantegna's frescoed Gonzagas."[19]

Not content to evoke just Shakespeare, Vernon Lee fancied the idea of having a "water pastoral, like the Sabrina part of 'Comus' " performed on the lake for the delectation of some Gonzaga duke.[20] This conceit so entranced her that a few years later she wrote a play about a performance of such a masque overlooking the lake, her closet drama, *Ariadne in Mantua* (1906), concluding with just such a water masque. Lee wrote it, she said, because the Ducal Palace obsessed her until she imagined an aria by the Florentine Caccini filling its corridors. Around Caccini's melody her play took shape. As Lee rightly saw, Mantua cries out for water pastoral, for where "now only the song of the frogs rises up from among the sedges and willows," one longs to hear Shakespeare and Milton resound across the waters.[21]

Few cities have elicited such contradictory reactions, and few haunt the imagination to the same degree. Mantua is Shakespearean in this, too. Although Milan has been rebuilt half a dozen times since antiquity, nowhere does it suggest the transience of all things human so poignantly as does the Ducal Palace of Mantua. The decay of *The Last Supper* seems modest by comparison.

Part Three
VENICE AND VENETIA

7
Venice, or Describing the Indescribable

COLOR TONALITIES

Where to begin with Venice? Where else but with color? The colors of Venice have elicited such glowing praise that it seems prudent to start in a low key. With his usual good sense, Charles de Rémusat made several observations that writers fearful of seeming naive have missed: The color of Venice is not the green of the lagoon or the apricot of a sunset, but rather the dirty white of Istrian marble. "From my first glance, I found Venice too white. I did not expect it, and I was counting on warm or dark shades, on black palaces which contrast with the pink or golden hues of buildings less severe. For me chalky white, which up close turns a dirty or grayish white, takes away from many Venetian buildings the air of antiquity and any effect of color. . . ."[1] The reputation of Venice for color Rémusat traced to the yellow and pink facing of the Doges' Palace. The rest of Venice looked as different from the Doges' Palace, he observed, as other churches did from Saint Mark's.

Rémusat's peer as a late-in-life newcomer to Italy, Jean Giono, made equally sage remarks about the colors and sounds. A city "surrounded by water and paved with water" is the only place in the world, he noted, where it is so elegant to wear black.[2] Since there is no dust, black is easy to keep clean, while formerly a lack of fresh water made linen difficult to maintain. Since mountain people associate death with a black bark, the gondola for him could portend only decay. In a city of floating coffins, he asked, why should anyone feel in a hurry? "Time is not money" in a city where the comedy is already over.[3] Giono pressed his paradoxes still further, for whereas most people came to feast their eyes, he delighted in being able to rest his ears.[4] In 1953, before motor boats had multiplied, he felt as though he were in a huge convent, where silence offered positive pleasure. Because the ears have so much to enjoy in Venice, it would be a splendid place, he concluded, in which to be blind!

Needless to say, no one else shared Giono's whimsy of trying to enjoy Venice without seeing it. If Rémusat found too many of the buildings white, while Giono delighted in black, Adrian Stokes hit upon a formula to link the two. His analysis of Venetian architecture, which we shall explore later, hinged on an interplay between black and white: "Venice excels in blackness and whiteness; water brings commerce between them. Italians excel in the use of black and white, white stone and interior darkness. Colour comes between, comes out of them, intensely yet gradually amassed, like a gondola between water and sky."[5]

Framing the black and white are the two elements in nature that change most often: sea and sky. It is effects of cloud and water that make Venice a city of ever-changing color. Many writers tried to render in prose the kind of subtleties that impressionist artists like Monet and Pissarro would render in paint. Of all such attempts, perhaps the most remarkable came before these painters had evolved their technique. While staying in Venice during December 1855, Jules and Edmond de Goncourt described colors playing on the water below their hotel window. Their enumeration of flashes of color suggests the English painter William Turner writing prose: "From our window (December, ten o'clock in the morning), the bluish sky turns opal at the horizon, and seems to float out there on the sea like a veil, of an unspeakably tender blue, drifting away.—Against this sky there are cupolas and campaniles, looking like oxydized silver.—Near the Giudecca one would say that the sun is skimming on the waves stones made of diamond and of fire, or shaking a coat of mail made of polished steel, ceaselessly restless and alive with twinklings. Against the Dogana in a warm shadow of violet, sails the color of tobacco catch a tawny light, and against the ball of gold that is the flaming sun the flying figure of Fortune is dazzling in its upward yearning."[6]

Although color photography did not emerge for another fifty years, the Goncourt brothers wanted to record colors much as a camera would, the evanescence piquing them to capture each fleeting sheen. As one savors the Degas-like quality of their prose, one realizes that they have stilled the mobile face of the water, freezing each instant into a timeless image. Not everyone, perhaps, will find the result pleasing, for one might not wish to linger beside water as lifeless as this: "The water is numbed, in a swoon, congealed, and the yellow masts of the boats and the pink palaces are reflected there, as though in an oil where the ribs of their lines drown in greasy liquid.— Seagulls navigate on these waters, like swans, or fly a little above, dipping their legs from time to time and letting drops of light rain down.—And the only noise is a distant hammer of a caulker, a groan of a pulley, a screech of a seagull."[7] If ever words aspired to turn into pigment, it is in the hands of these painters *manqués*, who used dashes like rests in music to crystallize each image. The young writers, aged twenty-seven and thirty-five, strove to combine effects from painting and music in a single passage, where colors and sounds interchange, while over everything hovers a form-riveting sun. Few passages fix the air of Venice so palpably as this one.

Henry James, who learned much from the Goncourt brothers, did not even try to rise to their pitch. As we saw in Turin, James loved to generalize, conflating a thousand impressions into one. Without evoking a particular view, he would capture the essence of many. Venice offered an ideal site for composites such as this: "The sea took on a thousand shades, but they are only infinite variations of blue, and those rosy walls I spoke of began to flush in the thick sunshine. Every patch of colour, every yard of weather-stained stucco, every glimpse of nestling garden or daub of sky above a *calle*, began to shine and sparkle—began, as the painters say, to 'compose.' The lagoon was streaked with odd currents, which played across it like huge smooth finger-marks."[8] From many glimpses, he composed a single image that sticks in the mind as effectively as that of the Goncourt brothers. While collecting impressions to fuse together,

James struck a note that has characterized Venice ever since he first arrived there in 1872: Already it had become a bazaar for tourists. Averring that "half the enjoyment of Venice is a question of dodging," he studded his essays with tips on how to avoid fellow tourists.[9] Venice was and is the only city in northern Italy to require such advice.

Maurice Hewlett, who felt more at home in Tuscany than in Venice, also took a crack at describing the colors he saw from his room. Like Stokes and the Goncourt brothers, he noticed how a spectrum of colors on the sea contrasted with the blotchy white of the buildings: "As I sit writing, I look out upon a broad sheet of sea, which is coloured in bands of grey, pink, bright green, dark blue, coral, and french grey: . . . Beyond that is a misty line of warm red (the houses of the Lido) out of the other window I can see a white domed church, if you can call a thing white which is stained with weather and warm with generations of sunlight."[10] Like Rémusat and Stokes, Hewlett did not know quite what to call the weather-beaten white of Istrian marble. He summed up his distress at the general dishevelment by deploring a pontifical high mass that he attended at Saint Mark's. It was so carelessly conducted as to make him lament, "These people have lost all their artistry and live upon their past like fungus on a fine old tree."[11] This abhorrent metaphor sounded a theme that pervaded writing about Venice: No amount of beauty could hide the decay. For a lover of Tuscan directness such as Hewlett, Venice became a Mantua writ large.

THE CHURCH OF SAINT MARK'S

No other city boasts so undisputed a center as the Piazza San Marco provides Venice, where the "Salon of Europe," as James called it, has enthralled strollers for hundreds of years. Writing in 1831, Valery captured its two-faced character with his usual trenchancy: "The Piazza di San Marco is unique in all the world. There the Orient and the Occident stand face to face, on one side the Doges' Palace, with its architecture of lace, its balconies, and its galleries matching those of Arab buildings, and Saint Mark's church, whose pointed facade and lead-covered cupolas recall a mosque in Constantinople or Cairo; on the other side are the uniform arcades and shops in the Palais-Royal [of Paris]."[12]

Alluring though the shops and cafés may be, the cynosure of all eyes can only be the Church of Saint Mark's. Already nearly eight hundred years old, it became a cathedral only in 1807, having hitherto served as the chapel of the Doges. There the Doge took his oath, and there the tomb of Saint Mark preserved bones carried off from Alexandria about 820. Saint Mark's ranks with the cathedrals of Pisa and Florence as being one of the few buildings in Italy to which nearly every writer responded. Foremost among these responses is the description that John Ruskin penned in *The Stones of Venice*. In a famous chapter, he conducted the reader along the streets from his pension on the Campo San Moïse to the piazza, retracing his own experience of discovering the church anew each day. The climax that lets the eye fall at last upon the facade is one of Ruskin's most majestic instances of a delayed crescendo. The first impression is of "a multitude of pillars and white domes, clustered into a long low pyramid of coloured light; a treasure-heap, it seems partly of gold, and partly of opal and mother-of-pearl, hollowed beneath into five great vaulted porches ceiled with fair mosaic, and beset with sculpture of alabaster, clear as amber and delicate as ivory. . . ."[13]

The enumeration builds for another page, delineating the sculpture and columns of the porches, the capitals, and the archivolts, until one reaches the pinnacles. There Ruskin preferred to adduce the crash of the sea, which pounds unheard above the four horses from Byzantium: ". . . the breasts of the Greek horses are seen blazing in their breadth of golden strength, and the St. Mark's Lion, lifted on a blue field covered with stars, until at last, as if in ecstasy, the crests of the arches break into a marble foam, and toss themselves far into the blue sky in flashes and wreaths of sculptured spray, as if the breakers of the Lido shore had been frost-bound before they fell, and the sea nymphs had inlaid them with coral and amethyst."[14] As happens on the facade, so in this passage, color and shape, vision and metaphor, combine into a dazzling whole.

The interior pleased him less because it employed every trick for fanning idolatry: "Darkness and mystery; confused recesses of building; artificial light employed in small quantity, but maintained with a constancy which seems to give it a kind of sacredness; preciousness of material easily comprehended by the vulgar eye; close air loaded with a sweet peculiar odour . . . these, the stage properties of superstition . . . are assembled in St. Mark's to a degree, as far as I know, unexampled in any other European church."[15] All this gimcrackery elicited not one comment from the Venetians, for whom the beauty of Saint Mark's is "unfelt, the language it uses is forgotten."[16] From such indifference Ruskin vowed to rescue the building, since evangelist that he was, he could not bear to let others ignore anything that thrilled him.

That he succeeded may be judged from Henry James's complaints in 1882 about the "restoration" of the exterior, where workmen had removed the patina of age while smoothing undulations in the floor of the nave. Having renewed the alarm about the destruction of Venice that Ruskin had sounded in 1845, how James might have gasped if his guide, like that of E. V. Lucas in 1889, had peddled pieces of mosaic that he chipped from the walls before his customer's eyes.[17] Yet nothing could prevent James from savoring the "glowing dimness" of the interior. Having declared it a place to visit for a few minutes each day so that you can discover its "beauty of surface, of tone, of detail, of things near enough to touch and kneel upon and lean against," he also warned that there is no beauty of "proportion or perspective; there is nothing grandly balanced or far-arching; there are no long lines nor triumphs of the perpendicular."[18] Quite devoid of the symmetry of a Gothic cathedral, this treasure-house of details beckoned like a "dusky cavern."

The most ecstatic hymn to Saint Mark's came from a voice that we have heard grumbling across Lombardy. André Suarès, the detractor of Milan and Mantua, lost himself in ecstasy upon glimpsing Saint Mark's. So effusive, not to say fulsome, was his praise of this "church of the Grail" that one can scarcely believe that the satirist of Mantua had found paradise at last. It was a golden paradise, whose incense wafted like a vapor of gold, conveying a dream crystallized in stone and colored glass, where four domes circling a fifth seemed to betoken a wisdom of a thousand years in this most "internal" of churches.[19] While golden shields dangling from the domes caught the light as in a pageant, Suarès imagined that he heard a choir singing amid the drifting perfumes in this "church of the spheres," whose domes revolved like planets around the sun. Indulging a kind of synesthesia that seized him nowhere else, he fancied himself to be standing in "a cosmic temple, a solar church," whose design disclosed "the secret of the ages, a thousand-year-old gnosis,"[20] in which four domes swirling around a fifth evoked strophes the Creator sang when he began the world.

In contrast to Ruskin, Suarès let musical images throng his pages. Indulging the sense of touch, he likened the marbles to velvet, or oriental rugs, or rather mirrors. No, they resembled instead the crystal of still waters. Every cranny from floor to ceiling shimmered with gold, just as every stone radiated light the way a human voice radiates speech. Rembrandt had labored all his life in vain to rival such a poem of light and shade. While Suarès strewed images almost frantically to convey his wonder at the whole, no one feature enchanted him so deeply as the interaction of all. Suarès's hymn brings to mind poetry by Rimbaud and Verlaine, with its appeals to all five senses, for it was not harmony of line or of perspective or of mass—things that James found wanting in the church—but of all these together that moved him. Since for Suarès the magic of Saint Mark's recurred whenever he entered it, he enjoyed that rarest of traveler's delights, an epiphany renewed.

A few years earlier, Walter Pater's disciple Arthur Symons had enjoyed a similar ecstasy. For him as for Henry James, the church spoke through color rather than shape. The impressionist in Symons burst out, when he called Saint Mark's the "most beautiful church in the world . . . because it has the changing colours of an opal, the soft outlines of a living thing. It takes the reflection of every cloud, and in certain lights, flushes into rose, whitens to a lily."[21] Any surface that changed color before his eyes captivated Symons, a man who prized iridescence because each shift of light caught a different facet of his soul: "The gold, when the light strikes it, glitters in one part like rock-crystal, in another like gilt chain armour. Rosy lights play upon it, and the very vault dies away in soft fire."[22] In days before motion pictures and strobe lights have made such displays commonplace, Saint Mark's must have seemed a fairy tale to a connoisseur of surfaces.

Such lyricism was bound to find a comeuppance. It did in the disdain of an English philosopher, Herbert Spencer, who stopped off in Venice in 1880 after a trip to Egypt. While he praised assemblages of buildings, which "placed without reference to effect, present everywhere charming combinations of forms and colors," he denounced Saint Mark's for pressing the ornamentation of flat surfaces to extremes.[23] Not one to mince words, Spencer wrote that Saint Mark's "is a fine sample of barbaric architecture. I use the word barbaric advisedly; for it has the trait distinctive of semi-civilized art—excess of decoration." Lest anyone doubt whether he considered the Venetians "semi-civilized," he repeated the point: "The characteristic of barbaric art is that it leaves no spaces without ornament; and this is the characteristic of St. Mark's."[24]

These diary entries, written less than thirty years after *The Stones of Venice*, betray invincible ignorance of Ruskin's message. Where no simplicity of structure matched the complexity of surface, Spencer could only deplore the air of instability that resulted. For this Victorian any building whose facade did not announce the structure behind was telling a lie. Venice, and least of all Saint Mark's, is no place for positivists. Still, the philistinism of the well-informed need not sound so silly as it does in this case, for one may legitimately find the facades of Venice tedious after a while. What is offensive is that Spencer found them so at first glance.

Astoundingly, the Goncourt brothers passed a similar judgment not on Saint Mark's as a whole but on its mosaics. With touching literalism they recorded their dismay at the "frightening nudities, grotesque maimings, hideous swellings" of the biblical figures, while they judged even more alarming the jumble of animals.[25] Unable to overcome a taste for realism, they objected to donkeys with huge ears, camels whose necks were elongated like those of reptiles, greedy heraldic birds, and hippogriffs that looked like bats and leeches. The blue sea seemed to be teeming with maggots, and the trees looked like old men. This outburst, which opens the brothers' pages on Venice, shows to what degree they preferred glimpses of contemporary life to impressions of medieval art, since they wanted to do in words what a contemporary like Gavarni did in drawings: to sketch vagaries of fashion. They sneered at the mosaics with words that anticipated Spencer's contempt for "barbaric art": "These mosaics—frightening caricatures with the ugliness of a primitive idol, of a fetish of savages—seem, in an embryonic art, the timid and dreaded impressions of a childish people before the divinity."[26] The language of positivism, based on undisguised contempt for "primitive" peoples, speaks through these lines. The Goncourt brothers were so eager to be up-to-date that they could see no merit in the medieval.

While French writers were busy refining one another's judgments, a different response came from an Englishman who shared the interest of the Goncourt brothers in mores of the eighteenth century. The Treasury of Saint Mark's delighted Osbert Sitwell with its bric-a-brac from Byzantium. The booty gathered in Saint Mark's and its treasury struck him as comprising the world's finest collection of Byzantine art. The Adriatic coast, he recalled, is strewn with objects that Venetian ships lost on the way home from Byzantium, while Saint Mark's itself is the chief storehouse of those that arrived. By a strange alchemy, objects that originated in the East have acclimated themselves here as nowhere else: "The incongruity of the exhibits is by one means or another banished until they become part of the building, grow in to it as an orchid flowers from a tropical tree, and even impart to this shrine a portion of the magic of the places from which they were wrenched."[27]

All the same, Sitwell denounced the sack of Constantinople in 1204, an act of envy whereby the Venetians ravaged a city that they ought to have cherished. Sitwell held their assault to have been in vain, for Haghia Sophia so triumphantly surpasses Saint Mark's as to make Venice seem "an upstart, a usurping poor relation grown rich through the plunder of those who should have been dear to her."[28] If Genoa was a city of pirates turned bankers, Venice was a city of pillagers turned connoisseurs.

OTHER CHURCHES: ZANIPOLO AND THE FRARI

Other churches in Venice have received far less attention than Saint Mark's. Writers were so eager to sketch outdoor life and ensembles of buildings that hardly any essayist surveyed even the major churches. Vaudoyer singled out the ceiling of the Church of San Pantaleone, which Zanantonio Fumiani decorated in the late seventeenth century. Foreshortenings make this one of the most spectacular frescoes in the city, but because the one-armed Fumiani painted only ceilings, museums ignore him. The fact that he taught himself to paint with his left hand after losing his right makes his feat border on the incredible. Vaudoyer extolled the colonnades, which rise above one another in a cascade that would have enthralled Eugène Delacroix.[29] The ceiling was a particular favorite with Henri de Régnier, who no doubt would have enjoyed dwelling in a decor such as Fumiani had envisioned.

Brushing aside such anomalies, Ruskin asserted that two churches besides Saint Mark's demand attention: the Dominican one of San Giovanni e Paolo, known affectionately as Zanipolo, and the Franciscan one of the Frari. Suarès went into dithyrambs over tombs of the doges in Zanipolo, tombs which Ruskin for once described more soberly. It is almost as though Suarès wanted to outdo Ruskin, having adopted his distinction between early gothic tombs and later ornate ones. Like Ruskin, the Frenchman castigated the Lombardi brothers for forgetting by 1500 that tombs ought to be simple. "Lombardi and the others are famous marble-workers, without doubt; they invented the bed of state, the everlasting scaffold where all the rich and powerful wanted from then on to be exposed. They put the dead to moulder in a theater. A stage-set is erected for each, a pillory. Grief has drawn a curtain of eloquence in front of the abyss."[30] These tombs prompted Suarès to discourse on the relative merits of gothic slabs versus ancient urns. Reproaching the urn for having suspended the dead on caryatids out of touch with the earth, Suarès praised gothic tombs for not gilding death. Gothic sculptors paid proper respect to death, while the Lombardi swathed it in finery.

In exhaustive detail, Ruskin had distinguished the doges' tombs of the fourteenth century that retained something of the "pure calmness of early Christianity" from those of the fifteenth that displayed "the beautiful pomp of the Renaissance faithlessness."[31] Ruskin called the tomb of Francesco Foscari, who died in 1457, the first important example of Renaissance art, which shows "the refuse of one style encumbering the embryo of another."[32] He anticipated Suarès in deploring how ostentation spoiled a sepulchre: "For exactly in proportion as the pride of life became more insolent, the fear of death became more servile."[33] The affinity between the two men's views suggests that in many ways Suarès was a Ruskinian in Barrèsian clothing. Like Ruskin, Suarès hated pomposity and acrobatics, such as the kind that marred Giulio Romano's works. While the two moralizers shared certain aversions, they did not always agree in their enthusiasms. Suarès detested the Scaliger tombs in Verona, which Ruskin adored, and Ruskin admired the Cathedral of Milan, which Suarès loathed. Still, a Ruskinian tenderness breaks out of Suarès more often than he admitted.

One of the spots both men adored was the statue of Bartolomeo Colleoni by Verrocchio, which stands on the piazza outside Zanipolo. A sly maneuver assigned this location in front of the School of Saint Mark, now a hospital, which abuts Zanipolo. Colleoni, having commanded the land forces of Venice for twenty-five years, bequeathed his fortune to the Republic on the single condition that it erect an equestrian statue to his memory—on the Piazza San Marco. Since no individual, not even Saint Mark, has a statue on the piazza, another location had to be found. Venetian cunning hit upon the stratagem of erecting the statue in front of not the Church but rather the School of Saint Mark.

In his diary of 1846 Ruskin saluted the displaced statue as the finest equestrian one he had ever seen: ". . . the set of it is the most living, muscular, and resolute conceivable."[34] He admired the foot turned down in the stirrup, the left shoulder flung forward, and the straight legs jutting out from the horse. The face, while "verging on fierceness," seemed from the right-hand side to be "almost mild."[35] Suarès, too, admired the statue's ardor. From a superb pedestal, the commander seemed poised to gallop through Venice, flaunting honesty before people unworthy of it.

No such un-Venetian accent mars the Church of the Frari, whose Franciscans vied with Zanipolo's Dominicans. Santa Maria Gloriosa dei Frari contains tombs more recent than most of those in Zanipolo, including one that Canova designed for Titian, only to have his pupils convert it into his own. The church also boasts a floor of red Verona marble alternating with white Istrian stone to reproduce the pinkish glow of the Doges' Palace.

Basking in this glow are paintings of rare merit. The sacristy to the right of the main altar contains a Madonna by Giovanni Bellini, about which Henry James exclaimed, "Nothing in Venice is more perfect than this, and we know of no work of art more complete."[36] To behold that particular Bellini in the half-light of a fourteenth-century building affords a chance to commune directly with Henry James, for here is a spot that he prized still sheltering a work of art that he adored. "It is impossible to imagine anything more finished or more ripe. It is one of those things that sum up the genius of a painter, the experience of a life, the teaching of a school. It seems painted with molten gems, which have only been clarified by time, and it is as solemn as it is gorgeous and as simple as it is deep."[37] Given James's tendency to inject a note of levity wherever possible, his gravity makes this Bellini stand out. Admirers of James should frequent it for the same reason that devotees of Pater should visit the Morettos in Brescia, for writers so polished seldom proclaimed an allegiance so absolute.

Since 1919 the Frari has housed two magnificent Titians, one of which, *The Assumption of the Virgin*, arrived there only after World War I. Having protested when it hung in the Academy that "its position is an inconceivable scandal," James would have rejoiced that relocation fulfilled its potential to be "one of the mightiest of so-called sacred pictures."[38] Vaudoyer declared of the *Assumption* hanging over the high altar that it dominates the nave like a "grand swell on an organ."[39] The view from the nave annuls the effect of two separate pictures, one of the Apostles swarming below, the other of the Virgin soaring above, for the scenes now blend together, as Titian intended, in a crescendo of red and gold.

Ruskin did not admire the Frari so unreservedly as he did Zanipolo, nor did Suarès write about it. Nevertheless, in 1879 Ruskin pronounced the other Titian in the church, the so-called *Pesaro Madonna*, the finest Titian in Venice.[40] Even more instructive is a comment on the late sixteenth-century tomb of Pietro Bernardo, the pomp of which prompted Ruskin to explain why he esteemed so few paintings and statues executed after 1500. He objected to what he called "posture-making," a tendency that having begun in Perugino triumphed in Michelangelo. It consists of a "painter's considering, in the first place, not how, under the circumstances, they [the figures] would actually have walked, or stood, or looked, but how they may most gracefully and harmoniously walk or stand."[41] While arranging figures gracefully, artists after Perugino forgot about naturalness, so that "ideal" posture banished veracity as a goal of composition. Although conceding that in Michelangelo the habit of "composing attitudes" produced noble effects, the critic held that in lesser men "it ends necessarily in utter lifelessness and abortion."[42] Predictably, Ruskin praised Giotto as the painter who best avoided this "infection," while lauding the Pre-Raphaelites of his own day for having shunned it as well. However unreliable Ruskin may be concerning the Baroque, there can be no doubt that pure posture-making can look as repellent as he says. It is what Suarès objected to in Giulio Romano, and when carried into theology, it inspired the contortions of Counter-Reformation thought. The Protestant in Ruskin and the Jew in Suarès objected alike to posturing as a substitute for truth.

Ruskin elaborated a similar point when he observed that between the thirteenth and the sixteenth centuries designers of tombs began to conceal the coffin. What had begun as a "gloomy mass of stone" became loaded first with religious sculpture and then with flower-work and Virtues to mask its shape: ". . . finally losing its four-square form, it is modelled on graceful types of ancient vases, made as little like a coffin as possible, and refined away in various elegances, till it becomes, at last, a mere pedestal or stage for the portrait statue."[43] The moralist in Ruskin revolted at such disguises: A tomb is a tomb and should announce the body within.

ADRIAN STOKES ON ENSEMBLES OF BUILDINGS

Notwithstanding all that has been said about individual buildings, no writer, not even Ruskin, did justice to the architecture of Venice as a whole. Various obstacles explain the gap. As soon as one leaves the Grand Canal, it is difficult to peruse a sweep of facades except from the lagoon, and, of course, the city lacks a plan. In this Venice is the antithesis of Turin. No Roman camp underlies its meandering lanes, no river bisects its mysterious quarters, and no mountains overlook its huddled houses. When glimpsed from the Campanile of Saint Mark's, Venice becomes a sea of roofs, where scarcely any water peeks through, and still less any plan. A dearth of bird's-eye views may explain why Venice had to wait for Adrian Stokes to bring some coherence into writing about the buildings.

If Rémusat stressed white, Stokes noticed how "Venice excels in blackness and whiteness; water brings commerce between them."[44] To emphasize the water, he examined what it means to glide past a building at canal level instead of to stroll past at head level. As we loll on water, we heed the immobility of buildings, and we descry recesses because water sharpens projections and etches depths more than air does. Tracing essential shapes back to Saint Mark's, he identified the ingredients of Venetian architecture as the oblong panel, the pointed arch, and the braided Byzantine curve. These shapes fuse together in the cylinders of gothic chimney-stacks, with their bell-like tops: ". . . the relationship of oblong, cylinder, and curve is the preeminent subject of Venetian Renaissance architecture, especially preoccupation with rectangular panel and oblong jamb to door and window. . . ."[45]

To show how Venice as we know it dates from the Renaissance, Stokes argued that the city takes its look from rectangles of stone covering campi and bridges. During the Renaissance, "the *liston*, the thin oblong of the most white Istrian stone, was set as an inlay everywhere, marking even the meanest apertures throughout the city."[46] From the traits of Istrian stone, which bleaches in sun and blackens in shade, Stokes explained the play of black and white. Sooty disks and circular holes allow dark interiors, framed by white or blackening stone, to peek through. "Since circular apertures suggest a ship," Stokes suggested that facades had been filled in rather like flanks of a vessel whose ribs show through. "There exists in the Gothic palace windows . . . a constant communication—and a musical one—between the inside and the outside world, as if flambeaux burnt steadily near the balconies and the palace lay open to the night music of the serenade."[47] On the Grand Canal especially, Venetian facades feature dark apertures that look enough like navels to invite prying glances from gondolas below.

Even more than apertures Stokes emphasized a lightness that derives from placing all effects of weight at water level: "So heavy are Venetian buildings at ground or sea level that they appear sometimes to be upside down, especially since it is rare that they are crowned with the usual projecting cornice. The untapering lightness of the upper stories, combined with the narrowness and sheerness of the whole, affords a minimum effect of weight."[48] Weight is so concentrated around the foundations that projections from upper stories resemble "incrustations at the mouths of caves raised above the sea."[49] No building betrays any effort to articulate a system of support. Columns project out beyond the beams they carry, capitals seem unrelated to the architraves above them, and arches spring so steeply from columns as to appear weightless. It is an architecture for fairyland, or rather for a city on water, where weight seems to vanish.

Prose-poet that he was, Stokes hit upon a metaphor to characterize this architecture: The buildings are cliffs, and their openings caves. Venice presents a picture "of rock and cave with strong bulwark at the base, with precipice and scattered encrusted orifice. As in a cliff there is no display of constructive *strength*."[50] These man-made cliffs attain coherence not from seeking to balance forces but from promoting "a commerce, and so an identification, between disparate units."[51] If one quibbles that Palladio injected balance into certain churches, he can be dismissed as a latecomer who perfected facades without altering the face of the city.

Having stressed the tendency of Istrian marble to blacken away from the sun, Stokes focused on the blackness of the gondola: "The gondolier's seaworthy serpent, we have seen, is black between water and sky."[52] Standing in silhouette, the gondolier looms black against an opalescent backdrop, while at the same time, "This solid blackness seems to have been extracted from the dark places of water which therefore now appear lighter."[53] The rhythmic strokes of the gondolier recapitulate "in an orderly succession the crowded flood upon which he works."[54] Although Stokes's writing tends to be compressed, almost telegraphic, his originality shines through. One wishes that he had written before, instead of after, Ruskin, James, and Suarès, so that they could have exploited his ideas. The tragedy of Stokes is that he found no successor, since, like Edward Freeman, he exemplified an amateur tradition that trained no disciples.

TINTORETTO: THE SHAKESPEARE OF VENICE

Of Venice's six greatest painters during the sixteenth century—Carpaccio, Bellini, Giorgione, Titian, Tintoretto, and Veronese—all except Carpaccio and Tintoretto grew up on the mainland, and all except Tintoretto and Veronese left their greatest works elsewhere. Titian painted for the courts of Europe; the greatest assemblage of his works is in the Prado in Madrid. Apart from the *Presentation of the Virgin,* which fills one of the walls of the Academy, and *The Assumption* in the Frari, Titian does not set the tone in Venice. The painter whose masterworks one must come to Venice to see is not Veronese either, but Tintoretto. Art lovers discover Tintoretto in Venice the way they discover Fra Angelico in Florence and Raphael in Rome. His pictures are so abundant as to make Mary McCarthy quip that in Venice the word "Tintoretto" rivals the word for "bill" (*il conto*) as the most frequently heard.[55]

An unlikely motif inspired Tintoretto's admirers all the way from Ruskin and James to Barrès and Vaudoyer: He reminded them of Shakespeare. As Ruskin stated in *The Stones of Venice,* the ungovernable imagination of the "Grotesque Renaissance" permeated the two greatest men (besides Dante) whom Italy produced, Michelangelo and Tintoretto, as it also permeated Shakespeare.[56] In his first travel essay on Italy, the twenty-nine-year-old Henry James chimed in: "You get from Tintoret's work the impression that he *felt,* pictorially, the great, beautiful, terrible spectacle of human life very much as Shakespeare felt it poetically. . . ."[57] In 1920 Jean-Louis Vaudoyer tried to specify wherein the similarity lies: "It would be tempting to try to make a parallel between Tintoretto and Shakespeare; to show in one and the other a blend of strength and grace, of mystery and affirmation, of transports and failures, of drama and fairy-play; a sort of divination amidst pain; and a background of robust sadness, which is never discouragement but is, if you will, a state of peaceful revolt, comparable to the mighty movements of the sea, to the pathos-filled games of clouds. . . ."[58] By inciting writers to forge the grandest images, Tintoretto reminds one of his younger English contemporary. The metaphors presuppose no parallels between scenes in Shakespeare and those by Tintoretto, for the comparison lies rather in similarity of overall impact. Both artists featured interactions of light and dark, both combined the grandiose and the intimate, and both overshot the mark from time to time in picturing extremes.

Maurice Barrès construed the parallel even more majestically when he added to the name of Shakespeare those of Michelangelo, Beethoven, and Balzac, calling them the "sublime rams" who had butted their heads against the ultimate barriers of human ignorance.[59] Having tried to imagine Tintoretto's deathbed vision, which he likened to Beethoven's desire to regain his hearing, he decided that no one mind could have conceived all the figures in Tintoretto's *Crucifixion*.

Of English writers, Ruskin was temperamentally best equipped to interpret Tintoretto. Two letters of September 1845, in which he recorded his discovery of the School of San Rocco, announced a passion that would last a lifetime: "He [Tintoretto] took it so entirely out of me today that I could do nothing at last but lie on a bench and laugh. . . . Tintoret don't [sic] seem to be able to stretch himself till you give him a canvas forty feet square—and then he lashes out like a leviathan, and heaven and earth come together."[60]

The enthusiasm ignited in that first encounter inspired fervent pages in *Modern Painters*, culminating in a twenty-five-page synopsis of the fifty-two paintings in the School of San Rocco, where he explained that the painter had executed these canvases to show in the dark.[61] Knowing of no other great master who had consented to paint for a room "plunged into almost total obscurity,"[62] he invoked the absence of daylight to explain the sketchiness of what he called "scene-painting." Ruskin marveled at the rapidity with which Tintoretto had worked, praising his ability to sketch a figure in ten strokes, a tree in two. Ranking San Rocco with the Sistine Chapel and with the frescoes of the Campo Santo of Pisa as the three greatest ensembles of wall painting in existence (he did not mention the Arena

Chapel by Giotto in this context), Ruskin poured out his affection in some of the most tightly argued of all his pages. His synopsis of the paintings leaves the reader as breathless as do the paintings themselves; the writing is an exercise in Tintorettesque gigantism. Yet, when he reached *The Crucifixion,* he concluded demurely, "I must leave this picture to work its will on the spectator; for it is beyond all analysis, and above all praise."[63] Coming from the most indefatigable of praisers, there could be no finer salute.

Having warned that Ruskin left nothing for others to say about Venice, Henry James took up the challenge by penning his own encomium to Tintoretto. What appealed to James was the painter's willingness to visualize a scene as though he were a novelist: "It was the whole scene that Tintoret seemed to have beheld in a flash of inspiration intense enough to stamp it ineffaceably on his perception; and it was the whole scene, complete, peculiar, individual, unprecedented, that he committed to canvas with all the vehemence of his talent."[64] Tintoretto possessed a literary imagination capable of dissolving the tension between real and ideal: "The homeliest prose melts into the most ethereal poetry—the literal and the imaginative fairly confound their identity."[65] However much one may admire Henry James, one must confess to a degree of surprise at his homage to Tintoretto. Since James was hardly given to depicting scenes on the scale of *The Crucifixion,* where in his fiction is one to look for traces of Tintoretto? Evidently it was not the outsized works as such, but rather intimate details within them, like the donkey cropping palm fronds behind the cross, that fascinated James. Although our ignorance about Tintoretto exceeds even that about Shakespeare, James, like Ruskin, declared the painter's life to have been "one of the most intellectually passionate ever led."[66] As with Shakespeare, Tintoretto provoked writers to read their own genius into his. And deservedly so, for James shared with Tintoretto a certain sketchiness, a fondness for odd angles and bizarre perspectives, a liking for contrasts of light and shade, and a focus on minor characters. The wonder of everyday things excited both artists.

Ten years later, James took another crack at describing the School of San Rocco. Having complained of the poor light and the lack of visitors, he pontificated, "Solemn indeed is the place, solemn and strangely suggestive, for the simple reason that we shall scarcely find four walls elsewhere that inclose within a like area an equal quantity of genius. The air is thick with it and dense and difficult to breathe; for it was genius that was not happy, inasmuch as it lacked the art to fix itself for ever. It is not immortality that we breathe at the Scuola di San Rocco, but conscious, reluctant mortality."[67]

The lament about Tintoretto's wrestling with mortality climaxes a page about the "fitful figures that gleam here and there out of the grey tapestry (as it were) with which the painter has hung all the walls."[68] It was typical of James to elide impressions from many pictures, focusing on none, while alluding to all. It is only too evident that he never read Bernard Berenson on how to describe pictures one at a time. Of the *Crucifixion* James wrote, "It is true that in looking at this huge composition you look at many pictures; it has not only a multitude of figures but a wealth of episodes; and you pass from one of these to the other as if you were 'doing' a gallery. Surely no single picture in the world contains more of human life. . . . It is one of the greatest things in art; it is always interesting."[69]

Although James may seem a miniaturist compared to Tintoretto, the novelist, too, contrived to fit many scenes into one composition. He, too, strove to be "always interesting," and if he knew less of ordinary people than Tintoretto did, he discerned light and shade equally well in those he did know. Tintoretto's ambition stirred James as deeply as did the prodigality and energy. To a young American dismayed by a certain effeteness in Europeans, Tintoretto brought a breath of fresh air, for this most visionary of Venetians was also the most down-to-earth.

Another gifted English essayist, the liberal historian John Richard Green, celebrated Tintoretto's love of the common man. Having observed the differences between the marble School of San Rocco and the brick Church of the Frari across from it, Green pointed out what they have in common. In the same way as the Franciscans rejected the "caste-spirit" of the thirteenth century, Tintoretto repudiated the caste-spirit of the late sixteenth century, a spirit that honored men for "aesthetic refinement and intellectual power," but not for common humanity.[70] Tintoretto glorified peasants in paintings from the gospel, infusing heaven into everyday life. Green saw in

Tintoretto not a titan wrestling to win a deathless reputation but a visionary striving to convey the message of the New Testament. In Tintoretto as in the Bible, "the poetry lies in the strange, unearthly mingling of the commonest human life with the sublimest divine."[71]

A more cautious approach came from the usually audacious John Addington Symonds. Whereas Tintoretto roused Ruskin and James to pen one purple passage after another, the painter moved Symonds to write as plainly as possible. Several times in the course of five pages, Symonds confessed that he could not specify how Tintoretto achieved his effects. The Christ standing before Pilate in San Rocco looks divine, but Symonds could not say why. He extolled the depiction of Jonah being belched from the whale's mouth—it seemed to anticipate William Blake—and he hailed the "indescribable hermaphroditic genius" who tempts Christ in *The Temptation of Christ*.[72] Having called *The Marriage of Bacchus and Ariadne* in the Doges' Palace "the most perfect of all modern attempts to realise an antique myth," he refused to expound its wonders because, "It is well to leave the very highest achievement of art untouched by criticism, undescribed."[73] Although Ruskin had likewise fallen silent before the *Crucifixion*, before the other pictures he unrolled one mighty period after another. One does not know which is more compelling, Ruskin's rhetoric or Symonds's reticence, for Tintoretto invites one both to rhapsodize and to fall rapt. In profusion and daring he surpasses what even the fondest expect of Venice, for he imagined a pictorial world to rival the real one. That may be why the Goncourt brothers and Suarès ignored Tintoretto; for them, the real city was enough.

As if to climax all these reactions, the novelist Richard Aldington told an anecdote about a visit to the School of San Rocco in the 1920s. Accompanied by a witty and ebullient friend, he expected his companion to wax flippant after they had toured the floors separately. All his friend could mumble was, "Let's go. I feel as if I'd read all Shakespeare's plays in an hour."[74]

MISGIVINGS

So powerful is the enchantment of a first-time visit to Venice that some visitors never tear themselves away. O'Faolain invoked the figure of Frederick Rolfe, alias Baron Corvo, to personify the spell of Venice turned Circe; people who decide to prolong a stay should beware of "going Corvo." As O'Faolain told it, in 1907 "Corvo was taken to Venice for a brief holiday; refused to leave it, piled up debts, was reduced to pauperdom; thrown out of his hotel; rejected by his friends; tramped around his beloved city in the winter night like a homeless cat; got pneumonia, recovered; died and left this, his last wonderful tribute to the Circe who had killed him."[75] The tribute is Corvo's novel, *The Desire and Pursuit of the Whole* (written 1909–10), which chronicles fear of conspirators who might force him to leave Venice. Too paranoid to make an observant writer, too monomaniacal to notice subtleties or to invent comparisons, Corvo stands as a warning against obsessive love of a single place.

A more attractive mode of Venice-mania seized another Englishman, Horatio Brown, only six years older than Corvo, who lived in Venice from 1879 until his death in 1926. Lore gleaned from his gondolier filled his *Life on the Lagoons* (1884), the first of his many works about everyday life in Venice. It was he who without having read Corvo's manuscript pronounced it unfit to publish because it insulted its author's benefactors.

Brown's lifelong attachment found a counterpart in that of the French novelist Paul Morand, who assembled jottings of sixty-five years in *Venises* (1971). Not a narrative like Régnier's *L'Altana*, but a collection of incidental pieces, the book includes some memorable aphorisms. About other cities aphorisms might seem an insult, but in Venice they emphasize the uniqueness. Here are three of them:

> "Squeezed in the *rii* of Venice like a bookmark between the pages; certain streets are so narrow that Browning complained that in them he could not open his umbrella."
>
> "The vultures of Venice are the cats."
>
> "The Venetian dialect is distinguished by its use of the letter Z; the Grand Canal itself forms a Z."[76]

Morand scoured Venice like a cat, gleaning scraps of meaning.

For Germans the exponent of ambiguity about Venice was Thomas Mann, who published his most famous novella, *Death in Venice,* in the year of Corvo's death. This story of the deliquescence of a German scholar amid the stink of Venice is the best-known warning about such perils. Gustav Aschenbach let a lifetime of discipline ebb away as he drifted along the canals and tasted the languor of the Lido. Infatuation with a beautiful Polish boy so upset him that he succumbed to disease from the East. Although Mann included passages worthy of a travel essayist, his archness and distance make him unreliable as a guide. His irony illuminates German self-doubt better than it does Venetian aplomb.

Mann's novella echoed the ambivalence that Vernon Lee felt toward this siren city. Her first and last collections of travel essays each contain a piece that expounds misgivings about the city. The essay in *Genius Loci* (1899) tells of a quest for one spot in Venice that would epitomize the city. She found her symbol in the leather coat of Admiral Francesco Morosini, which abides in the Arsenal Museum among other relics of his campaign in Greece during the 1680s. It was during his victorious assault on Athens in 1687 that a Venetian shell blew up the Parthenon. As Lee pondered the labels about capture of cannon and conversion of Turkish prisoners, it dawned upon her that Admiral Morosini had contrived Venice's last success in the East. Being the last outpost of the Alexandrian world, Venice lost her *raison d'être* when she surrendered the Peloponnesus to the Turks in 1715. "From that moment, and despite all lingering independence and Doges and Councils, Venice was merely a dead city from past times—a provincial town, differing in beauty and oddity only from those of the mainland; ready for Austrians; preparing for Cook and his tourists."[77]

The deficiencies of the lagoon permeate an essay of her final collection, *The Golden Keys* (1925). Writing just before World War I, she summed up generations of misgivings about Venice in a sentence that oozes along like the watery state it describes. Twenty-five years before Jean-Paul Sartre, she evoked what he would call the "viscous," that gelatinous condition between liquid and solid which for her typified Venetian laxity: ". . . all the dead greatness and the happiness which has never really been, and the crumble of endless neglect and the creepy life of obscure baseness, seem all to be in their ooze [of the Venetian waters], never thoroughly rinsed by the storms and the tides and sending up faint miasmas in which the soul fevers and dissolves, as it rocks to and fro, vaguely queasy with the faint lurch of the gondola and its inhumanly slow progress."[78] The city was too liquid, too full of "shimmering colours and sliding forms," in a word too viscous, for her to grasp any of them with the fixity that pleased her.[79] Venice sapped any desire to impose form.

A brilliant summing up came from William Hazlitt, who concluded his trip of 1825 in Venice. Juggling opposites with aplomb, he discerned in Venice a precarious balance between elements that elsewhere never joined. The artificiality of the setting instilled artifice into the city's soul. "Man, proud of his amphibious creation, spared no pains to aggrandize and embellish it, even to extravagance and excess. . . . Venice is loaded with ornament, like a rich city-heiress with jewels. It seems the natural order of things. Her origin was a wonder: her end is to surprise. . . . Herself an anomaly, she reconciles contradictions, liberty with aristocracy, commerce with nobility, the want of titles with the pride of birth and heraldry. A violent birth in nature, she lays greedy, perhaps ill-advised, hands on all the artificial advantages that can supply her original defects. Use turns to gaudy beauty; extreme hardship to intemperance in pleasure. From the level uniform expanse that forever encircles her, she would obviously affect the aspiring in forms, the quaint, the complicated, relief and projection. The richness and foppery of her architecture arise from this. . . ."[80]

"The richness and foppery of her architecture"—Ruskin and Stokes expounded this theme with endless inventiveness. "Her end is to surprise"—this is the motif of Suarès and Régnier, of James and the Goncourt brothers. Ornament as the "natural order of things"—this summarizes the objections of the prude Spencer and the realist Rémusat. "Intemperance in pleasure" alarmed Thomas Mann and repelled Vernon Lee, while the "amphibious" character of marble built on water fascinated everyone. The oddities of Venetian existence boiled down to a necessity for humans to supply all needs in a city whose only resource is water. Only by exalting what is man-made could such a city survive: "The want of simplicity and severity in Venetian taste seems owing to this, that all here is factitious and the work of art: redundancy again is an attribute of commerce, whose eye is gross and large, and does not admit of the *too much;* and as to irregularity and want of fixed principles, we may account by analogy at least for these, from that element of which Venice is the nominal bride, to which she owes her all, and the very essence of which is caprice, uncertainty, and vicissitude!"[81]

"Caprice, uncertainty, vicissitude"—these catchwords recall Venice for all who distrust her watery ways. Suarès stated the notion succinctly when he called the Grand Canal "a liquid meadow in the Champs-Elysées of Neptune."[82] Although as a Frenchman he must have had in mind the Champs-Elysées of Paris, he was also imagining Venice as a kind of Elysian Fields on water. For others, like Vernon Lee, the waters seemed more mephitic than paradisical. More than any other city, this one evokes not debates but epiphanies.

8

Tuscan Art on the Venetian Plain: Padua

CITY OF THE BULL

Padua is the only major city in northern Italy that virtually no foreign writer has loved. It is a city that invites carping, raillery, and downright satire, notwithstanding its possession of three or four supreme works of art and one of the most venerable universities in Europe. Padua disappoints partly because it seems so different from Venice. Earthy Padua, the City of the Bull, displays little of the water-born poetry of its neighbor. It is as though travelers coming to or from Venice reserve their capacity for reverie for the City of the Lagoons, so that the dominant note of writing about Padua is deprecation, even disdain. The only writer who preferred Padua to Venice was Stendhal, when in 1817 friends at the Caffè Pedrocchi amused him better than those in Venice. This confirms yet again that Stendhal was not a sightseer of wide range; a *bon vivant* rather, to whom Italy meant above all his beloved of the moment and the dazzle of opera.

Although Padua has inspired no lyrics, it has prompted plenty of satire. Suarès waxed eloquent making fun of the city's ponderosity: "Heavy and doltish, Badova rather than Padova—the Paduans do have something Batavian [i.e., Dutch] about them—Padua is under the sign of the Bull; the university is named 'il Bò.' How they must eat here! The horse of Gattamelata himself belongs in a butcher shop."[1] Although many of Suarès's grievances apply equally to Bologna, another earthy city of learning, somehow a lesser Bologna next door to Venice offends in a way that the larger one astride the

Via Emilia does not. Suarès sneered at the arcades of Padua for featuring short, thick pillars, which look like wool mufflers guarding abandoned chapels.[2] All of the buildings huddle, he complained, the only vertical accents being feeble minarets among the domes of Il Santo and Santa Giustina. This heaviness he saw reflected in a native son, the Roman historian Livy, whose "slow, thick, solemn, and solid" prose shows lots of muscle but few nerves.[3] Hardly what one would expect from the university town of Venice! It is as though Padua wants to proclaim affinity to the earth in contrast to Venice's marriage to the waters.

On a visit to Petrarch's home at Arquà, Vernon Lee unloosed one of those backward glances at which she excelled. She recounted how moisture from the canals permeated a spring day: ". . . the returning heat has sucked fogs from all this soaking green country of reclaimed swamp and never-ending canal, making the pavement of Padua wet till noon, and the great loggias of its public palace clammy as with historical horrors; and wrapping the fields at sunset, and our souls also, with a dank cere-cloth of cold vapours."[4] The earthiness of Padua had something to do, she implied, with warding off an encroaching swamp.

SUARÈS ON DONATELLO

"That cauldron of brick, the *Santo*, bubbling with silver domes," Maurice Hewlett called the church that is the principal pilgrimage site of northern Italy.[5] There on any day of the week one may witness the lame, the sick, and the helpless thronging the altar of a wonder-working saint, who in the 1220s dared challenge the tyrant Ezzelino. Valery noted a quaint detail to emphasize the drawing power of the saint. Even though the French had sacked the church in 1797, thirty years later it had accumulated enough new treasure to require two Dalmatians to serve as watchdogs, who in June 1826 had just nabbed a thief, who had hidden in the church at closing time.[6] Because thousands more masses were requested than altars or priests could accommodate, a papal bull had authorized giant masses (*messoni*) to be said near the end of the year, each to count for a thousand ordinary ones.[7] Upon glimpsing the tongue of Saint Anthony, Valery commented that, even if less eloquent than that of Cicero, it had aroused far more devotion.

Il Santo might be a mere curiosity did it not house around its main altar a dozen masterworks by Donatello. Already in his sixties, from 1443 to 1453 Donatello labored to complete castings for the high altar of Il Santo, which was dismantled in the mid-seventeenth century only to be reassembled in the nineteenth. Tucked away in what must be the most unlikely abode of any supreme masterpiece, these reliefs scarcely get noticed. Kenneth Clark, at least, had the wit to affirm that they "seemed equal to the Giottos [of the Arena Chapel], and with the Masaccios of the Carmine [in Florence], to be the bedrock of European art."[8]

Most of the writers who might have extolled these works did not. Although Ruskin admired Donatello in Florence and wrote at length about the Giotto frescoes a mile away, he never mentioned these works of comparable importance. Symonds and James bypassed Padua, as did Barrès and Régnier. In 1913 a German art historian making his first trip to Italy succumbed to Donatello in Padua. Although, as we shall see in Verona, Karl Scheffler disliked most Renaissance art, he applauded the tension between medieval fervor and Renaissance grace that he saw in Donatello's reliefs. His notion that Donatello was half-German helped him to recognize the uniqueness of the rose-marble *Entombment* behind the high altar. He proclaimed it "beautiful and strong enough to kneel before; the heart's blood of a mighty primitive is in it, the great German-Gothic fervor."[9] However extravagant the rhetoric, at least Scheffler knew how to use his eyes, for Donatello's *Entombment*, itself entombed near the saint's relics, is one of the most expressive reliefs in European art.

Apart from Scheffler, it fell to the satirist of the City of the Bull, André Suarès, to laud Donatello's reliefs. For him Donatello was a Rembrandt of sculpture who enclosed "the soul in bodies in order to make it easier to touch."[10] Suarès, who seemed so often to fly off on a tangent, here voiced what ought to have been a consensus: "In the Church of Il Santo, which gleams with abusive wealth, Donatello in his old age left the world's most beautiful bas-reliefs. Art can go no further. A work without peer in all of sculpture, in which the supreme modeller shows what a painter he could be in bronze or stone."[11] No other bas-reliefs reminded Suarès so forcibly of painting; Mantegna drew inspiration from them, while those masters of line, Verrocchio and Pollaiuolo, might as well have. No flat sculpture attained the intensity expressed in the *Entombment* until Auguste Préault modeled his *Massacre* in the 1830s. Donatello inscribed on the Virgin's face a grief that can only be called expressionistic. "It is a solid painting, which has all the depth it needs. The crowd, the action, the passions, the characters, everything is seen in relief; everything is declared with gestures; the inner mystery is revealed by movement; in a word everything is incarnated into matter. Or rather, there is no matter any more, to such an extent the energy of life has light and naiveté."[12] Here Suarès announced his ideal of having energy become sheer light so as to incarnate itself in matter.

As if one tribute were not enough, Suarès also looked at Donatello's statue of Gattamelata with fresh eyes. The Frenchman had the unique good fortune to arrive when workmen were cleaning the bronze, so that he could scramble up to look Gattamelata in the face. This is what he saw: "Out of Gattamelata Donatello made the old Roman general who lacks genius, as he lived in every century, Vespasian or Fabius the Cunctator, Crassus or Sforza. To begin with, he wanted him to be of peasant stock: an old ploughman on horseback, aged about sixty, when the man of ambition has no mercy left. A huge square head, with thick bones, vulgar ears, no doubt hairy with couch-grass: neither intelligence nor pride prevail in this face, but rather invincible stubbornness."[13] Donatello's talent as a military portraitist came into focus when Suarès commented on the sagging cheeks of the old general, the cheeks of a man who drinks. The mouth lacks teeth. The fat, sensual nose, narrow at the nostrils, and the thin upper lip above a fat lower one suggest a man who is "tired and strong like an old rock, long battered by the tide. He has no pity. He has no cruelty. . . . Amid the cries and flames of slaughter, on the evening of a sack, he drinks a double pint of old wine. He is implacable and sweet-tongued. And that perhaps is why Erasmus of Narni was given the name of Gattamelata, which means Honey-Cat."[14] Donatello's skill at portraiture found an equal in Suarès, who was always alert to a psychological nuance that proclaims genius. To stand face-to-face with Gattamelata epitomized for him what Italy, and only Italy, could offer.

Suarès grew sarcastic in the nearby Church of Santa Giustina, which boasts four bulbous domes not unlike those of Il Santo. "An idea of fierce raillery grabs the imagination, beset by the pompous ugliness of this church, coiffed with minarets and turbans. One envisions Monsieur de Sade installed as guard of a seraglio by Napoleon himself: he makes his entrance into this bathhouse of blinding brilliance at the head of black ulemas, greeted by a guild of white eunuchs."[15] The idea of Napoleon striding into this church, in which the Marquis de Sade supervises a harem, is too delicious. Lofty Corinthian columns meet in arches that suggest a well-lighted prison by Piranesi, making it just the sort of place that the Marquis de Sade deserved as an asylum. And the luminous grandeur makes it no less suited than the cathedral of Milan to house Napoleon's ego.

Suarès's sally against the "mosque" of Santa Giustina caused him to overlook the remarkable floor, which stretches in lozenges of black, red, and white marble for almost a hundred meters. Having quoted President de Brosses's remark of the 1740s that this is perhaps the most beautiful, or at least the best preserved, floor in Italy, Rémusat wryly added that such would still be the case if the Austrians had not stabled the horses of a cavalry regiment here for six months in 1848.[16] Suarès was too busy looking up at the well-lighted columns to notice the splendor at his feet, nicked though it still is by those unwelcome hooves. Nor did he notice an altarpiece by Veronese, which Vaudoyer deemed that artist's most beautiful, "a festive painting, which spreads its huge bouquet of warm colors above the High Altar and gladdens the whole church."[17] For all his acumen, Suarès perceived only what struck his fancy or goaded his wit, so that like his model Barrès he could overlook works of stunning beauty that did not fit the metaphor of the moment. Fortunately, he chanced upon the Donatellos of Padua at just the right moment to convince us that they had been waiting four and a half centuries for his visit.

FRESCOES

If Padua does not advertise Donatello's reliefs, the same can no longer be said of Giotto's frescoes in the Scrovegni Chapel near the Roman Arena. Ever since Ruskin wrote a picture-by-picture account of them in the 1850s, they have received all the acclaim one could wish.[18]

Yet it was not always so. In 1857 Rémusat had to sidle past laundry drying on fruit trees in order to contact a servant of the orchard's owner.[19] Even more disconcerting is Ruskin's report of 1846 that "at Padua the rain beats through the west window of the Arena chapel, and runs down *over* the frescoes."[20]

Far from extolling all the frescoes, Ruskin dismissed half a dozen of them as barely worth noticing. Of *The Massacre of the Innocents* he wrote, "Of all the series, this composition is the one which exhibits most of Giotto's weaknesses. All early work is apt to fail in the rendering of violent action: but Giotto is, in this instance, inferior not only to his successors, but to the feeblest of the miniature-painters of the thirteenth century; while his imperfect drawing is seen at its worst in the nude figures of the children."[21] Ruskin's admiration for Giotto the Naturalist rested on the assumption that in most of his work he showed "a juster understanding of the probable facts than most other painters."[22]

The climax, written in 1860, sounded a warning that would pervade Ruskin's writings for the next twenty years. Giotto reminded the Englishman of everything that was wrong with modernity: "The work to which England is now devoting herself withdraws her eyes from beauty as her heart from rest; nor do I perceive any revival of great art to be possible among us while the nation continues in its present temper. As long as it can bear to see misery and squalor in its streets, it can neither invest nor accept human beauty in its pictures. . . ."[23]

Ruskin would not concede that Giotto might have witnessed ugliness and cruelty to match any that beset Londoners in 1860. His oversight was corrected by a scholar of Irish and Italian descent, who delighted in anecdotes about Giotto. Walter Starkie collected stories not only from Vasari but also from Dante, some of which deserve retelling. One day when Dante came to watch Giotto at work in the Scrovegni Chapel, he noticed the painter's children playing on the ground and commented, "They were as ugly as himself, and I wonder that the creations of his brain were so much more beautiful than his own children."[24] Equally telling is Giotto's remark after being knocked off his feet by a herd of pigs: "The pigs are quite right; when I think how many thousands of crowns I have earned with their bristles, without ever giving them a bowl of soup."[25] Likening Giotto's "gentle roguishness" to that of Boccaccio, Starkie observed that Giotto worked best whenever scripture was vague enough to allow him to envision his own scenes. The angels weeping over the Entombment, flying "hither and thither like frightened birds before the storm, and their bodies twisted in agony," recurred to Starkie even in moments of gaiety.[26]

Karl Scheffler believed like Ruskin that the first discoverers of any vision express it more purely than successors can. Having gazed long and hard at the Arena Chapel, he pronounced all subsequent Renaissance painting, and especially that of Mantegna, incapable of addressing the soul. Yet he noticed that the Arena Chapel disappoints at first glance because it lacks unity; it is too motley to cohere.[27] One must examine individual frescoes to discover what a revolution Giotto wrought: He made pictorial space compete with real space. Scheffler hailed this as the first wall painting to be anything other than decorative. For the first time walls bore framed pictures that did not enhance the architecture but rather competed with it, the pictures aiming not to divert the onlooker but to instruct him.

Scheffler showed his immersion in German categories when he construed Giotto as the first "sentimental" artist, in the sense that Friedrich Schiller had contrasted with "naive." Giotto's figures betray a self-awareness that lacks the divine un-self-consciousness of ancient art. They stand ready to "sentimentalize" a world that the ancients had naively accepted. As Scheffler put it, "Earlier man was in the world, now the world is in man."[28]

Scheffler's appraisal seems all the more haunting when one considers that already in 1912 he detected the beginnings of industrial renewal that would spoil the medieval atmosphere. The following sentences from before World War I ring like a prophecy: "It seems as if Italian cities like Padua, in which a strong reflection of the Middle Ages is still alive, will become more or less Americanized in the next decades. One already sees in the mind's eye factories and worker's suburbs. In Italy this development will produce many unpleasant effects because of the glaring contrast between the old loveliness and the new ugliness."[29] Not even Suarès waxed so prophetic as this.

A brief tribute to Giotto came from another refugee from modernity, Evelyn Underhill, who sought in Italy a beauty England could no longer offer. True to her talent as a miniaturist, she reduced the overall impression of the Scrovegni Chapel to essentials: ". . . the whole chapel is perhaps the most satisfactory bit of colour I have ever seen. . . . Their first impression is of marvelous blueness, tempered by a very gentle gold; and then of serious persons, substantial and yet unearthly, who are static in a blue world."[30] Underhill, who in Brescia and Bologna showed herself very sensitive to sculpture, judged the bronzes of Donatello in Il Santo to be "superb but unemotional," while reserving her ultimate praise for the women of Padua: "The handsomest race of women I have ever seen. They grow old beautifully, many of their faces looking like carved ivory; and they drape their heads like ancient Greeks."[31] Even she did not realize how unique is Padua's claim to possess in Giotto and Donatello two of the supreme masterpieces of Tuscan art, works which in Kenneth Clark's phrase form the "bedrock of European art." Only Florence can make a similar assertion.

9
Verona, Epitome of Italy

CONTRADICTIONS

All travel writing probes the interaction of opposites. The cities that fascinate writers most are those in which opposites intermingle unexpectedly: water and marble in Venice, civilization and decay in Mantua, wealth and poverty in Genoa. Verona offers a veritable fireworks of commingled opposites, for as one German art historian put it: "Verona is a city of the mountains and lies in the plain. Verona is a city of the North and lies in the South. Verona has a double soul: it is a city of coldness of the will and it is a city of warmth and of beauty at the same time."[1] Arthur Moeller van den Bruck, who went on to proclaim German uniqueness, wrote this about a city that has inspired many such remarks.

Verona reminded northerners of home more than did any other city in northern Italy, putting them in mind of their own culture and prompting them to propound lessons for England, France, and especially Germany. After Ruskin recommended that Verona's palaces be imitated in Victorian Britain, Scheffler grumbled that they had been too much imitated in Bismarck's Germany. Freeman made the Roman Arena and the Porta dei Borsari an occasion to deplore the transitional character of Roman architecture, dismissing most of it as a thousand-year-long stagnation between Greek and Romanesque practices. Maurel denounced Verona's loyalty to various German masters, from Theodoric the Ostrogoth and Alboin the Lombard to Pepin, Berengar, Otto I, and the dreaded Ezzelino. Verona was for him a Pisa—another city with a superb location, which had kept selling out to German conquerors only to fall into the hands of Florence, just as Verona had succumbed to Venice.

Why should Verona have inspired such uneasiness, when Turin, Milan, and Venice did not? Verona owes some of its uniqueness to its being a gateway city. Germans, especially those arriving from Bavaria or Prussia, have usually entered Italy via the Brenner Pass, which debouches in Verona. It was here that many Germans, such as Goethe, first glimpsed Roman ruins, red-tiled roofs, and a city built of marble and brick.

As if hints of places further south were not enough, Verona boasts ensembles of buildings that prompt comparisons among disparate epochs. Verona is preeminently a city of ensembles. The Piazza dell' Erbe, with its faded outdoor frescoes, its market stalls, and its town hall, is one such. The bridges over the Adige form another ensemble, and so do the outdoor tombs of the Scaliger family. Most compelling of all is the Piazza Brà (whose name derives from the Latin word *pratum*, for meadow, as in Padua's Prato della Valle) with its Roman arena, Roman gate, and several stunning Renaissance palaces. The compactness of this ensemble awed the historian Thomas Babington Macaulay, who described it in a letter of 1856: "You have an amphitheatre which very likely Pliny may have frequented; huge old palaces and towers, the work of princes who were contemporary with our Edward the First; and most charming and graceful architecture of the time of Michelangelo and Raphael; and all this within a space not larger than Belgrave Square."[2]

Of all pronouncements that Verona has elicited, none is more stirring than a passage composed by Ruskin for a lecture of 1870. Ruskin's love of Verona dated from his summer alone in Italy in 1845. Already in September of that year he could write to his father that about Verona he had always felt "there is more poetry than about any other city whatsoever in Europe—Venice itself not excepted, for Venice at its best, had a twang of manufacture and trade about it which noble Verona was free from. . . ."[3] In the spring of 1869 Ruskin spent two months there collecting materials for a work to be called *The Stones of Verona*. Unfortunately, this companion piece to *The Stones of Venice* never advanced beyond the twenty pages of a lecture entitled "Verona and Its Rivers" (1870).

The lecture opens with a description of a hilltop view from northeast of the city: "Now, I do not think that there is any other rock in all the world, from which the places and monuments, of so complex and deep a fragment of the history of its ages can be visible, as from this piece of crag, with its blue and prickly weeds. For you have thus beneath you at once, the birthplaces of Virgil [near Mantua] and Livy [Padua], the homes of Dante [near Verona] and Petrarch and the source of the most sweet and pathetic inspiration of your own Shakespeare [*Romeo and Juliet*]; the spot where the civilization of the Gothic kingdoms was founded on the throne of Theodoric, and where whatever was strongest in the Italian race redeemed itself into life by its league against Barbarossa. You have the cradle of natural science and medicine in the schools of Padua; the central light of Italian chivalry in the power of the Scaligers; the chief stain of Italian cruelty in that of Ezzelin; and, lastly, the birthplace of the highest art; for among these hills, or by this very Adige bank, were born Mantegna, Titian, Correggio, and Veronese."[4] In this passage Ruskin fudged geographical accuracy in order to emphasize historical scope. He knew that the Berici Hills block Padua from view, as they do Petrarch's home in Arquà; he knew that Titian was born out of sight in mountains far to the north of Venice; and he knew that Correggio was born south of the Po. Rhetoric obscures certain historical niceties as well. In calling the Scaligers the "central light of Italian chivalry," he could have meant only the first two of that race, for one of the last two was debauched, while the other murdered his brothers. Nor did he mention other places that Verona scans: Cremona, the home of stringed instruments; Parma, the site of Correggio's glory; Bologna, the mother of universities; or Ferrara, the nurse of epic poets. Yet, if Ruskin's examples are sometimes faulty, his thesis is not: The view across the Lombard Plain embraces a wider range of cultural achievements than perhaps any other in Europe.

What Ruskin admired above all in Verona was its palaces. In lectures delivered at Manchester in 1857, he commended the palaces of Verona as a model for the merchants of England to emulate. They should invest their wealth the way merchants of Verona had done to produce "the loveliest Renaissance architecture of Italy, not disturbed by pride, nor defiled by luxury, but rising in fair fulfillment of domestic service, serenity of effortless grace, and modesty of home seclusion; its richest work given the windows that open on the narrowest streets and most silent gardens."[5] The industrialists of Manchester, most of whom would hear of Verona only from Ruskin, knew that he was delivering lessons learned during long years in Italy. Yet they must have been surprised that not Venice but Verona was the city he chose to embody those lessons: ". . . if I were asked to lay my finger in a map of the world, on the spot of the world's surface which contained at this moment the most singular concentration of art-teaching and art-treasure, I should lay it on the name of the town of Verona."[6]

The Stones of Venice anticipated the sermon to the merchants of Manchester when it praised "the effect which would be produced upon the comfort or luxury of daily life by the revival of the Gothic school of architecture."[7] In a passage that refers equally to Padua, Vicenza, and Verona, Ruskin rejoiced that a visitor to Verona can "still stand upon the marble balcony in the soft summer air, and feel its smooth surface warm from the noontide as he leans on it in the twilight; he can still see the strong sweep of the unruined traceries drawn on the deep serenity of the starry sky, and watch the fantastic shadows of the clustered arches shorten in the moonlight on the chequered floor. . . ."[8] To an unsympathetic ear, this may sound like a schoolboy girding himself to recite *Romeo and Juliet*. Yet it shows Ruskin's sensitivity to changes of temperature no less than of light, and reveals, as does nearly all his writing, his delight whenever the past obtruded upon the present.

The hard-to-please art historian Karl Scheffler likewise found much to ponder in Verona's architecture. Published in the same year as Moeller van den Bruck's *Die italienische Schönheit* (1913), Scheffler's diary reads like a rebuttal of Moeller's effusions. Although Scheffler never quoted Ruskin, he denounced Verona's palaces for being a compromise in which neither the Gothic nor the Renaissance element prevails. Seeing in them a model for the style that German office buildings and apartment houses had adopted during the 1870s, he regretted that "the triviality of imitations" already afflicted the originals.[9] This aversion did not prevent Scheffler from admiring the arcaded courtyards of the churches, and like Rémusat, he lauded the fortifications of Sanmichaeli for showing a "seriousness" that Verona otherwise lacked.[10]

The wittiest cultural critic to interpret Verona was the Irish novelist Sean O'Faolain, who climaxed his *A Summer in Italy* with a thirty-page disquisition on Verona as an epitome of Italy. O'Faolain might have chosen for his motto a line from Henry James: "There are other things in Verona to make it a liberal education to be born there, though that it *is* one for the contemporary Veronese I don't pretend to say."[11] A gap between the education that monuments proffer and natives' disdain of it galled O'Faolain unbearably. Torn between a desire to visit art galleries and a preference for the present, he dramatized the conflict in a dialogue between two aspects of himself. The voice of conscience that he called his *Doppelgänger* looked like "an Oxford don, with a soft full beard that reminded me of A. E. or William Morris or John Ruskin."[12] After a brief encounter at the start of his stay, the don returned in the guise of the Tempter, Beelzebub himself, to discourse on Ruskin. Beelzebub stated that, for all Ruskin's "divine English" and "X-ray eyes," he "loved everything that idealized reality. Byzantine formalisations and Gothic idealisations were right up *his* street. And all that probably came from the fact that he was a mild, lymphatic, shy, poor chap, with no least capacity for human friendship; or, as we know, for love."[13] The Irishman chided Ruskin for mentioning the poor of Venice only once and for alluding to the Austrian siege of 1849 only to lament that a "cannon-ball tore a hole through a Tintoretto."[14]

Even this tirade could not quiet O'Faolain's obsession with the gap between Then and Now. No amount of goodwill could square the vulgarity of contemporary Catholic art with the magnificence of the past, for religious kitsch defied all connection with the grace of San Zeno or the mystery of Sant'Anastasia.[15] The Irishman simply gave up trying to reconcile contemporary vulgarity with medieval or Renaissance perfection. On the one hand, he deplored Ruskin's preaching because it sounded no less sentimental than the most sugary kitsch, and, on the other hand, he found no consolation in the wisdom of the folk, at least not in northern Italy. Verona typified a country where past and present clash forever.

After rejecting all the idols that Italy-worshipers have erected, O'Faolain fell back on equating Italian reality with Italian art. His sightseeing culminated in a visit to the gallery of Verona, in which he scanned faces of Madonnas and saints for resemblances to everyday Italians. "I am quite sure a great, if not the greater, part of the pleasure these pictures gave to the people who first saw them was on the lines of 'Will ye look at Beppo in an angel's wings! The dead spit of him'."[16] Without minimizing the role of idealization, O'Faolain hailed realism as a kind of magic that transformed "a simple wench . . . into a Madonna."[17] Having for centuries wrought such transformations, today Italian artists no longer do so. That was the nub of O'Faolain's disappointment.

VERONA MARBLE

Mere argumentativeness cannot overshadow the appeal of Verona's buildings, for the city ranks right behind Venice and Milan in the quality of architectural writing it has inspired. This is owing partly to the variety of the buildings and partly to the uniqueness of Verona marble. No other building material roused English writers to quite the degree of enthusiasm as did this pink stone. Quarried north of Verona, the marble is so plentiful as to provide the city with gutters, a fact that astonished Arthur Symons.[18] A generation earlier, J. A. Symonds had exclaimed over the grain of the marble, noting that its name, *mandorlato,* derives from a resemblance to the pink of almond blossoms. Emphasizing its range of colors, he explained why it complements terra-cotta so superbly: "But it [mandorlato] is far from having the simple beauty of a single hue. Like all noble veined stones, it passes by a series of modulations through a gamut of associated rather than contrasted tints. Not the pink of the almond blossom only, but the creamy whiteness of the almond kernel, and the dull yellow of an almond nut may be found in it."[19]

Only Adrian Stokes has described the veining of marble as precisely as Symonds, and even he did not see the white of an almond kernel or the yellow of a nut in this "almonded" stone. In his earliest book, Stokes praised the salmon tint of Verona marble so lavishly that one almost recoils at the sensuality of his language. At sunset the Verona marble of Venice suggested both fire and "the rich pinky flesh of succulent fishes."[20] Some of the most distinctive effects of Venice's buildings he ascribed to "the live colors [of Verona marble] amid the blackening stone,"[21] where the marble supplies what can only be called flesh tones. When used for carving, however, the stone works less well because its surface needs to be polished in a process that removes sharp edges. This made the nimbus above a certain Madonna so chunky as to resemble "an eatable rather than a metal."[22] Stokes's language became even more lush when he compared reflections off darkish stone to those off chocolate. Properly polished Verona marble glows in a way that outshines Carrara stone "with the disconcerting *pointillisme* of its crystals."[23] Although the "eruptive smoothness of good polished Verona" resembles a flower in bloom, its fault lines bar its use for small objects.

Ruskin anticipated both Symonds and Stokes in appreciating Verona marble but differed from both by evoking the mountains that bear it. Standing on his promontory above Verona, he reviewed the regions from which various types come. Nearest to Verona, the stone hardens "first into a limestone having knots of splendid brown jasper in it, as our chalk has flints, and in a few miles more into true marble, coloured by iron into a glowing orange, or pale warm red—the peach-blossom marble, of which Verona is chiefly built: and then as you advance farther into the hills, into variegated marbles, so rich and grotesque in their veinings, and so fancifully lending themselves to decoration, that this last time of my stay at Verona I was quite seriously impeded . . . by involuntary misgivings whether the churches were real churches, or only museums of practical geology. . . ."[24] It was typical of Ruskin to trace marble back to its source and to see in carved stone a lesson in geology. In gliding between natural history and art history, he kept alive the many-sidedness we associate with the Enlightenment. Although a similar breadth of interests animated Charles de Rémusat and Jules Michelet, Ruskin, born a generation later, was the last of the breed. After him, science and art went separate ways.

ROMAN ARCHITECTURE

Veins of color that intertwine in Verona marble recall layers of history that the city has accumulated. From Roman ruins to Theodoric's Palace, from Romanesque churches to the palaces that delighted Ruskin, Verona preserves notable works of art from every period except the Lombard. Such continuity prompted writers to philosophize about the ups and downs of culture. The theme of decline and rebirth focused naturally around the Roman Arena, which boasts the best preserved interior of any after that of Nîmes. For several centuries now, visitors have attended theater performances there. Rémusat delighted so much in the outdoor theatricals that he recommended they be adopted in Paris. Henry James savored a performance in "the vast stony oval [that] rose high against the sky in a single clear, continuous line, broken here and there only by strolling and reclining loungers."[25] This spectacle contributed not a little to the liberal education that he felt Verona offered to all comers. Fifty years earlier at the Congress of Verona (1822), John Hobhouse was dismayed at the alacrity with which the Veronesi had erected a huge statue of "Madonna Verona" inside the Arena to welcome guests of the Austrians.[26] He found this a trifle feckless in a people who had changed rulers three times in the previous twenty-five years.

That connoisseur of church architecture, Edward Freeman, waxed eloquent when he beheld the Arena and the Roman gateway nearby, the Porta dei Borsari. In the Arena he commended the absence of Greek excrescences, praising "the genuine Roman effect" of its massive arches and what he called the "stone carpentry" that supported its "vast and cavernous recesses."[27] The gateway, however, impelled Freeman to expound what he held to be the faults of Roman architecture. He contrasted this second-century gate unfavorably with a fourth-century one, the Porta Nigra of Trier, noting that between the two had come the invention of the arcade. Around A.D. 280 architects of Diocletian's Palace in Split had devised the arcade to solve a problem that had perplexed their predecessors for five hundred years. Until then, Roman architects had found no way to couple Greek columns organically with Roman arches; instead of placing arches atop columns, as at Split, they had plastered Greek pillars onto the face of an arch, where they had no function. Since the arch carried all the weight, Greek fittings reminded Freeman of outdated appurtenances on railroad carriages: "In the Verona gate the Greek features are still there, masking the Roman construction; over the actual openings, over the windows above them, we get unmeaning entablatures and pediments, stone pictures, so to speak, of real entablatures and pediments, like the survivals of the shape of the old post-chaise carved or painted on the modern railway-carriage."[28] "Stone pictures" of Greek elements no longer defaced the Porta Nigra of Trier, where "the remains of the columnar system, the half-columns or pilasters, have sunk into the subordinate place which they hold in Romanesque buildings."[29]

Freeman went on to state his "heretical view that classical Roman architecture is only a transitional stage between one consistent form of construction and decoration in the shape of Greek art and another consistent form of construction and decoration in the shape of Romanesque art."[30] This contention rests on the premise that the arcade solved the problem of how to combine Greek columns with Roman arches so that both carry weight. In the arcades of Split, Romanesque style was born, to be incorporated almost at once into the basilicas from which Christian churches sprang. Impelled, like others in Verona, to generalize to excess, Freeman used the Arena and the gateway to contrast the strengths and weaknesses of Roman architecture. No one else has imputed such depth of meaning to these venerable structures.

And yet the ever-provocative Karl Scheffler was not to be outdone. He fell in love with the Arena because it displayed an "engineer's beauty" from which breathes the anonymity and "transpersonal" identity of an entire people.[31] In Scheffler's eyes Freeman could not have been more mistaken. Not only did Roman architects not copy models, but their originality enabled them to embody a community's will. Whereas Renaissance architects conceived a city in terms of separate classes, individuals, and institutions, only Roman architects knew how to build for an entire people. Such disdain for the individualism of the Renaissance echoed doctrines current in the school of German thought known as *völkisch*. Scheffler lauded the Arena of Verona because it seemed to express the impulse of a whole people, whom it helped to unify. Whereas Jacob Burckhardt had extolled Renaissance individualism for facilitating communal celebration in towns, if not in nations, Scheffler denounced it for hastening the breakdown of society. He yearned for a unity that he saw incarnated in Roman buildings.

THE SCALIGER TOMBS

Just as the Arena is the largest Roman monument left standing north of Rome, so Verona boasts another unique ensemble. The tombs of the Scaliger family stand outdoors at street level behind the Piazza dei Signori. Their placement in the open air impressed even Lord Byron, who remarked to Hobhouse that "such a sepulchre renders the contemplation of death less dreadful than our dreary deep and underground vaults."[32] The young Henry James, who at first found the tombs difficult to comprehend, conceded that "even to the hurried and preoccupied traveller the solemn little chapel-yard in the city's heart, in which they stand girdled by their great swaying curtain of linked and twisted iron, is one of the most impressive spots in Italy. Nowhere else is such a wealth of artistic achievement crowded into so narrow a space; nowhere else are the daily comings and goings of men blessed by the presence of *manlier* art."[33] Written before the sojourn in Rome and Florence that would produce his first novel, this passage owes much to Ruskin.

For the true poet of the Scaliger tombs was none other than the English seer. In the last volume of *The Stones of Venice* he surveyed the four della Scala rulers and their outdoor tombs, tracing a correlation between the growing wickedness of the family and the increasing elegance of their tombs. Instead of fretting over this affront to his belief that great art promotes moral virtue, Ruskin relished all three arrays of statuary. Beholding the tomb of Can Grande, he exulted in the equestrian statue of 1329, whose original was removed in 1910 to the courtyard of the Scaliger Fortress. Like Scheffler after him, Ruskin marveled at "his helmet, dragon-winged and crested with the dog's head, tossed back behind his shoulders, and the broad and blazoned drapery floating back from his horse's breast,—so truly drawn by the old workman from the life, that it seems to wave in the wind, and the knight's spear to shake."[34] Ruskin loved a statue to vibrate.

Praising the inconspicuousness of the tomb, which tops the portal of the church, he enunciated his view of morality in art: "It is not the question whether his wars were just, or his greatness honourably achieved; but whether, supposing them to have been so, these facts are well and gracefully told upon his tomb."[35] It is the sincerity of the artist and not the purity of the subject that elevates art above the common level. This same criterion would lead others to admire the Charterhouse of Pavia and the Malatesta Temple at Rimini, built for monsters by artists of genius. To illustrate Can Grande's modesty, Ruskin pointed out reliefs that recorded victories at the siege of Vicenza and the battle of Piacenza. A century later such scenes would have monopolized an artist's attention, but here they subserved a recumbent statue that expressed its prince's "hope of resurrection."

Ruskin pronounced the tomb of Can Mastino II to be as exquisite as that of his father, except that a statue of Fortitude tended to overshadow the Crucifixion. Otherwise, the array of statues around the canopied figure satisfied the critic's demand for a program of meaning. The final tomb, that of Can Signorio, who was, as Ruskin noted, "twice a fratricide, the last time when he lay upon his deathbed," saw statues of the virtues increased from one to six. This bit of effrontery did not prevent its being "the stateliest and most sumptuous of the three . . . a many pinnacled pile, surrounded by niches with statues of the warrior saints."[36]

Adverting almost twenty years later to Can Signorio's tomb, Ruskin drew a moral from that ruler's obsession to promote his sons at the expense of his brothers: "a prince who had in every way benefited and cared for the city" ordered his two brothers killed so that his children might reign, the second order coming from his deathbed.[37] The outcome belonged in a morality play: "And the end of all was, that one of these children murdered the other, and was driven himself from the throne—so ending the dynasty of the Scalas."[38] Having ceased by 1870 to be a writer on travel and art in order to become a sage, Ruskin proceeded to scold his contemporaries with a bluntness that had been missing from *The Stones of Venice:* "We fancy we are so very sincere ourselves; but the Christian avarice of London commits more murders in a day, than the worst Christian ambition of the Scalas did in their two centuries of power at Verona."[39] As was his wont, Ruskin infused a sense of purpose into an otherwise bewildering monument, so that the Scaliger tombs seem to radiate wisdom. Whatever O'Faolain may say, on this one occasion Ruskin sided with Renaissance vigor against medieval piety. The Jewish feuilletonist Israel Zangwill, who usually sounded as banal as he was pretentious, stated the paradox aptly: "The Scaliger street-tombs in Verona are at least artistically laudable, however ironically their Christian ostensiveness compares with the record of the Family of the Ladder, whose rungs were murdered relatives."[40] If Ruskin all but excused those murders because their perpetrator commissioned great art, the Jewish moralist did not.

Karl Scheffler also took unexpected pleasure in these statues, which seem so un-cemetery-like. The equestrian figure of Can Grande evoked an unlikely comparison: "Something almost clownlike, a kind of circus grotesque has been elevated into a sublimely architectonic and psychologically monumental creation. In exuberant fullness of life the rider chap laughs down from the sarcophagus at the beholder . . . astride a fantastically garbed horse, which has something drolly uncanny about it, something bizarrely monumental."[41] Scheffler's enthusiasm makes Ruskin's seem almost demure.

Scheffler's homage to the Germanic spirit of these statues only confirmed French aversion to them. Both Maurel and Suarès detested the Scaliger tombs as intrusions of German art, which looked as out of place in Italy as Verdi would sound at Bayreuth.[42] Maurel huffed that the later Scaligers lacked "the minimum of taste which would forbid one to climb church spires on horseback."[43]

As might be expected, Suarès proved even more scathing. After denouncing Germans who flocked to Verona, he unleashed his wrath on the Scaligers, who, "with their names of dogs, reigned by the power of rabies."[44] Having chanced upon the tombs at night after a light snowfall, he borrowed from the snow an image that would have appalled Ruskin or Scheffler: "There must be, somewhere in hell, a similar spot for the damned of pride and violence, where the only glimmer is the fire of the snow, those funereal rays which extinguish all color, which disclose the blackness to itself, light which numbs hope and does not warm."[45] Once set baying, Suarès could not call off the hunt. In the "cemetery of the Big Dogs," he envisioned Can Grande as a hunter, whose helmet resembled an eagle that is strangling both its master and the city of Verona.[46] The malevolent bird even turned into the two-headed eagle of the Habsburgs. This hellish vision climaxed with snow burying the burial place of the Scaligers under a blizzard that portended the end of the world. After Ruskin's delight in beauty and James's pleasure in manliness, Suarès conjured up a scene out of Dante. Incapable of provoking a mild response, the Scaliger tombs pushed each writer toward his point of least resistance, Ruskin toward panegyric, Scheffler toward *völkisch* trumpeting, and Suarès toward vilification.

ECSTASY AMONG THE CYPRESSES

Assorted impressions of Verona cohere as in a powerful lens during a stroll in the Giusti Gardens. Their cypresses, which overlook the city from the northeast, so enchanted Goethe that he carried a branch of one through the streets. He adored a tree whose every limb he felt to be striving toward the sky.[47] French writers discerned in the beds and slopes of the gardens not only a haven from change but also a symbol of Italy. Gabriel Faure experienced an almost religious awe before the cypresses, some of which dated back five hundred years. The notion that the upper ones have stared across the plain for all those centuries made them seem guardians of the battlefields that surround Verona. From atop the Giusti Gardens, the peaceable Frenchman recalled the struggle of Constantine against Maxentius, of Theodoric against Odoacer, of Charlemagne against the Lombards, and of the French against the Austrians at Solferino, whose tower may be spied from Verona's heights. As he watched a mist rise from the river to envelop the roofs, essentials stood out. Whereas others exalted the sunshine of Italy for clarifying outlines, Faure lauded the mist for obscuring details.[48]

The stillness of the Giusti Gardens cast a similar spell over Henri de Régnier when he visited them in 1924. The cypresses suggested "something monastic and warlike. They have grown stiff in a kind of vegetable discipline, immoveable in their green without season. I think of their brothers in the Villa d'Este, of their brothers in the great cemeteries of Scutari and Eyoub [near Istanbul]. They exhale a bitter odor."[49] In his calm way Régnier narrated an epiphany of his own atop the gardens: " . . . and suddenly, leaning on the stone balustrade, I feel flooded by an obscure and deep joy, by a kind of happiness composed of that sky and those trees, of that weak plaint of the fountains, of a trembling of foliage, of the damp taste of the air I breathe, made of that solitude and of that silence, and of being there. . . ."[50] Such simple ingredients helped Régnier to grasp the abiding elements of Italy.

Even André Suarès curbed his gall when he entered this sacred precinct. The cypresses, exuding a perfume bitter and "incorruptible" from five hundred years of reaching hungrily for the sky, enthralled him. Foliage brushing statues unveiled bizarre effects: Branches caressed balustrades, three leaves rested on a nymph's bare shoulder, and a maple stroked a bare bosom. "Green water smiles oddly, like a faun, in a basin. Three dolphins, covered with moss, throw high a thread of pure and fresh water. And the damp freshness spreads like a sound in the twilight."[51] The climax of Suarès's stroll, one of the high points of his tour in northern Italy, unrolled as he crested the upper terrace. The city below looked like a dream he had just left behind, while the belvedere itself, when viewed from below, looked like a cap on a colossal head, "a sculpted monster who grimaces at the top of the ascent and who stands out on the hill between the stairways. Caliban has been tamed. He carries lovers and a rare beauty."[52] A sunset put the sky on fire like a forge, while in a bed of flame the river smoked like a sword pulled from an enemy's body: "Verona burns like a pyre of desires. The bells are still. The flames of the star lick the roofs of brick. The city is a torrent of light, which comes to die among the fingers of cypresses."[53]

Just as Verona is a place where historians traced contradictory forces, so the Giusti Gardens seemed to reconcile clashing opposites. The conflicts that streak Verona's history like veins in its salmony marble recede in this place of damp calm. If travel writers need such places in order to focus their impressions, Verona's Giusti Gardens must rank as a favorite retreat. It is a place that helps one understand why Epicurus, the philosopher of refined pleasure, chose to live in a garden.

Part Four
EMILIA-ROMAGNA

10

Literary Ghosts in Parma

STENDHAL IN THE CITY OF CORREGGIO

The task of describing Parma has fallen mainly to the French. From the arrival in 1748 of the Spanish Bourbons, who were in fact half-French, Parma and Paris have shown a special affinity. During the 1760s a French prime minister, Tillot, brought the Enlightenment to Parma, while Parma's ambassador in Paris, the Count d'Argental, was a close friend of Voltaire. Millot, a Jesuit tutor of the crown prince, wrote a textbook of French history that remained standard in France until the 1830s. The abbé de Condillac, philosopher of the primacy of the senses, also served as tutor to the crown prince during the 1760s.

These previous Gallic influences fade beside that of the novelist Stendhal. By choosing Parma as the site of his *Charterhouse of Parma* (1839), he mesmerized all subsequent French visitors. Barrès relived favorite scenes from the novel wherever he turned. Maurel and Faure fell prey to the same excitement, while Jean-Louis Vaudoyer as late as 1950 tried to locate the buildings depicted by Stendhal, including the charterhouse north of the city where the novelist consigned his hero.

A master at elevating disappointment into art, André Suarès defined the malaise that Parma awakens in lovers of Stendhal: "In Parma, one conjures up a First Empire of the provinces. One might say it is the work of a grand duke who wanted to imitate Napoleon and who had drawn up, following the *Memorial of Saint-Helena*, plans for the ugliest, best ordered, most useful and boring city in the universe: a metropolis which occupies the midpoint between a barracks, a hospital, a warehouse, a prison, and a ministry of war. The Farnese were the Napoleons of a huge village."[1] The Parisian could not bear to find in Parma a checkerboard city designed to please a small-town Napoleon. Surely Stendhal must have had something more august in mind. Like other Frenchmen, Suarès searched in vain for traces of Stendhal's characters in a garrison town, whose brownish yellow recalled all too well its famous cheese.

English travelers, by way of contrast, enjoyed Parma as the city of Correggio, a painter whose frescoes scarcely exist anywhere else. Symonds, Hutton, and even Robert Browning went there in quest of Correggio. These two schools of connoisseurship met in André Maurel, who, by delighting equally in Correggio and Stendhal, noticed affinities between them: innocence in pursuit of unattainable love, attraction to youthful beauty, and pioneering of artistic feats, in which Correggio's frescoing of cupolas matched Stendhal's deepening of introspection in fiction. The two masters also concealed sources of their art, while displaying a common faith in the senses. Although Stendhal was far more analytical, introspective, and modern than Correggio, the experiences that he scrutinized were ones that we associate with that painter: sensual love, masculine images of female bodies, and obsession with women as saviors. Vaudoyer confirmed Stendhal's fascination with Correggio by citing a letter that the novelist wrote to Balzac after the latter had reviewed the novel: "The whole character of the Duchess Sanseverina is copied from Correggio (that is, she produces on my soul the same effect as Correggio)."[2] Vaudoyer clinched his argument by observing how a title like *The Charterhouse of Cremona* or *The Charterhouse of Modena* would have fallen flat. Only the city that everyone linked with Correggio could have suited this novel.

As luck would have it, Stendhal attended *lycée* during the years from 1795 to 1799, when the newly founded secondary schools of France taught the philosophy of Condillac in an abbreviated form known as "Ideology." As an adolescent, Stendhal imbibed the notion of the primacy of sensory experience, a notion which as an adult he would see embodied in paintings by Correggio. By an odd coincidence, Parma had hosted Condillac as tutor to its crown prince; even the court printer Bodoni, as he refined the impact made on the eyes by fonts of type, was reflecting Condillac's philosophy. Still another affinity existed between the French painter Pierre-Paul Prud'hon, who studied Correggio in Parma in the 1780s, and Stendhal. Both men elaborated boudoir art into something at once more analytical and more dreamlike. The reveries of female bodies that Correggio painted and Prud'hon emulated inspired some of the obsessions of Stendhal's hero, Fabrice. The two painters and the novelist concurred that our senses shape everything. If intellect merely arranges what the senses have absorbed, no mist of metaphysics will obtrude between what gets observed and what gets depicted.

A similar directness animated another great artist who grew up near Parma. Giuseppe Verdi was born just twenty-five kilometers to the northwest and lived there nearly all his life. Verdi knew how to pour feeling into melodies in a way that echoes Correggio. Verdi's early operas display an exuberance that suggests the tangle of bodies that Correggio painted in the cupola of the cathedral; those angels could be singing a chorus by Verdi. They soar with a virility that foreshadows Verdi's melodies, and both exude an innocence that recalls Fabrice in prison atop the fortress of Parma. Perched above the plain, Stendhal's hero rediscovered a boyish innocence of the kind that permeates the frescoes and streams through Verdi. Something in the air around Parma must induce male spirits to soar. Although Goethe could not have had Correggio in mind when he wrote that the "Eternal Feminine draws us upward," Parma, a city that he never visited, inspired three other artists to make this notion palpable: in paint, in words, and in music.

In his *Life of Stendhal* (1946), the American biographer Matthew Josephson told an eye-opening story about the inception of *The Charterhouse of Parma*. For years Stendhal had enjoyed perusing an Italian manuscript about the Farnese family in the sixteenth century. It told the following tale. As a young man, Alessandro Farnese, the future Pope Paul III, required the protection of his aunt, Vanozze Farnese, to save him from prison. Vanozze was mistress of Cardinal Roderigo Lenzuoli, a favorite of Pope Alexander VI. After the young Alessandro had attacked the escort of his beloved, killing one of the servants and carrying her off for a month, he went to prison, from which he escaped with the aid of his aunt and her lover, who had a rope smuggled to him in the Castel Sant'Angelo. After living in hiding, he won pardon, thanks to intrigues by his aunt, and was duly appointed cardinal at age twenty-five in 1493. He then fell in love with a Roman lady, Cleria, by whom he had two children. Only after her death many years later did he alter his way of life and become Pope Paul III (1534–49), who launched the Counter-Reformation and installed his descendants as rulers of Parma.

Josephson summed up the way in which Stendhal transformed these historical characters: "In *The Charterhouse of Parma* the little Duchy of Parma replaces Rome: he takes the historical figure of Vanozze Farnese and makes her the Duchesa Sanseverina, or 'Gina'; Cardinal Roderigo becomes Count Mosca, Minister to the Prince of Parma and lover of Gina; the handsome young Alessandro Farnese reappears as Fabrizio del Dongo, nephew of Gina; Cleria, of the Farnese annals, turns up again as *Clélia* Conti. But the singular thing is that all these characters and their adventures typifying the sixteenth century are carried over by Stendhal into the nineteenth century; we are asked to believe that the despotism and debauchery of Rome in 1500 could reappear in the little Italian principality of Parma in the 1820's."³

Josephson added that Stendhal spiced his sixteenth-century tale with touches from the nineteenth-century Carbonari. In prison Fabrice reads Silvio Pellico's memoir about imprisonment in Milan, Venice, and Brünn. By juxtaposing elements three centuries apart, the novel interweaves past and present in a way calculated to bewitch visitors to Italy. *The Charterhouse of Parma* is a traveler's fantasy about *cinquecento* Rome come to life in early nineteenth-century Emilia. However implausible such anachronism might seem elsewhere, in Italy it seems utterly natural. A whole chorus of French travelers from Valery and Rémusat to Barrès and Vaudoyer testified that they, too, experienced Italy as a palimpsest in which past and present change places when least expected.

THE ECSTASIES OF MAURICE BARRÈS

Parma's wealth of literary associations makes it the right place to weigh the contribution of Maurice Barrès to writing about Italy. A man of letters to his fingertips, Barrès lived and breathed for the art of writing, yet in an *oeuvre* of more than twenty volumes, his essays on Italy constitute portions of just two books, one published in 1894 and the other in 1903. Although these essays exerted untold influence, their author was anything but likeable. Barrès lacked the bonhomie of Valery, the balance of Rémusat, and the grace of Vaudoyer. In place of these winning qualities, Barrès glorified his ego, which he paraded through some of the most attractive sites in Italy. Through sheer energy of mind, Barrès could change forever how a reader feels about a locale.

Like any other Frenchman, Barrès came to Parma to pay homage to Stendhal. Unlike the others, however, he had followed Stendhal's hero Fabrice first to the shores of Lake Como and Lago Maggiore before pursuing him to Parma. There as a matter of course he connected Stendhal with Correggio: "I know very well why Stendhal situates his novel in Parma. He often came here to admire the voluptuousness of Correggio, which he must have felt with extreme intensity, since he could enjoy Italian opera; and in his mind the name of Parma remained tied to that search for happiness through fond feelings to which he dedicated that immoral and passionate hymn: *The Charterhouse*."[4] Barrès knew by intuition how his predecessor had adored Correggio, adding in a touch worthy of Vaudoyer that fondness for Italian opera may nourish a passion for that painter. Barrès showed to what extent Stendhal and Correggio fused in his mind when he lauded the women of Parma for flashing the smiles of Stendhal's Clélia above bosoms painted by Correggio.

As he roamed the ramparts under trees too young for Stendhal to have seen, Barrès supposed that it must have been on this very terrace that Fabrice brooded about Clélia after a year without seeing her. In a typical leap, these thoughts predisposed Barrès to forgive Marie-Louise for having preferred Count Neipperg to Napoleon: "What a beautiful little city is Parma, partaking of an almost German sentimentality, under a gray blue veil of October! At this moment I can almost pardon Marie-Louise, sweet soul who lived only in mid-body."[5]

In keeping with a day spent contemplating the dead, Barrès ventured into the cemetery, the only writer to do so. He marveled at how the marble tomb of Paganini, who died while on concert tour in Parma, contrasted with the other graves, which were covered only by grass or in spring by Parma violets. The "sad and stale odor of cemeteries" wrung from him a cry that confirmed his love of literature: "Ah, these dead are more dead than Fabrice del Dongo, Count Mosca, la Sanseverina and la Crescenzi, who never existed."[6]

Although Barrès wished that his own novels might cast a similar spell, it is not his ability to create character but rather to make places live that commands respect. He concluded his stroll in the cemetery by musing on the transience of exaltation: "What a delight to wander in the city of Correggio while yielding to the music of tender thoughts! It is a fatal pleasure to suffer willingly on tiptoes, to know that our life is ebbing away, that it gets lost in vulgarities."[7]

So Stendhal might have written had he been in Barrès's place. Barrès's eagerness to identify with his mentor exemplifies what might be called apostolic succession among travel writers. By frequenting certain spots that he reckoned must have appealed to Stendhal, Barrès hallowed these spots in the eyes of successors, so that Suarès, Maurel, and Vaudoyer felt obliged to frequent them as well. Although Barrès might have disliked the metaphor, he promoted pilgrimages, urging others to linger where he had communed with still others before him. For Barrès travel meant encounters, not as for Ruskin with beauty or wisdom, but rather as for Stendhal with genius, to be savored on its terrain. Just as a religious pilgrim longs to partake of a saint's grace, so Barrès pined to participate in an artist's genius. He desired not to be moved by a work's beauty but rather to be transfigured by its energy. Barrès is the patron saint of mental energy.

OSBERT SITWELL ON THE TOY COURT

Barrès's prestige makes it all the more surprising that the jauntiest writer about the Frenchness of Parma turns out to be not French but English. Sir Osbert Sitwell published a charming essay about Parma in his *Winters of Content* (1932). Just as he loved to imagine what early nineteenth-century Naples or Palermo must have felt like, so he delighted in imagining the atmosphere of Marie-Louise's Parma. He envisioned the streets twittering with soldiers and ambassadors: "Through them pranced the most Velasquez-like carriage-horses, drawing behind them equipages of a lovely, but rather bucolic elegance, while officers, in uniforms of a magnificence unparalleled even in the other lilied domains of Spain and Naples, strolled slowly up and down, clanking their spurs and twirling their dark moustachios."[8] Sitwell was only too aware that the "toy courts" of Parma and Modena used ceremony to screen out reality, for Napoleon's rule had terrified the princelings into esteeming trifles more than ever. "The nearer it drew to its end, the more exacting of etiquette was the Court, as though by the dismissal of a chamberlain for not bowing low enough all political discussion and all disturbance could be stifled and thus cured. As things grew worse, it clung more and more to this ramshackle, gilded refuge."[9] Sitwell held Prince Ranuce-Ernest, the "mischievous and spiteful, because frightened, little tyrant" of Stendhal's novel, to be an accurate depiction of the toy courts in decline.[10]

Sitwell even had a kind word for Marie-Louise, who had the good sense to have herself sculpted by a genius like Canova. Likening Canova to his contemporary Ingres, Sitwell predicted in 1932 that the sculptor would one day again win favor, a prophecy that came true in the 1960s. Sitwell quoted at length from Lady Morgan's account of a visit in 1819 to the attic of the Pilotta Palace, where she beheld bric-a-brac of Napoleon. Ormolu tripods, mirrors, quilts, and morocco boxes surrounded the cradle of the King of Rome, now stashed away from prying eyes. Valery reported that in 1816 the French Crown had sold these mementoes to Parma, where their gilt mocked the drab palace that housed them.

Sitwell's affinity with the Parma of the Bourbons climaxed in a chance visit in the mid-1920s to the "Royal Botanic Garden." In an enclosure known only to a few, he found a garden out of the early nineteenth century, tended by a grizzled gardener who could hardly speak. Awe at happening upon a secret nook at the season when it was most lovely, coupled with delight in finding a spot that corroborated something he had read about but never witnessed—these ingredients combined to awaken a sense of unrepeatable wonder. Sitwell opined that travelers derive their best tales from such moments.

Much better known, the Public Garden fascinated Sitwell through its contrast with the hidden Botanic Garden. Brooding on the past of the former yielded a lovely image of two eras brought into conjunction: "Even now, when this garden has been somewhat municipalised, when tall waste-paper baskets, those wire skeletons at the feast of democracy, have been placed at the telling angle of each vista, as formerly were statues in green niches, and when the unshaven dustman in his broad-brimmed, cavalier hat, brushing moted clouds of germ-laden glory into the peaceful air, has been substituted for the brocaded ladies and their velvet-coated *cicisbei*, it is perfection as a place to wander."[11] Trash baskets supplanting garden statues—what a way to symbolize the transformation of Europe in the hundred years from Marie-Louise to Mussolini.

The beauty of shade, statues, and water in a park devoid of flowers led Sitwell to muse on the advantages of Italian gardens. Because they rely on organization of space rather than of blossoms, their beauty lingers longer into autumn than does that of northern gardens, while in summer they furnish shadows and "the slow, rippling flash of water over stone" to soothe overheated citizens.[12] Where color floods down from sky and sun, it would be impertinent to add flowers. Viewed in winter, such a garden displays an "austere confidence in things that endure and do not wither with the seasons," making it a bracing place in which to anticipate spring.[13] Even a garden that might last for centuries took on fresh glints as a golden haze playing around the statues made everything unfamiliar. The gardens of Italy, which to the uninitiated look monotonous, disclosed to a connoisseur something unexpected year-round.

Osbert Sitwell, who adopted Parma as his favorite city in northern Italy, found charming things to say about every aspect of it, and not least about the facade of the cathedral. In evoking the lions that support pillars at all four entrances, he combined affection with persiflage, for he knew the sights so well that he could afford to speak of them like old family acquaintances: "The Cathedral . . . specialises, outside its four entrances, in those lovely but ludicrous lions of the special Romanesque breed always to be found angrily balancing pillars upon the small of the back, in front of the cathedrals of northern Italy; beasts that are obviously of a mixed Pekingese [*sic*], poodle, and lion ancestry."[14] No one else had noticed the all too obvious resemblance to Chinese lions. Sitwell's knack for domesticating unfamiliar sights carried over into his appreciation of the "Noah's-ark-like creation" of the Baptistery, with its reliefs of "delightfully improbable animals."[15] He remarked that every child born in Parma between 1294 and the 1920s was baptized in this one building. Perhaps he wished he had been himself.

With characteristic balance, a quality not always found in writing about Parma, Edith Wharton hailed the uniqueness of the Baptistery: "The ancient octagon of the Baptistery, with its encircling arcade and strange frieze of leaping, ramping and running animals, is outwardly one of the most interesting buildings in Italy; while its interior has a character of its own hardly to be matched in that land of fiercely competing individualism."[16] She lauded the vehemence of the frescoes, little aware that Lady Morgan had compared the painting of the Virgin to that of a "large female baboon, feeding her young."[17]

At first glance the cathedral looks less distinctive, although Rémusat deemed it, together with the Baptistery, the loveliest religious building that he saw in northern Italy.[18] No less a judge than Freeman extolled the eastern exterior, declaring that "few architectural objects can be nobler than the present effect of the absidal east end and absidal transepts joining to support the octagon cupola."[19] Unfortunately, the superb composition does not carry over into the interior, which shows merely "the genuine pier-arch, triforium, and clerestory, just as we might have seen them in England or Normandy."[20] Freeman preferred the interior of the cathedral of Modena, which approaches northern forms more beguilingly. In the cathedral of Parma the main attraction is of course not brickwork as in Modena but rather Correggio's frescoing of the cupola to produce what Wharton called "the maelstrom of his heavenly host."[21] His paintings constitute the climax, and for some the only reward, of a visit to Parma.

APPRAISALS OF CORREGGIO

Parma belongs to one painter more conspicuously than any other city in northern Italy. For centuries visitors came here for the sole purpose of seeing Correggio's two cupolas, as well as frescoes in the Convent of Saint Paul and several canvases now in the National

Gallery. Without Correggio, Parma might be as seldom visited as Modena, except by the French. Today's visitor may well feel astonished that not only was Correggio one of the three or four most admired of painters, ranking with Raphael and Michelangelo in the eyes of Stendhal and the Blashfields, but he was also one of the most controverted. This virtuoso, who never put a thought into a face, has excited more acrimony than many a lesser artist.

Correggio's admirers included Stendhal, Symonds, Maurel, and the Blashfields. Berenson, Osbert Sitwell, and Vaudoyer also praised his work. His detractors included Ruskin, Dickens, Rémusat, Wharton, and above all Suarès. Berenson admired him for "unconscious" painting, that is, for ignoring how his foreshortenings might stir controversy, and for rendering flesh.[22] Seeing him as a precursor of the Baroque, Berenson suggested that with a little prodding Correggio might have developed all the way to the rococo of Boucher and Nattier in the eighteenth century.[23] Berenson did not mention the uncanny resemblance between Correggio's nudes and those of a French imitator, Pierre-Paul Prud'hon. With his usual judiciousness, Berenson conceded Correggio's inadequacy at composing stationary figures but believed this to be outweighed by mastery in depicting movement.

Berenson's attempt of 1907 to strike a balance among controversialists was more cautious than that of Edith Wharton. She claimed that, whereas a hundred years earlier Correggio had been prized as a painter of "sentiment," by 1900 he could be esteemed solely for technique: "It is the defect of Correggio's art that it expresses no conviction whatever. He offers no clue to the *état d'âme* of his celestial gymnasts. They do not seem to be honestly in love with this world or the next, or to take any personal part in the transactions in which the artist has engaged them."[24] Wharton belittled the figures of Correggio as models who attitudinize, the artist having lacked the power to transmute their poses into anything sublime. For her, Correggio fell between the two stools of religious painting on the one hand and decoration on the other. The room that he decorated as a young man for the abbess of Saint Paul's lacked the "ethereal quality which is supposed to be the distinctive mark of Correggio's art. . . . The masses of foliage are too uniform and the *putti* too fat and stolid for their skyey task."[25]

The objections of Wharton seem churlish next to the plaudits of Symonds. While conceding that Correggio was no intellectual and no moralist, he devoted ten pages to expounding the "Correggiosity of Correggio," partly through allusions to music. Symonds compared Correggio's image of the Three Fates as "young and joyous Bacchantes" with Rossini's *Stabat Mater:* Both artists executed "voluptuous renderings of grave or mysterious motives."[26] The Englishman hailed the adolescent loveliness of Correggio's angels: "They belong to the generation of the fauns; like fauns, they combine a certain savage wildness, a dithyrambic ecstasy of inspiration, a delight in rapid movement as they revel amid clouds or flowers. . . ."[27] Delight in these "genii disimprisoned from the perfumed chalices of flowers"[28] reflected all too openly a yearning to be released from the chalice of Victorian morality. Where Wharton saw models preening, Symonds supposed Correggio to have invented a new race of mortals, for whom no models ever existed, not even in the court of a Roman emperor or a Turkish sultan. In a flight of fancy he supposed that Cherubino in Mozart's *Marriage of Figaro* "seems to have sat for all of them. At any rate they incarnate the very spirit of the songs he sings."[29]

The perfervid rhetoric continues concerning the apostles in the dome of San Giovanni, who gaze at Christ in "wild half-savage joy, as if these saints also had become the elemental genii of cloud and air, spirits emergent from ether, the salamanders of an empyrean intolerable to mortal sense."[30] Symonds's conception of the Renaissance as a fusion of pagan and Christian motifs found apotheosis in the paganism and homoeroticism of Correggio, who showed "earth straining upwards to ascend to heaven in violent commotion—a very orgasm of frenetic rapture."[31] Together with Maurel, the sexually troubled Englishman was the only writer to avow the sexual frenzy that pervades Correggio's two cupolas.

Having acknowledged the orgy, Symonds enumerated certain defects as well: The Christ of San Giovanni is "a sprawling figure which irresistibly reminds one of a frog."[32] If the clouds are too solid, still more distressing are the children, who "crawl upon these featherbeds of vapour, creep between the legs of the apostles, and play at bopeep behind their shoulders."[33] Correggio's use of light lacked tragic contrasts. There is none of Tintoretto's sublimity or Rembrandt's mystery in this botched chiaroscuro, which provides rather "the laughter of morning light, in a world of never-failing April hues."[34] Symonds could not conceal a yearning for Correggio's world when he summed it up: "Wantonness, innocent because unconscious of sin, immoral because incapable of any serious purpose, is the quality which prevails in all that he has painted."[35] Correggio evoked in Symonds nostalgia for the innocence of adolescent males.

If Symonds's rapture invites debunking, Suarès obliged in full, for he detested Correggio. There is no contrast in his work: Everyone flashes the same silly smile, nudity runs rampant, and the light is either too bright or too dark. Correggio lacks subtle gradations: His women are stupid and soft, having no bones, while his men have no character. Instead of painting from a model, he improvised, while forgetting that because "man is a clothed animal" nudity should be approached with awe and not allowed to proliferate, since nothing is more monotonous than lots of bare bodies.[36] The acrobats of the two cupolas reminded Suarès first of a circus and then of bravura singers in Wagner and Gounod, there being nothing at all of Bach in Correggio.

As a virtuoso, Correggio showed too much facility and not enough taste. The *Madonna with Saint Jerome*, perhaps the most admired of the canvases in Parma, shows the Magdalen as "an actress in courtly dress, not even a sinner," while Saint Jerome is "a sort of shepherd Daphnis, a galant faun" whose lion is made of paper.[37] Bodies in the cathedral cupola are neither male nor female, neither children nor adults. In a telling juxtaposition, Suarès compared the bearded apostles of San Giovanni to the portrait of Aristotle in Raphael's *School of Athens*: "At San Giovanni, a troop of curly Aristotles has left the School of Athens in order to dance a minuet on the ceiling."[38] These displaced Aristotles gaze without seeing, screaming at the top of their lungs, and have a breeze in their hair as they swim naked through clouds, while children climb their legs, pinch their backs, and scratch their shoulders. One can only call such works "the sublime form of the pretty."[39]

The conceit of a bevy of unseeing Aristotles strikes to the heart of Correggio's failings. By doing away with intellect, he appealed to a zest for the senses that the sophisticated can only deride. This most one-sided of great artists anticipated the sensuality of the Baroque, enshrining a split that would soon sunder human faculties. Correggio erected a monument to the splitting off of sensuality from the rest of life.

This may be why Correggio appealed to Stendhal, who believed he was reintegrating intellect and eros when he was in fact merely dissecting their conflict. In desiring to have a beloved in whatever city he visited, Stendhal was as badly torn between intellect and sensuality as Symonds. In December 1816 Stendhal admitted as much after passing through the painter's birthplace, the town of Correggio, northwest of Modena. Like Symonds in his reference to Cherubino, Stendhal, too, associated the painter with Mozart: "Yesterday I turned off the direct road to visit Correggio. Here was born in 1494 the man who knew how to depict in colors certain feelings which no poetry can attain and which after him Cimarosa and Mozart knew how to fix on paper. I noticed in the streets of Correggio the faces of women who recall the madonnas of this great painter."[40]

A no less biased attitude animated Ruskin, who visited Parma in 1845. Instead of scrutinizing the frescoes, he singled out the *Madonna with the Magdalen and Saint Jerome*. In contrast to Symonds, Ruskin had no use for a painter who appealed so directly to sexuality: "I never saw such desecrations of sacred subject. One of them, a Madonna with Christ on lap, painted for a widow lady—pleased her very much, say the traditions—and I daresay it would, for the Christ kicks and crows in a most lively and healthy manner, and the angel who is teaching him to read laughs at him. . . . Add to this the most lascivious young Magdalen conceivable—all the sensuality of [William] Etty refined and beautified and white fleshed and soft and golden haired till it is quite poison. . . ."[41] The seductiveness of the Magdalen so alarmed Ruskin that no amount of virtuosity in depicting landscape and especially leaves—he particularly admired the oak leaves in the *Antiope*—could redeem the affront. Young Ruskin must be one of very few who ever preferred painted leaves to painted flesh.

Ruskin's visit to Parma led him to remark in *Modern Painters* how the sun in southern climates imparts to the body a "firmness and sunny elasticity very different from the silky softness of the clothed nations of the north, where every model necessarily looks as if accidentally undressed."[42] Twenty-five years later Ruskin changed his tune, when, in comparing Tintoretto with Michelangelo, he grouped Correggio with the Venetian as being among those who had studied the human body while it was alive, in contrast to Michelangelo and Raphael, who had dissected it while it was dead.[43]

As if supporting the later Ruskin, Osbert Sitwell lauded Correggio for posing no problems and raising no issues, except how to enjoy natural beauty. Reproaching critics who, "spoilt by Michelangelo and Beethoven, insist on trouble in art as much as in life," Sitwell hailed Correggio as the "most restful and refreshing of great artists," who painted solely for his own joy and that of others, a characteristic usually reserved to lesser masters.[44] Because he provided so little to ponder, Correggio fell into disfavor among those who could not take beauty straight, or so Sitwell believed.

"A very peacock among painters," Correggio manifested originality to Sitwell chiefly as a decorator.[45] Although the connoisseur deplored the "bloated and boring babies" of the cathedral,[46] he extolled the "garlanded and scalloped apartments" of the Convent of Saint Paul's for having won from posterity the ultimate accolade: that of being taken for granted.[47] So numerous are imitations of the garlands in these rooms "that we do not pause to think of the genius of their creator, but have come to regard them almost as being spontaneously developed, like vine or olive-tree, in this environment: but none existed until Correggio evoked this one."[48] Construing Correggio as the antithesis of a tormented Romantic, Sitwell coined yet another metaphor to praise effortless creativity. Of any struggle to translate "natural into terms of pictorial beauty . . . he gives us no sign, taking the ground easily, like a well-bred racehorse, allowing himself no mental puffing or groaning. Indeed, there is something excessively aristocratic in his attitude, in his radiance and lack of complaint."[49]

An American fresco painter, Edwin Blashfield, brought the discussion back to earth by focusing on Correggio's technique. An ability to achieve silvery color while avoiding the overpainting that dulls fresco astonished the American. Correggio composed with light the way Michelangelo did with "muscular expression," shunning repose in order to depict perpetual motion.[50] Correggio's saints, even in altarpieces, undulate to the point where they wobble on their feet.

Study of the cupola of the cathedral transformed Blashfield's estimate of Correggio, whose gallery pictures he continued to belittle. The American mounted the gallery below the cupola and then ascended a staircase inside the pendentives: "The guide pulls open with an echoing rattle a small door in the thick wall; light bursts in; below you is an awful depth; two iron bars, strong, but slight to the imagination, are between you and it, and beyond the bars and the abyss, the smiling giants of Correggio float lightly over a dizzy gulf that makes your spinal marrow creep."[51] Answering Jacob Burckhardt's question, "What good could we expect from these creations if they came to life?", Blashfield saw sublimity in the profusion, the smiles, and the lack of restraint, sheer size imparting grandeur to a work whose details disappointed him like everyone else.

A still more exuberant appraisal came from André Maurel, who projected onto the painter the youthfulness that radiated from the fourteen-year-olds in the cupolas. Maurel pictured Correggio as an Adam who had rediscovered the art of painting, one who painted everything as the first man might have seen it. Intoxicated by sun and flesh, Correggio delighted in improbable postures.[52] *The Assumption of the Virgin* in the cathedral cupola Maurel extolled as a nuptial flight, an etherealized sexual dream. The Frenchman's refusal to admit defects in Correggio, when he spotted them so well in Giulio Romano, can be traced to a need to idealize youth. He who detested the Farnese princes needed to revel in something as naive as Correggio's art.

Sophisticated writers bubbling with enthusiasm for Correggio were venting a boyishness that bore rich fruit in other contexts. Stendhal's ability to portray a young man's hopes, Symonds's capacity to sketch a landscape, and Maurel's willingness to probe a hundred different cities owed much to a buoyancy that one might call Correggian. Italy no more resembled Correggio's visions than Parma did Stendhal's. But thanks to these two, the one endowed with too little intellect, the other with too much, Parma haunted travelers to a degree that few cities could match. Only sixth-century Ravenna and sixteenth-century Venice have inspired comparable fantasies. The real prince of Parma was not a Farnese—he was Correggio.

11

A City with Sunset in Its Walls: Bologna

ARCADES

As befitted a city devoted to learning, eating, and worshiping, Bologna attracted writers who admired solidity more than display. Valery pronounced it one of the most attractive cities in Italy, as did Thomas Grey and Lord Byron before him. Rémusat admired a decor that suggested a setting for Boccaccio's novellas, while the German journalist Albert Zacher considered it an annex of Rome. Bologna did not, however, draw scintillating writers except for Barrès, whose comments on Bolognese painting could as readily have emerged in Paris or Rome. No one evoked Bologna as trenchantly as Michelet did Genoa or as scathingly as Suarès did Milan.

Every visitor rejoiced at the arcades, which proliferated after 1500, bringing Roman vaulting to the humblest street. Just as Bologna's university trained civil servants to carry Roman law throughout the Papal States, so the city's miles of arcades carried the rounded vaults of the Roman forum into every quarter. Arcades unified the streets, making the city one vast courtyard, whose arches sheltered conversation and beggary, strolling and sloth.

William Hazlitt, a perceptive stroller, noticed how the winding streets differed from the avenues of Parma. Without mentioning gardens, he made Parma seem a French or Italian one, while Bologna disclosed the surprises of an English one: "At Parma (as well as Turin) you see a whole street at once, and have a magical and imposing effect produced once for all. At Bologna you meet with a number of surprises; new beauties unfold themselves, a perspective is gradually prolonged, or branches off by some retired and casual opening, winding its heedless way—the *rus in urbe*—where leisure might be supposed to dwell with learning."[1] This passage does more than describe two kinds of streets, for a more apt portrayal of Hazlitt's prose style and of the familiar essay that it helped to pioneer can hardly be imagined.

A few years earlier Stendhal and Shelley visited Bologna, where they commented on the optics of the arcades. In 1816 Stendhal voiced an opinion that remains almost unique: He urged that arcades be confined to one side of a street, as in Modena, lest they appear "deserted and dark."[2] Noticing a sinister air, Rémusat suggested that from one of these houses might sally forth some brother or husband bent on revenge.[3] Shelley caught the operatic mood when he commended moonlight on colonnades, marveling that the leaning towers threw such spooky shadows that "you might almost fancy the city is rocked by an earthquake."[4]

Vernon Lee noticed something different about the towers, remarking how rain improved their color: "And against the pure washed sky I noticed for the first time that the two leaning towers, which one thinks of as frowning dark, are really of an unsubstantial rose-colour weathered lilac, a colour like that of the leafless woods on the Apennines above Bologna. . . ."[5] Only an impressionist would have noted how the color of the Apennines in early spring rhymes with the lilac of the towers.

The supreme impressionists in Bologna were the Goncourt brothers, for anything to do with play of light or color fascinated them. Trying to paint in words, they observed how arcades create an effect of chiaroscuro. Having spotted chiaroscuro wherever flecks of light penetrate the arcades, they overlooked a more obvious instance: gloom under an arcade adjoining brightness in the street. Connecting the city with one of its painters who used contrast dramatically, the pair lamented how Guercino had ruined his canvases by using a glaze that crumbled and left the surface black. The Goncourt brothers, Jules in the lead, squeezed all these insights into three sentences: "In this city, the arcade takes possession of every street and puts a shadow under these vaults in the manner of [Francois-Marius] Granet, a shadow where narrow light filters here and there onto the greenish hues of the walls, making this city of sunshine the city of *chiaroscuro*. It is indeed the country of the talent for chiaroscuro of Guercino, who after daubing his canvases with a preparation of powdered marble, itself covered with a glaze, earned the repute of being the magician of color. But after fifty years, the preparation fell off, and Guercino is no longer anything but the colorist of night."[6]

If the Goncourt brothers were the only observers to associate arcades with chiaroscuro, Osbert Sitwell devised a different but equally apt comparison during the 1920s. Endless perspectives, such as Hazlitt had described, predestined Bologna to inspire receding vistas in baroque stage drops. While many derived from winding streets, not a few reflected Bologna's courtyards and staircases: ". . .everywhere one observes grand and beautiful courtyards and staircases, for most of the later palaces were constructed with an eye for the view of them to be obtained from the doorway, and in Bologna the art of such effects was especially well understood. Thus each vista here prophesies or reflects something of the lost theatrical traditions of the eighteenth century, and is near in feeling to the accustomed columned backgrounds of the Bibbienas."[7]

Sitwell's benignity contrasted with the argumentativeness of Karl Scheffler as he pondered the layout of Bologna. The cantankerous German, ever on the lookout for northern motifs, enjoyed the arcades in spite of himself. Comparing the covered sidewalks to corridors, he commented that one glimpses the city from inside an enclosure, with each view framed beneath a Roman arch. He applauded the city plan, in which two "gate streets" that stretch from north to south and east to west meet in the Piazza Maggiore.[8] Since streets radiate from there at unexpected angles, Bologna resembles a medieval town rather than a *Residenzstadt*, where all streets had to converge on the palace. The squares of Bologna combine intimacy with monumentality, even though clergy, nobility, and bourgeoisie erected their own buildings without a common plan. A need to huddle behind protecting walls held such cities together more effectively than any ruler's will. The German patriot marveled at what Italian builders could achieve notwithstanding the absence of a ruler to coordinate their efforts.

No such scruples bothered Goethe during his three days in Bologna in October 1786. Upon arriving, he carried out his customary initial act of climbing the city's tower. Utterly enchanted by the view from the Asinelli Tower, he had the good fortune to be able to see clear across the Po Valley to the Alps, the Adriatic, and Parma. The watchman boasted that the clear air kept moss from covering the roofs but complained that in recent years haze had begun to obscure the telescope view of Vicenza almost one hundred and twenty kilometers away.[9] Little could Goethe have guessed how familiar this lament would sound two hundred years later! The slant of the tower offended the German's taste, leading him to suppose that it had been designed to lean after perpendicular towers had begun to pall. In imputing a kind of rococo playfulness to its builders, he showed a certain fondness for eccentricities of his own time.

PAINTERS

Like most of his contemporaries, Goethe was drawn by the Bologna school of painters, the city being famous above all for painters and professors of law, both of whom showed much in common. Then as now, law professors aimed to synthesize earlier rules into digests, which arranged preexisting elements into new patterns. That is exactly what the painters of Bologna had aspired to do between 1580 and 1660. They acted like law professors, seeking, as Symonds put it, "to revive art by recomposing what lay before them in disintegrated fragments."[10] The notion that painters should incorporate the best features of earlier masters illustrates the syncretism native to Bologna. Pope Gregory XIII applied the same principle to codifying church law, and so did Aldrovandi in classifying plants. A city that promoted their kind of academicism nurtured painters who aspired to combine what was best in their predecessors, "the voluptuous charm of Correggio, the luminous color of Titian, the terribleness of Michelangelo, and the serenity of Raphael."[11] Yet what succeeds in a classroom will pall in painting, where disparate elements tend to clash in the absence of genius to control them.

The Bologna school began with Lodovico Carracci, who in the 1580s enlisted his two cousins Annibale and Agostino in an academy, which taught students how to imitate the best features of the previous hundred years. When Annibale moved to Rome in 1595, he had already studied Correggio in Parma and Titian and Veronese in Venice. In Rome he trained Bologna-born Domenichino and Guido Reni, the latter going on to spend most of his last thirty years in his native Bologna. Youngest of the group was Guercino, who was active in Rome, Modena, Piacenza, and Bologna until his death in 1666. His use of marble dust would make him an object of pity to the Goncourt brothers. These six painters mastered an art of *haute vulgarisation*, pioneering the high style that the English pundit Sir Joshua Reynolds hailed as the pinnacle of Western art. During the eighteenth century, English lords on the Grand Tour revered Bologna the way Ruskinians would later adore Venice and Florence. Academic painting, for which Raphael is sometimes blamed, originated with the Bolognesi, who counteracted mannerism by teaching that a masterpiece could be cobbled together out of the "best" of earlier masterpieces. Still enjoying acclaim from Stendhal and Lord Byron, only after 1840 did the Bologna painters begin to lose favor.

For that shift of taste, Ruskin was largely responsible. His invective against Domenichino in the first volume of *Modern Painters* shows what a violent hater he could be, for he called the colors and execution "coarse and feelingless," the whole endeavor deceptive, and its taste corrupt.[12] Because a major goal of *Modern Painters* was to discredit the Bologna school in favor of the "modern" J. M. W. Turner, Ruskin could not allow himself to relent. Of a painting that Byron had adored, Guercino's *Hagar in the Wilderness*, he wrote, "The grief of Guercino's Hagar, in the Brera Gallery at Milan, is partly despicable, partly disgusting, partly ridiculous; it is not the grief of the injured Egyptian, driven forth into the desert with the destiny of a nation in her heart; but of a servant of all work turned away for stealing tea and sugar."[13]

More sensible was the criticism of Goethe, who frequented the Carracci, Guido and Domenichino, during his three days in 1786. He objected to "degrading objects" that filled the pictures: corpses, criminals, and fools, with a pretty woman to stare at them, and a saint who looked paralyzed beneath a gorgeous cape.[14] The great humanist pronounced the subjects inhumane and the portrayal grotesque: "There is nothing which gives a human touch, out of ten subjects there is not one which ought to have been painted, and that one the artist could not take from the correct side."[15] The incongruity of using masterly technique to depict repulsive subjects bewildered Goethe and only reinforced his admiration for Raphael. To a picture of Saint Agatha by Raphael, which the poet happened upon in Bologna, he imputed the face of Iphigenia at a time when he was revising his play *Iphigenia auf Tauris* (1787). In a touching aside he promised to "read his play" to her image in his mind, pledging not to let his heroine utter anything that Saint Agatha could not have said.[16]

Goethe's aversion got renewed thirty years later by Percy Bysshe Shelley. Writing to Thomas Love Peacock in 1818, Shelley raged against the mortification of the flesh that he saw in Guercino's *Saint Bruno*. Whereas Ruskin would condemn such a painting as contrived, Shelley regarded it as all too sincere, so that for him it discredited not only Catholic piety but Christian belief itself: "I never saw such a figure as this fellow. His face was wrinkled like a dried snake's skin, and drawn in long hard lines: his very hands were wrinkled. He looked like an animated mummy. He was clothed in a loose dress of death-coloured flannel, such as you might fancy a shroud might be, after it had wrapt a corpse a month or two. It had a yellow, putrefied, ghastly hue, which it cast on all the objects around, so that the hands and face of the Carthusian and his companion were jaundiced by this sepulchral glimmer. Why write books against religion, when we may hang up such pictures?"[17] Shelley's aversion to death-praising paintings climaxed several years later when the fresco "The Triumph of Death" in the Campo Santo of Pisa goaded him into rejoining with a poem, "The Triumph of Life."

Deeper insight into the painters of Bologna came from Maurice Barrès. The emotional extremes in Bologna's pictures fascinated Barrès, who compared their psychological probing to that of the modern novel. If he had any contemporary in mind, it must have been Paul Bourget, a positivist who became an analyst of sin. Bourget liked to depict pathological obsessions, especially in young men.[18] A syncretist of psychology, who adored harsh contrasts of light and dark, Bourget made characters seem stiff in the same way as did Guercino or Reni. To link Bourget with these artists was already a stroke of genius, but Barrès saw still deeper when he connected the Bologna painters with the *Spiritual Exercises* (1522–23) of Ignatius Loyola. The founder of the Jesuits had aspired to induce in believers a semblance of mystical passion, even if the real thing was lacking. As Barrès put it, "Bolognese art seeks systematically what extreme situations it can combine in order to place persons in a state out of the ordinary. Painting and sculpture become the portrayal of persons of fixed character in a particular catastrophe."[19] The notion of portraying "persons of fixed character in a particular catastrophe" fits equally well a novel by Paul Bourget.

Barrès introduced a further note from the Paris boulevards when he compared figures of the Virgin in Bolognese painting to "a great lady whom people seek to amuse,"[20] while attending angels became pages who foretold Cherubino courting the Marquise. To render mystical states, "The painter places his personages in an action where they can display exactly that degree of confusion and weakness which we require in order to be moved and informed."[21] Barrès concluded his disquisition on what might be called the "Spiritual Exercises of the Bolognesi" by chiding critics who objected to the elegance of these angels, saints, and martyrs. The painters preferred courtiers as models, and this for the same reason that analysts like Bourget featured women of fashion.[22] Today the concocting of such scenes repels as strongly in Guercino or Reni as it does in the fiction of Bourget or Barrès himself. Was there not something Jesuitical in Barrès, something that welcomed contrived plots and whipped-up emotion? Because Barrès the novelist did not hesitate to manipulate his readers, he could see through painters who had performed similar tricks. Barrès exposing the Jesuitism of the Bolognesi illustrates the maxim "It takes a thief to catch a thief."

With his usual nonchalance, Kenneth Clark threw new light on all this when he recounted his first visit to the gallery of Bologna in 1925. The old building, since entirely renovated, exuded a gloom consistent with that of its paintings. A museum that André Suarès called a "labyrinth of illustrious crusts" impressed Kenneth Clark as a labyrinth of shadows: "I therefore set off down the arcades in high hopes, enchanted by the shouting, the hooting and the Michelangelesque torsos of the young men painting the stucco. I needed all my elation, for entering the Museum was like entering a dark, stuffy and loveless mausoleum. Provincial museums in my youth were the most dismal spots on earth (they still are in France). They seemed to be the revenge of the impotent on passion and creative joy. In Bologna the authorities had the advantage of material that had lent itself to the gloomiest and most ponderous presentation. . . ."[23] Although earlier visitors had taken the gloom for granted, after it was gone perhaps only Vaudoyer would have missed it. Disliking the clinical air of most renovated galleries, he would have saluted the darkness of the old museum as befitting the Jesuitical finesse of its paintings.

CHURCHES

Bologna's earthiness is enhanced by the apricot, orange-brown, pink, and other gaudy hues that enliven walls as far as the eye can see. The Strada Maggiore, which carries the Via Emilia across the eastern portion of the city, presents a fairy tale of colored arches, whose like exists nowhere else, not even in neighboring Modena. Although that city also displays cheerful oranges and pinks, they seem but a foretaste of the earthy reds, pinks, and vermilions that splash the inner city of Bologna. Yet what may be the most richly colored city in Italy has found few to praise its apricot flush. Possibly, colors that glow freshly today languished under grime in the nineteenth century. In any case, it fell to Freya Stark to coin a phrase for these streets of orange and pink: They look "as if sunset were built into the walls."[24]

Most observers noticed something else, not the sprightly but rather the strenuous side of Bologna, as if they could not rid their minds of the muscularity dear to the painters. Fulsomeness resides most conspicuously in certain churches, whose rotundity recalls that the city once vied with Florence and Siena to build the grandest edifice in Europe. San Petronio, sadly marred by an unfinished facade, was planned in 1390 to be the largest church in Christendom. Its transept having never been built, the huge space that we see was meant to be only the nave. Amateur though he was, Rémusat spotted the defect of San Petronio when he noted that the vaults span too great a distance between piers to achieve a genuine pointed effect.[25] Although the vast size did not leave the Frenchman unmoved, he observed that the nave impresses only at first glance, there being little to please a seeker of detail.

The same can be said of the burial church of Saint Dominic, the Spanish founder of the Dominican order, whose members in 1232 inaugurated the Inquisition. A contemporary of Saint Francis, Dominic died in Bologna in 1221, having returned there ill from a journey to Hungary. Evelyn Underhill underwent one of her transports when she beheld Dominic's tomb: "It is lovely, a fairy house in white marble, much too bright and joyous in its beauty for the stern old Saint of the Inquisition."[26] She who had noticed the incongruity of having Peter Martyr buried in the Portinari Chapel in Milan detected a similar impropriety here, where the church is too large and the carving too sprightly. The panels by Niccolò Pisano inspired her to comments that, written at age twenty-seven, show English amateurism at its most ebullient. She praised Niccolò as "the true father of sculpture in Italy," who, "with only Byzantines to guide him, swung round from their stiff symbolism, to this Greek revelry in the beauty of humanity."[27] Having caviled that no one was allowed to be ugly in Niccolò's world, she rejoiced at the rebirth of sculpture: "His people live, and yet they recognize that they are a marble people, and must not be too violent and unstatuesque."[28]

An even more diverse agglomeration accumulated in the seven churches of Santo Stefano, built around a tenth-century baptistery atop a temple of Isis. A cluster of "three brick churches, a crypt, two cloisters, and various chapels and excrescences"[29] enchanted Underhill to the point where she exclaimed, as she would later at Ravenna, "These churches really add a new thing to one's mental inheritance."[30] Columns from the temple of Isis, supplemented by brick columns with Lombard capitals, thrilled her.

In her old age, Vernon Lee published an essay on the Seven Churches. As a child she used to stop off in Bologna on her way home to Rome, and even then the Seven Churches had bewitched her. Forty years later she described her awe at their "maze of low-roofed basilicas, chapels, crypts and shrines; cloisters also, and damp monastic yards under belfries, and mysterious corridors, with graves and tabernacles, tucked away in them; barrocco *Gesù Mortos* shelved where you expect only broken chairs and derelict besoms, and the Three Kings, huge black Gothic chessmen. . . . Sanctuaries of all kinds, and one within the other, smelling of bats and rats, in which I also seemed to breathe the pent-up centuries."[31]

With her flair for myth, Lee felt the Seven Churches to be a repository not only of disused religious objects but of scenery such as Wagner might have conceived for *Parsifal*. The Templar's Church, known as the House of Pilate, loomed as "a place of indescribable mystery and awe, compared with which Wagner's Grail-Music is scarcely less futile a sham than his cardboard architecture. It is a place whose appropriate sounds would not be plain-chants even, however archaic, but mutterings and wailings and solitary footfalls; a building which has the shuddering nightmare quality of the moments before a wintry dawn."[32]

Lee's ability to intuit the past by injecting myth into places sprang to life in the crypt of the Temple of Isis. When an old woman showed her the "Sacred House of Loreto" behind an altar, Lee mused, "Is not the subterranean worship of the Nile-goddess still hidden in those churches and crypts and cloisters? May it not be the loin-cloth of ever-murdered, ever resuscitating Osiris which hangs vague and white over the arms of the cross on that staircased sepulchral altar, under the dome of Pilate's House?"[33]

As she plunged deeper, the House of Pilate became a relic of primitive religion, a place that seemed to "be oozing with the mysteries of times long before Christianity, or even paganism: the terror and sorrows of a nether world and the nethermost soul."[34] She touched bottom, as it were, in the lowest reaches of the House of Pilate, "muddy and full of pools." It required interaction between childhood memory and adult perception to recognize that the Seven Churches "seem like the lairs, the hidden resting-places, where mankind has cowered in silence and darkness with its broken limbs and sores and fever visions, resting and healing itself between the real miseries of this world and the imagined terrors of the next."[35]

Only Vernon Lee could have discerned in the bowels of Bologna a depository of ancestral fears. Her gift for amplifying personal memories into collective images shone at its best in a city that others tended to regard as prosaic. Having detected the air of a stage set that impressed Rémusat and Sitwell, she linked it with the aspect of a storehouse that struck Valery and the prevalence of poverty that shocked the Goncourt brothers. All these images flowed together in a climactic vision of the House of Pilate. This most poetic of all passages about Bologna evoked a stage set under the earth, where ancestral attitudes elbowed one another like ghosts. Lee envisioned something like a magic-lantern show of early man at worship: "The church itself was dark but for what came from the ill-lighted cloister within; and the great altar with its stairs and balconies, its look of being a temple, and a triumphal stage, and yet at the same time a pillory of some sort, loomed white in the dusk. At its foot, in an embrasure, flickered the only lamp, a glass cup with a nightlight, flat on the marble slab. There, I felt, was *It. It*. What? The something whose white drapery hangs limp like a corpse over the arms of the cross on the top of that church inside a church. The whole place was full of *It: It*, a vague terror and sorrow."[36] This experience of a *mysterium tremendum*, as Evelyn Underhill might have called it, infused a stage set worthy of the Bibbiena with visions of earliest Christian worship and even of pagan worship. No other traveler wrote anything quite like this hymn to the restorative power of darkness in the depths of the earth.

12

Ravenna, Tomb of Tombs

AN ISLAND IN TIME

Ravenna has inspired much beautiful writing, nearly all of it wistful. No one deemed this relic of the expiring Roman Empire cheerful, and most found it downright sad. A place of death and short-lived rebirth, Ravenna perplexed writers all the more because it contains almost no Renaissance art. Comparisons to Renaissance and Baroque cities ring hollow in a town whose most famous names date from the fifth and sixth centuries. A museum unto itself within the larger museum of Italy, Ravenna is, as Vogüé put it, the tomb of tombs.

Writing about Ravenna proceeded in two veins: Valery, Rémusat, and Freeman, on the one hand, eschewed pathos in order to describe monuments as soberly as possible; Vogüé, Barrès, and Blashfield, on the other hand, bewailed the contrast between the abandon of Ravenna in their day and the splendor of the last capital of the Roman Empire in the West. Nearly all writers began by narrating the history of the fifth and sixth centuries, when the last Western emperors huddled in a swamp-girt city whose port gave access to still-flourishing Constantinople.

The 150 years between Alaric's capture of Rome in 410 and Justinian's conquest of the Gothic kingdom of northern Italy witnessed no fewer than three major attempts to restore a semblance of Roman rule to Italy. Two children of Emperor Theodosius, Honorius and his sister Galla Placidia, dominated until 450, the latter erecting the church of San Giovanni Evangelista as well as her celebrated tomb.

A second epoch saw the rise of the Ostrogoths under Odoacer and his conqueror, Theodoric. Writers as diverse as Freeman, Gregorovius, Vogüé, and the Blashfields extolled Theodoric for having given Italy, in Freeman's words, "such a season of rest and prosperity as she had never had since the days of the Antonines, such as she has never had again till our own times."[1] The third endeavor came under the generals Belisarius and Narses, whom the Byzantine emperor Justinian dispatched to conquer and rule in his name. Lombards invading under Alboin overturned their success by the year 570, confining the Byzantines within a small territory that bequeathed its borrowed name of Rome to modern Romagna. English, French, and German writers concurred that Italy would have fared better if Ostrogoths under the likes of Theodoric or Lombards under the likes of Desiderius could have continued ruling, with no Eastern emperors or popes to plague them. Ravenna stimulated North Europeans to imagine how a civilization as orderly as their own might have prospered in an Italy purged of Byzantine and papal intrigue. Of course, who can say whether such a civilization would have enticed subsequent travelers?

Freeman was most outspoken in lauding Theodoric, who built "the earliest civilized monuments of our own race"[2] and whose reign, apart from the murder of Odoacer with which it began and that of Boethius with which it ended, was "like a kind of dream, like the romantic ideal of a beneficent ruler turned by some spell into true history."[3] The Victorian applauded the Arian king's steadfastness in tolerating orthodox worship alongside that of his Arian tribesmen. It is owing to Theodoric's toleration that Ravenna boasts churches both for Arians and Orthodox. In the sixteenth century his statesmanship would be mocked by Counter-Reformation bigots who scattered his bones.

No less remarkable was Galla Placidia, who may rightly be called "daughter, sister, wife, and mother of Emperors." Visitors to southern Italy who happen upon the supposed site of Alaric's grave in a riverbed at Cosenza, Calabria, seldom recall that this invader had carried off from Rome the Western emperor's daughter, Galla Placidia. As told by Rémusat, she soon won the love of Alaric's lieutenant, Altauf, only to see her husband die in Spain, whereupon she returned to the palace of her brother, the emperor Honorius, in Ravenna.[4] Having married his general, Constantius, she proceeded to embellish the city. Her brother and her husband share her tomb, while Altauf supposedly lies buried in a chapel of San Lorenzo in Milan. Having failed to persuade the Eastern emperor, Theodosius, to accept Constantius as his successor, Galla Placidia died in Ravenna, one of the few women of antiquity who helped rebuild a city.

Not only is Ravenna, as Rémusat said, one of the few cities of northern Italy that kindles no desire to look at paintings,[5] but it is one of very few whose history interlocks with faraway places like Constantinople, or Spain, where Galla Placidia might have lingered if her first husband had lived longer, or Aachen, whither Charlemagne shipped the marbles of Theodoric's Palace. That is why Dante's burial in Ravenna seems so fitting: He took refuge in a city that had witnessed the first efforts to unite Italy under post-Roman auspices.

FRENCH ELEGISTS

Three French writers caught the atmosphere to perfection. The most moving piece came from Eugène-Melchior de Vogüé, who had written with similar pathos about the Near East in the 1870s. During the spring of 1893 he visited Ravenna, which stirred him to one of the finest elegies ever written about an Italian city. Likening the survival of this mud-locked town to that of cities of the pharaohs beside the Nile, he called Ravenna "the sweet corpse, the Western Byzantium."[6] In a detail missed by everyone else, Vogüé noticed how in the morning monks and beggars gathered outside the few houses of the well-to-do, like clients of a patrician in ancient Rome, waiting to accompany the lady of the house to mass.

While bidding farewell to the city from the pine forest, Vogüé felt he was gazing at a giant cemetery: "One does not leave Ravenna; it leaves you. It is she who takes refuge in her past; this gossamer vision cannot be renewed. In order to overcome one's doubt of the real, of the sense of evanescence and fluidity which Ravenna insinuates into one's mind, one must include in one's final glimpse the one stone which speaks of life among these tombs: the French stone in the baptistery, with its comforting phrase, *In Hope of God*."[7] A

French soldier under Gaston de Foix in 1512 had presumably inscribed this motto of hope among the tombs. Using rhetorical flourishes that recall Chateaubriand, Vogüé remembered that Dante had placed the entrance to his Earthly Paradise in the pine forest of Ravenna, a spot whose lack of humans made it seem worthy of the honor. In an image straight out of Chateaubriand, Vogüé noted how trees spared by a recent fire stood like columns from a ruined temple.

Two generations earlier the pine forest had aroused Valery to an equally expressive climax. Valery dubbed the trees "illustrious" because "ancestors of these pines served to build the fleets of Augustus; as ships of Venice, they carried the crusaders from Europe to Asia. Now their unhappy progeny, allotted to the naval paymasters of neighboring states, have become Austrian brigantines which protect the Turks, or tiny papal ships which Barbary pirates pillaged and insulted until France liberated Greece and defeated Algiers."[8] Valery underlined the mood of desolation by recalling the battle of Ravenna on April 11, 1512, when Gaston de Foix lost his life at age twenty-two defeating troops of Julius II and of Spain. This meaningless battle, which did nothing to secure Italy, was watched by three of the most famous writers of the day: the courtier Castiglione, the poet Ariosto, and the future pope Leo X, who was then papal legate to the Spanish. The carnage enlivened battle scenes that Ariosto put into *Orlando Furioso* a few years later. A battle more remarkable for the writers who saw it than for any issue it settled symbolized the futility of post-Byzantine Ravenna.

A city so rich in death could not fail to move Maurice Barrès, who arrived a year after Vogüé. No other pair of writers reinforced one another's impressions to the same degree as these two, whose eloquence suited those whom Barrès called "the deadest dead of Italy."[9] Barrès began by asking, "Is it a flat village of Brittany? Under the rain, is it a desolate plain of the Camargue?"[10] The incongruity between past and present assaulted Barrès at the tomb of Theodoric, whose custodian seemed a pensioner puttering in a suburb: "He is Theodoric the Arian, but he is also a retiree in the suburbs. He comes from the sixth century, but also from Neuilly. When I rang at the gate, the custodian was grafting roses."[11] The abandon of the monuments invited Barrès to savor "the acrid pleasure of losing interest in everything."[12] Water welling up in the crypt of Sant'

Apollinare in Classe supplied a metaphor for the whole city: "Everywhere in Ravenna, things are tired of holding themselves up and want to go where the people already are: under ground. They aspire to descend into the grave, at last to decay."[13]

The plain leading to the pine forest prolonged communion with the dead: "There is no beauty, no pleasure, but rather a violent and indefinable feeling which grips the soul and makes it feel serious."[14] The pine forest had burned in 1890, leaving only a few trees, whose isolation enveloped them in eternity: "Their indestructible character, the stagnant water which surrounds them, and the moaning of the Adriatic instil in the stroller an idea of eternity. From here life is nothing more than a distant sound of yapping dogs."[15]

Anticipating his essay on Venice, Barrès appraised four figures who had received monuments in Ravenna. The portrait of the Empress Theodora, the tomb of Dante, the column erected to Gaston de Foix, and the cabin in the pine forest where Garibaldi hid in 1849 (and where his wife died)—all convinced Barrès that deeds speak louder than shrines. Whereas Dante and Garibaldi are remembered for what they achieved, Theodora and Gaston de Foix are recalled only because someone built them a monument. Freeman expressed an identical reaction when he admitted, "in the presence of the tomb of Theodoric and the tomb of Dante, we have no mind to tarry by the column which commemorates the death and the useless victory of Gaston of Foix."[16]

Upon returning from the pine forest, Barrès tossed off one of his most haunting remarks. After glimpsing several brickmakers hip-deep in mud, he reflected that slime dried into blocks has outlasted whole civilizations.[17] Building blocks of dried mud survived, while the marbles of Rome were sacked and those of Aquileia burned. Cities that gleamed too brightly attracted looters, while Ravenna's brick did not. To compound the irony, mud flats that furnished the brick also bred malaria, thus improving the protection. Even in Rome more remains of ancient brick than of ancient marble.

CHURCHES WITHOUT FACADES

The earliest of the mosaicked buildings of Ravenna, the tomb of Galla Placidia built in the 440s, has inspired remarkable descriptions.

The exterior shows a blandness that suited a religion just emerging from persecution; the brick building, which measures barely ten by twelve meters, reminded Maurel of a fire station.[18] Henry James recommended it to the lover of "dusky architectural nooks," likening it to a "narrow low-browed cave, shaped like a Latin cross," where loom "three enormous barbaric sarcophagi" in a space that "might be a small natural grotto lined with glimmering mineral substances."[19]

The images on those glimmering walls interested James less than they did Evelyn Underhill, who was enthralled by the similarity to classical figures. She waxed lyrical over the naturalness: "The people are slender, supple; they move and bend freely; they are descended from the paintings of Pompeii. . . . The whole of this ornament, with the doves drinking at a vase, so naturalistically rendered, to the stags at the river, though afterwards freely used in Romanesque architecture, came, I believe, from Rome, not Byzance."[20] In her enthusiasm for Rome, Underhill would have been thrilled to learn that, as Rémusat reported, this tomb is the only spot on earth where a Roman emperor, Honorius, still inhabits his original tomb.[21] Unfortunately, the body of Galla Placidia on its cypress throne was burned four centuries ago when inquisitive children thrust a taper into her sarcophagus, itself once covered in silver and gold.

The plain exterior of Galla Placidia's tomb extends to the fronts of sixth-century churches, showing that early Christian architects had not learned how to boast of their faith. Edward Freeman deemed the basilicas of Ravenna among the most significant buildings in Europe because they show Christian architects adopting the arcade, which had emerged just two centuries before in Diocletian's Palace in Split. Like "spoils of heathendom," long ranges of columns march toward the altar, with mosaics filling the space where later would fit triforium and clerestory. Freeman, who had studied churches perhaps more closely than anyone else of his generation, declared Sant' Apollinare Nuovo to be the noblest of all: "Few of man's works are more striking than that long procession of triumphant virgins headed by the Three Kings—not stiff conventional forms, as in the later Byzantine work, but living and moving human beings—bearing their gifts to their Lord on the knees of His Mother."[22] Freeman saluted Theodoric for having built this church for his Arian coreligionists while permitting the Orthodox a church and baptistery of their own, Justinian having added the mosaics to celebrate the return of the basilica to Orthodoxy.

Vogüé shared Freeman's reverence for the procession of virgins in Sant' Apollinare Nuovo, its figures haunting the rest of his stay. Constituting a Christian equivalent of a panathenaic procession to the Parthenon, "these women in white, who move in uniform rhythm, these motionless eyes which converge above ours" escorted Vogüé in a cortege that would not leave him as he tramped the empty streets, the virgins providing him a bevy of clients the way beggars and monks did wealthy ladies of Ravenna.[23] The only dissonance came when a custodian at San Vitale boasted how Sarah Bernhardt had come to copy Theodora's costumes.

Writing in 1873, Henry James evoked the helter-skelter of Ravenna's buildings, reacting with disbelief to the sarcophagi, whose abundance startled Vogüé and Blashfield as well. The basilica of Sant' Apollinare Nuovo furnished "a magazine of early Christian odds and ends; fragments of yellow marble encrusted with quaint sculptured emblems of primitive dogma; great rough troughs, containing the bones of old bishops; episcopal chairs with the marble worn narrow by centuries of pressure from the solid episcopal person; slabs from the fronts of old pulpits."[24] The "odd, knowing, sidelong look" from the eyes of the white maidens made James eager to "murmur a defensive prayer or so were I to find myself alone in the church towards dusk."[25] James was the only writer who responded to Ravenna with drollery.

André Suarès, who detested the mosaics of San Vitale, reacted differently to those of Sant' Apollinare Nuovo, where he fell in love with an image of Christ seated above the arcade near the altar, flanked on either side by a pair of angels. Scrutinizing the face as closely as he had that of Gattamelata in Padua, Suarès declared the figure to embody everything that he desired in a portrayal of Christ: beauty, gravity, and sadness. Writing as though he had climbed a ladder to behold the face, he exclaimed, "Eyes, he is all eyes; the pupils and the eyebrows redouble them. The entire body has the arc of a long pupil. In the oval face, with thin cheeks, and pointed beard, all the lines run to the eyes. . . ."[26] This avowal stands out because Suarès did not often mention depictions of Christ, and he found the rest of Ravenna revolting.

Four or five kilometers south of present-day Ravenna stands the sole remnant of the port of Classis, the basilica of Sant' Apollinare in Classe. Although Rémusat pronounced it the most beautiful basilica anywhere, it had suffered grievous losses, Sigismondo Malatesta having pillaged marble facings from the lower walls. Mosaics that had once glowed above them had also vanished. A frieze of 128 bishops of Ravenna seemed a provincial travesty of the heads of the popes that had decorated Saint-Paul's-Outside-the-Walls in Rome before it burned in 1823. To make matters worse, Rémusat had to overlook a farmhouse built in the courtyard, not to mention water welling up from the crypt.[27] Despite these intrusions, he preferred the design to that of Sant' Apollinare Nuovo, built forty years before, since the abundance of light illumining Byzantine mosaics recalled a Greek temple. Freeman took a different view of the provenance of these buildings. Noting that inscriptions in Ravenna use no language but Latin—the same was true of Justinian's codification of law—Freeman emphasized the preponderance of Rome. As late as the year 600, emperors, even in Byzantium, scorned any language but Latin.[28] Only centuries later did Saint Mark's of Venice allow Greek inscriptions to creep onto mosaicked walls.

Edwin Blashfield had the good fortune to visit Ravenna in springtime, when the "pestilential" marshes burst into bloom. On his way to Classe he saw nature reproduce "the color scheme of the Byzantines in the blue of the waters and in the tender green of the young blades of rice; while tamarisks, lilies, orchids, blossoming flags and rushes, suggest the more vivid hues of the mosaics."[29] Arthur Symons could not have sketched a unison of color between nature and art more cunningly. Less happily, spring weather also sucked water into the basilica, where "the scummy surface of its gilded pools appears to mock the color of the mosaics."[30]

Arriving a few years after Blashfield, Evelyn Underhill formulated in this church one of those succinct visions in which her diary abounds. In place of scummy waters, she experienced a "sense of majestic ritual; space, dignity, absolutely faultless proportions,"[31] her pleasure anticipating that of more recent tourists, who see the church clean and dry. For her the building conveyed a sense of "something rhythmical, elastic, alive almost . . . an effect of balanced line and mass, quite independent of the coloured mosaic."[32] Like Freeman she rejoiced at glimpsing what classical Rome must have looked like. "The just size of the columns, strong and delicate, the charming span of arch, the great sense of spaciousness and ease, are classical characteristics. I had not imagined a basilica to be such a lovely thing. One should dream of them always filled with grave, stately people, who move slowly and lift their hands in ceremonial gestures."[33] Only too evidently, Underhill wanted to people the basilica with women in white like those who ring Sant' Apollinare Nuovo.

ALADDIN'S CAVE IN SAN VITALE

The one truly Greek church in Ravenna is San Vitale, where, as Vogüé put it, Byzantium glided between the rectangle of the pagan basilica and the spire of the Gothic cathedral to interpose squat curves, where "maniacal and subtle thought turns ever about itself."[34] In this church Edwin Blashfield's admiration for Greece led him to belittle Roman architecture in the manner of Edward Freeman. As we saw in Verona, Freeman denounced Roman architecture as a transitional phase between Greek and Romanesque, in which Romans applied as ornament elements that Greeks had treated as structure. Blashfield likewise praised Byzantine Greeks for having discarded the ornament of the Romans as soon as the incubus of the Empire had lifted: "But the heavy cornices, which once under a roof protected nothing from a rain which did not fall; the super-imposed orders, with their pediments and colonnettes, stuck unmeaningly upon structural masonry,—he [the Greek] rejected unhesitatingly, substituting surfaces with but slight projections, lightly though richly carved, where the columns were true weight-bearers, and there were no useless members."[35]

Blashfield lauded Justinian for having employed Greek artisans who introduced to Italy the pattern of the Madonna that would prevail for eight centuries. The Church of San Vitale, erected between 526 and 547, is the oldest domed church in the West, one boasting a dome "raised by Greek workmen long after Italy had forgotten the cunning which curved the cupola of the Pantheon and vaulted the baths of Caracalla."[36] Blashfield could not say enough to commend the colors of the mosaics, which mirrored the "gold of Byzantium, the purple of Caesar, the blues and greens of the chariot factions" of Byzantium.[37] Blashfield esteemed the mosaics of San Vitale above those of Saint Mark's in Venice, especially for skillful use of gold and gradation of color.[38]

Saluting mosaic as the supreme form of wall decoration, Blashfield emphasized its imperishability. Whereas fresco flakes, blackens, or mildews, glass cubes look as though they had been applied yesterday. Dispensing a rare piece of information, the artist noted that the glint derives from the impossibility of affixing cubes on a level plane, each adhering at a slightly different angle to the ground of powdered travertine and linseed oil: ". . . the result is the varied tonality produced by a thousand different degrees of reflection, giving an indescribable richness of surface . . . ," enhanced by the fact that each color may include as many as twelve shades.[39] In a climax worthy of the Goncourts, Blashfield admitted that the color of San Vitale went to his head like strong wine, "provoking all sorts of impossible analogies."[40]

Another inebriate of color, Arthur Symons, delighted in the decay of San Vitale, which reminded him of an excavation whose columns had just emerged from the earth. Since the "covering of rough red brick" seemed a "mere shell" spread over these "royal palaces built for God and the saints," the contrast awakened a yearning for hidden treasure.[41] Symons remarked how hues in the mosaics reflected "certain purples and reds and bluish yellows" that he would later see streaking a sunset over the marshes.[42] Even more bewitching was a single column of green marble "veined with more colours than I have ever seen in marble: agate, porphyry, malachite, and I know not how many other precious substances. Looked at against the light it is like a great mottled green snake, dully alive, and standing rigid. Overhead, in the dome, there is a sky which is like the neck of a peacock, flowered over with patterns of leaves and beasts and birds. . . ."[43]

Evelyn Underhill reacted less favorably to the mosaics of San Vitale, which she deemed inferior to those in the Baptistery of the

Orthodox. Even though the choir of San Vitale shone "like some deep jewel," for her it exuded no joy, only a "morose magnificence."[44] Vogüé added a piquant note concerning the portrait of Justinian, which stands facing that of Theodora. This depiction of the emperor as a man in the prime of life contrasts with one in Sant' Apollinare Nuovo that endows the emperor with sagging jowls. In San Vitale the emperor appears a leader of men, while in the second he has become a bureaucrat hunched over his files, a contrast that reminded Vogüé of two types of portraits of Napoleon: the slim consul and the corpulent emperor.[45]

Itching to rebut whatever others said, Suarès lambasted the portrait of Theodora. Having begun *Vers Venise* with a satire on Milan, Suarès ended it with a hatchet job on Theodora. At first sight the stiff figures reminded him of epileptics about to suffer an attack, or rather of the dying tricked out in finery to await the end: "A world of strange beasts welcomes this procession of mummies set on their feet: gaunt does, birds with beaks of sharks, dogs covered with scales, peacocks with claws. . . ."[46]

Gradually Suarès saw through the finery to glimpse sexual desire. Justinian and his courtiers lust after the courtesans who stare back from the opposite wall. Showing neither breasts nor hips, yet steeped in orgies, Theodora glares at us with the eyes of an owl. Wallowing in desire, she displays "the surface of slumbering water, on a soul bare like a viper, hot like a panther, akin to a den of sins."[47] Although others saw in the image hints of Theodora's career as an adventuress, no one else vilified her as a whore in heat. Eager to mate with her are the fleshless bodies of Justinian and his entourage, whose eyes dilate as if they have just taken belladonna. To them Suarès imputed the same lust as to Theodora, all of them bodies without bones, mere lips and pupils. As the invective mounts, one begins to suspect that not Justinian or Theodora but Suarès had a brain teeming with unmentionable desires.

As if to restore common sense after Suarès's vagaries, Karl Scheffler enjoyed in San Vitale one of the ecstatic moments of his Italian trip. As he raised his eyes from watching barefooted men and women sweep out the mud, he beheld an "eastern fairy-tale," in which the very flowers and vines betrayed deeper feeling than many later Madonnas. "A visit in this isolation that glows with colors and forms, inside an abandoned, fever-ridden old church is an unforgettable experience. One glimpses rising out of the morass, out of the fragility of life, the miracle of human idealism, of human rapture over beauty, and of the human instinct to worship. It is not astonishing that in such churches Christians learned to believe in paradise."[48] Scheffler's glimpse of paradise and Suarès's vision of courtesans span the attractions of an interior that sent one critic of the Renaissance into ecstasy while it drove another to distraction.

13

Reminiscences of Rome in Rimini

AN INHUMAN HUMANIST

A traveler coming from Ravenna or Bologna must cross the Rubicon fifteen kilometers before reaching Rimini. The boundary between Cisalpine Gaul and the Roman Republic marked for Julius Caesar, as it still does for us, a step from which there is no returning. The ancient Romans made Rimini a key junction, where the Via Flaminia from Rome ended and the Via Emilia for Piacenza began. Stretched between a bridge of Tiberius and an arch of Augustus, the old town recalls the Roman camp that it once was, its Roman monuments vying with a masterpiece of the fifteenth century, the Malatesta Temple designed by Alberti and decorated by another Florentine, Agostino di Duccio. One savors Florentine genius more palpably here than in any other city of northern Italy except Padua.

Men of letters could not help bringing to this coastal city memories of Dante's verses in the fifth canto of the *Inferno* about the tragic love of Francesca da Rimini for her husband's brother Paolo. But even their plaint fades beside the deeds of another wayward lover three centuries later. Sigismondo Malatesta, the epitome of a criminal on a throne, riveted attention in a city that he beautified, winning acclaim from moralists as diverse as Symonds, Hutton, and Maurel, who condoned his crimes in order to exalt his panache. Maurel praised Sigismondo's refusal to veil his crimes, marveling at the scoundrel's zeal to build a pantheon to honor both Greek scholars and his third wife. Maurel was the only visitor to evoke the library that Sigismondo ordered built for his brother in neighboring Cesena. Modeled on Michelozzo's library at San Marco in Florence, this building of about 1450 remains the second oldest library of the Renaissance and one of the loveliest.[1] The contradictions of this murderer turned scholar take the breath away.

Suarès brought his usual acerbity to bear upon the vainglorious rogue, noting that not for nothing does Rimini smell more of marshes than of the sea.[2] Likening condottieri to bad actors, he saw their posturing foreshadowed by Nero, who in contrast to Renaissance swaggerers dazzled not just provincial towns but a whole empire. Suarès's tirade against village Neros reads like a foreboding of Mussolini, who was born in the Apennines not fifty kilometers from here. Like many others in this region, Mussolini probably descended from Roman soldiers whom Augustus dispersed in Romagna, so that il Duce came by his Roman gestures honestly. It defies belief that it was in 1910 and not 1930 that Suarès wrote, "They [Renaissance princes] have the vanity of mountebanks who possess public favor. They make themselves up as Roman Caesars; they grease their cheek with all the paints that imitate power. . . . Clowns are tragic, when they reign and get hissed. At their slightest whim, these little wretches aped great passion. Of Nero the Magnificent they had only the shifty eye and the insolence."[3] Mussolini did the tricks of a village mountebank wearing the trappings of an emperor.

Yet, when Suarès proceeded to list the crimes of Sigismondo, Mussolini appears paltry by comparison: "The tyrants of Rimini played Nero shamelessly. . . . The ugliness of this prince [Sigismondo] strikes me, carved on an admirable medal: debased pride, a solemn impudence, a self-indulgent resoluteness; cruelty in search of praise; he collects beautiful manuscripts, and he kills a woman in order to violate her dead body; he reads the insipid Terence; he loves Greek which he does not understand; and at a scoffing word he stabs one of his friends as they rise from table."[4] The conjunction in Sigismondo of virtue and vice answered a rhetorician's dream, goading writers to unfurl the paradoxes of the textbooks in order to evoke a criminal turned scholar. Devotees of classical probity could imagine no harsher epithet than "inhuman humanist."

THE MALATESTA TEMPLE

However beguiling may be the enigma of Sigismondo "Wronghead," most travelers focused not on the man but on the temple that he commissioned. Leone Battista Alberti was asked to transform a Gothic Franciscan church into a memorial to his patron that would also honor scholars. The effrontery notwithstanding, Sigismondo's decision to transform a church dedicated to Saint Francis into a temple to his own love affair produced one of the most admired works in northern Italy. It has stimulated a body of writing no less juicy than did its patron.

Topping all these is a book by Adrian Stokes, whose reflections debuted in T. S. Eliot's journal *The Criterion*. Written between 1925 and 1931, *Stones of Rimini* (1934) ranks as one of the most original essays on Italian art ever published by an Englishman. It comes as a shock, therefore, to learn that Stokes did not like Rimini, which he dismissed as "a town of cobblestones, in no way picturesque; a country-town that sprawls in the northern manner of industrial suburbs."[5] Treasuring his first glimpse of the temple's facade, he emphasized how the centrality of the door made each piece of Istrian marble merge into the whole: ". . . see how the pilasters are *grown* from the wall-space, grown steadfastly like a flower, without palpitation; see how incrusted is the effect of this most classical pediment within the central arch. You can no longer distinguish architectural members. The thing is organic, one, everlasting."[6] The parts disappeared into a whole, so that the emblems of intertwined roses and elephants that celebrate Sigismondo and Isotta seemed to grow from the stone. Letting his imagination run riot, Stokes coined a metaphor that suited Sigismondo to perfection: "The Malatesta rose is a tropical growth in miniature, an immense trunk with huge subsidiary shoots such as would stifle a deserted town within a year. It belongs to the foraging kind of vegetation that is almost animal."[7] Stokes never wearied of evoking the "forest" of roses that Sigismondo ordered to shelter his heraldic elephants: Fibers loop outward, while "the sheath's end . . . curls up and divides into flukes or scrolls."[8] From these curves derived the conceit of inserting a letter S to form what looks like a dollar sign.

Inside the temple, Stokes rejoiced to find the dollar sign placed among stunning colors: "There is elephantine foliage around the Gothic arches to the chapels: the predominant colours, blue and gold amid the stone hues, look personal and keen, interspersed in vault and spandrel above the porridge-coloured Greek marble of the reliefs: everywhere there are coloured disks nailed to wall-fronts; centres of gravity like navels."[9] Stokes went on in this vein for forty pages, examining each of the chapels and reliefs. Agostino di Duccio, who carved most of the reliefs, was known for his ability to render in stone diaphanous fabric so as to recall paintings by Botticelli. As Mary McCarthy put it: "Sheer chiffon veils, sometimes drooping over the soft cheek of a Virgin, sometimes rippling across a dimpling naked body, became, in the late *quattrocento*, almost a signature of the Florentine school. They are often seen in low relief, particularly in the work of Agostino di Duccio, that most voluptuous of Florentine sculptors, who botched the block of marble known as 'The Giant,' which Michelangelo, later, made into the 'David.'"[10]

Whereas McCarthy associated the drapery of Agostino with Botticelli, as Symonds did with that of Burne-Jones, Stokes linked Agostino with the watery matrix from which marble had congealed. Marble is compressed limestone, which embalms movements of the water where deposits once settled. As we noted in Verona, Stokes deemed marble the most watermarked of stone. Currents of lime-laden mud, out of which the stone had solidified, resumed pulsing beneath the chisel of Agostino, and nowhere so triumphantly as in the Malatesta Temple. Reliefs in the Chapel of the Planets depicted "every plane of waters," impelling Stokes to recount how in the temple he came to see "Mediterranean countries as water and water-life congealed into stone: I saw the elements in flux and trees growing from a crested marble wave. . . . The topmost wave is smooth, without a ripple. It is the shapely mountain side. On one summit there grows a myrtle tree, the aromatic evergreen shrub of limestone soil. The rose flowers in a valley of intermediate swell."[11] Better than any other sculptor, Agostino understood that marble is water congealed, water that longs to resume its "primeval eddies."[12]

Stokes could and did choose other towns besides Rimini to expound the watery pattern of limestone. He wrote earlier on Florence, later on Venice, and he could have written equally well about fountains in Viterbo or mantelpieces in Urbino. Instead, he exalted the Malatesta Temple because its carvings mimic water playing on sand, recalling the process whereby residues from animals turn into rock. Agostino had envisioned the water out of which stone had come. In a choice insight, Stokes discerned in the gray Verona marble used by Agostino a luminosity that seemed ideal for depicting astrology: "This Verona is hard, can be cut to a fine point. It is neither bright nor dull. No other marble is as luminous. Forms sculpted there are distinct yet suffused. The parallel is to objects seen in moonlight and to the curious magnetism of the moon mingling sea and earth."[13] A lunar glow filling the temple makes one forget that the marble itself was rifled from the interior of Sant' Apollinare in Classe at Ravenna. Startling as it is to find Florentine finesse imparted to Verona marble in a city built largely of brick, it is even more exhilarating to read the prose-poetry that Stokes fashioned out of this encounter.

For most others, the hero of the temple was neither Agostino nor Sigismondo but rather its architect Alberti. Symonds eulogized a man who seemed to have come fifty years too early, a genius whose feats of physical and mental prowess would awe Pater as surely as they did Hutton. Unfortunately, Alberti squandered his mature years in the study of the law, which Symonds in a Miltonic phrase called, "then as now, the quicksand of the noblest natures."[14] Alberti's sojourn in Rimini came midway in his career, after he had beautified Rome for Pope Nicholas V and before he went to Florence to do the same for the Medici. Symonds lauded the exterior of the temple as "perhaps the most original and graceful of the many attempts made by Italian builders to fuse the medieval and the classic styles."[15] In the interior Alberti had left "a strange medley of medieval and Renaissance work, a symbol of that dissolving scene in the world's pantomime, when the spirit of classic art, as yet but little comprehended, was encroaching on the early Christian taste."[16]

The wall ornaments enchanted Symonds for their spontaneity, gaiety, and pictorial skill. Like his contemporaries Boiardo in poetry and Botticelli in painting, Agostino combined Christian feeling and pagan ease in just the right proportions: "It was a happy moment, when art had reached consciousness, and the artist had not yet become self-conscious."[17] Neither hasty nor labored, these reliefs embodied the qualities that set mid-fifteenth-century art apart.

Even before the temple impelled Stokes to rethink the aims of sculpture, Aldous Huxley had weighed in with a dissent. Huxley decried Fascist intrusions upon Renaissance domains, having happened upon Rimini on a day when Fascists, escorting the right arm of a Jesuit saint, Francis Xavier, to sanctuaries throughout Italy, had reached Rimini. The obscenity of having Fascists parade a relic (the rest of whose body remained in Goa) inside a church that Sigismondo had wrested from Saint Francis prompted Huxley to confront the two saints with the two builders. The Englishman saw in Alberti's facade hints of protest against the incongruity of what converged here: "Grave, restrained and intellectual, Alberti's classical facade seems to deplore the *naïveté* of the first St. Francis and the intolerant enthusiasms of the second, and, praising Malatesta's intelligence, to rebuke him for his lusts and excesses."[18] No judgment could be further from Stokes's view that everything harmonizes in this building.

Huxley noticed how the triumphal arch of the facade presents a nobler version of the nearby Arch of Augustus, while in niches on the sides bones of scholars repose in unadorned sarcophagi. Huxley deemed such a "hymn to intellectual beauty" too severe to suit the blustering Sigismondo, who deserved rather the pomposity of the Baroque. "Alberti's monument, on the contrary, is a tribute to intellectual greatness. As a memorial to a particularly cunning and murderous ruffian, it is absurd."[19]

The French writers whom Huxley may be said to resemble paid both more and less attention to the temple than he did. Suarès, on the one hand, did not linger over Agostino's sculptures except to wonder what "the most graceful and feminine among the children of Donatello" was doing consorting with the monster Sigismondo.[20] Jean-Louis Vaudoyer, on the other hand, devoted to the temple his first major essay on Italy. Conceding that many would willingly trade the temple in order to have Sant' Apollinare in Classe intact, Vaudoyer, at age twenty-six, already displayed a knack for psychology: "The walls of this temple bear a strange, mysterious people, who seduce the imagination and lead it into a new world. Here, more than anywhere else in Italy, one best perceives the thick perfume of the early Renaissance: Clumsy, excited children have just discovered antiquity . . . they are not very learned and what they do not know they invent by copying nature. What other allegorical art is so lively, so naive?"[21]

A TURNING POINT ON THE JOURNEY TOWARD SELF-RENEWAL

However much Sigismondo, Alberti, and Agostino may monopolize attention, they cannot eclipse Rome in Rimini. For when Julius Caesar crossed the Rubicon from his province of Gaul into the forbidden territory of the Republic, he did so fifteen kilometers northwest of the city. Suarès flew into ecstasy when he stood on the very spot where Caesar had, in his own words, thrown the dice of history.[22] To savor a sense of dice being cast, the poet swirled pebbles in his mouth, relishing the knowledge that he still had central Italy to conquer. Suarès, a worshiper of acts of will, concluded *Vers Venise* on the banks of the Rubicon.

Rimini's chief reminder of ancient Rome is its location at the head of the great highway that Consul Marcus Emilius completed in 187 B.C. to connect the Adriatic Sea with the strategic city of Piacenza. As we have seen, the principal east-west streets of Parma and Bologna belong to the Via Emilia. It is awe-inspiring to stand on the narrow Roman bridge whose five arches of Istrian limestone span the River Marecchia and to realize that this one lane inaugurates the great thoroughfare of northern Italy. For more than two millenia, cities like Milan, Mantua, and Verona have funneled traffic through this bottleneck at the edge of Rimini. The bridge at Rimini abides as one of the most useful objects descending from antiquity, and also one of the most graceful.

Roman Rimini found apotheosis at the climax of the essay that Vaudoyer wrote in 1909. After a day savoring Roman relics and still more the temple, he strolled to the beach past ramshackle hotels. As he gazed at these flimsy structures, the contrast between their tawdriness and the majesty of Rome oppressed him with an urgency such as Ruskin must have known: ". . . ashamed of my epoch, I felt a sterile sadness devoid of beauty. Julius Caesar [he means Augustus] and Malatesta, one in his Arch, the other in his temple, still live in Rimini, where in their hurry the living work only for death. Under the arches of the temple, time was conquered, but, here, amid these fragile and sordid wrecks, an oblivion without grandeur has already settled."[23]

Weary with lugubrious thoughts, Vaudoyer returned to his hotel, only to encounter someone whom he had not seen for years. His acquaintance, a dandy from Paris, related traipsing all over Italy in order to behold portraits of Renaissance women. The boulevardier, a sort of picaro of impossible loves, imagined himself enamored of various heroines, beginning with Medea the daughter of Colleoni and ending as a matter of course with Isotta. As Vaudoyer's friend recounted Platonic "affairs" with these women, he exuded a certain high-mindedness, regretting that Medea had died before she could have known love and asserting that Isotta had deserved someone nobler than Sigismondo. Smacking of a novel by Henri de Régnier, such fantasies seemed to breathe life into the Renaissance, so that one almost wants to admire their audacity. But then one learns how after an evening of conversing Vaudoyer went to meet his friend's mistress, who had been left in the hotel. The dandy from Paris cohabited with a deaf-mute from Avignon, whom he required to model costumes of the women he adored. Needless to say, that evening she donned the robes of Isotta. This anecdote recalls tales such as the kind the novelist Villiers de l'Isle-Adam might have imagined. To encounter in the city of Sigismondo and Isotta caricatures out of fin-de-siècle fiction left Vaudoyer speechless, for the dandy was perverting something the writer adored.

By sexualizing the aura of places, Vaudoyer's acquaintance debased a process that has enriched countless others, for the goal of trips to Italy was and is self-renewal. Nearly all the writers featured in this book came to Italy seeking revival or even rebirth, and most of them found it, if not always in the form they had wished. Those who kept returning, like Ruskin, James, Maurel, Régnier, and Vaudoyer, matured through repeated contact with a beloved second country. They could watch themselves grow middle-aged and then old in communion with cherished places. Those who having settled in Italy also toured frequently, people like Berenson, Lee, and Hutton, derived equally profound refreshment from revisiting favorite spots.

Adrian Stokes's choice of Rimini as a place to focus his vision of the meaning of marble emphasized that city's role as a pivot, for it connects sea and land, past and present, North and center. The most dazzlingly original English writer on Italy since Ruskin devoted an entire book to explicating one building in a transitional city. Stokes found renewal by contemplating veins of marble, displaying an eye for stone that rivaled that of the sculptors he admired. Stokes's encounter with the stones of Rimini epitomized the power of Italian places to refresh, for Italy inspired him to discover something inside himself the way a sculptor divines a design inside a block of marble. Stokes's celebration of the stones of Rimini, like Ruskin's celebration of those of Venice and Verona eighty years before, represents a pinnacle of travel experience. Any city and any country that can inspire their degree of insight must be worth knowing.

Rimini, with its two-thousand-year-old bridge heading northwest into the Po Valley and its Arch of Augustus beckoning southward, is a fitting place to pause between two regions of this revivifying peninsula. Whatever fantasies Italy instilled in these its lovers, Rimini marks a dividing line between Italy north of the Apennines and Italy in the heart of those mountains. One phase of acquaintanceship with Italy ends here, where another begins. With its temple nestling between a bridge and an arch, Rimini embodies a land in which Roman ways reshaped themselves time and again. Just as travelers have come to renew themselves, so Italy has renewed its own inheritance time and again. A spectacle, repeated across two millenia, of a culture shedding one Roman skin, only to grow another, presents an image of life made new. The land of the Renaissance becomes a land of personal awakening, in which rebirths of ancient values foretell rebirth in oneself. To travel in the country of renaissances is to travel toward renewal of the self.

Notes

DNB   *Dictionary of National Biography*. 67 vols. (London: Smith, Elder, 1885–1901) and Supplements (London: Oxford University Press, 1927–).

RDM   *Revue des Deux Mondes* (Paris, 1831–).

Except where indicated all translations are my own. Further particulars about works cited appear in the Bio-Bibliography.

CHAPTER 1

1. Paul Fussell, *Abroad: British Literary Traveling Between the Wars* (New York: Oxford University Press, 1980), p. 203.
2. Ibid.
3. Ibid., p. 210.

CHAPTER 2

1. Bernard Wall, *Italian Art, Life and Landscape* (London: William Heinemann, 1956), pp. 5–6.
2. Henry Bordeaux, "Piémont-Ligurie," in *Le visage de l'Italie* (1929), ed. Gabriel Faure (Rome: Ente Nazionale Industrie Turistiche, 1934), p. 15.
3. William Hazlitt, *Notes of a Journey Through France and Italy* (1826), in *Complete Works* 10 (1932): 195–96.
4. Ibid., pp. 194–95.
5. Ibid., p. 196.
6. Charles de Rémusat, "Un voyage dans le nord de l'Italie," *RDM*, 2 pér., 11 (1 October 1857): 469.

7. Friedrich Nietzsche, Letter of November 13, 1888, to Franz Overbeck, in *Werke* (Munich: Hanser, 1966) 3:1330.
8. Jean Giono, *Voyage en Italie* (Paris: Gallimard, 1953), pp. 25–26.
9. Ibid., p. 26.
10. Henry James, "From Chambéry to Milan" (1872), in *Italian Hours* (Boston: Houghton Mifflin, 1909; reprinted New York: Grove Press, 1959), p. 86.
11. Edith Wharton, *The Valley of Decision* (New York: Scribner's, 1902), pp. 118–19.
12. Ibid., p. 110.
13. Ibid., pp. 111–12.
14. Antoine Valery, *Voyages en Italie* (Paris, 1833/1838) 3:434. On scientists' study of the Shroud see John H. Miller, *Report on the Shroud of Turin* (Boston: Houghton Mifflin, 1983).
15. Friedrich Nietzsche, Letter of April 7, 1888, to Pater Gast, in *Werke* 3:1283.
16. Ibid., Letter of April 14, 1888, to Carl Fuchs, in *Werke* 3:1287–88.
17. Italo Svevo, "Pagine di diario e sparse," in *Opera omnia* (Milano: dall'Oglio, 1968) 3:842.

CHAPTER 3

1. Antoine Valery, *Voyages en Italie* (Paris, 1833/38) 3:377.
2. Henry James, "Italy Revisited" (1877), in *Italian Hours* (1909) (New York: Grove Press, 1959), p. 114.
3. Adrian Stokes, *Quattro Cento* (1932), in *Critical Writings* (1978) 1:60.
4. Sean O'Faolain, *A Summer in Italy* (New York: Devin-Adair, 1950), pp. 40–41.
5. Ibid., pp. 41–42.
6. Ibid., p. 44.
7. Charles Dickens, *Pictures from Italy* (1846) (London: Deutsch, 1973), p. 79.
8. Thomas Hardy, "Genoa and the Mediterranean" (1887), in *The Complete Poems* (New York: Macmillan, 1976), p. 100. W. W. Collins included a watercolor of such a scene in *Cathedral Cities of Italy* (New York: Dodd, Mead, 1911), p. 180.
9. Heinrich Heine, *Reisebilder* (1828), in *Sämtliche Werke* (Leipzig: Meyer, 1893) 3:283.
10. Edith Wharton, *The Valley of Decision* (New York: Scribner's, 1902), pp. 355–56.
11. Jules Michelet, "Gênes" (1854), in *Le banquet: papiers intimes* (Paris: Calmann-Lévy, 1879), p. 15.
12. Ibid., p. 16.
13. Ibid.
14. Ibid.
15. Ibid., p. 17.
16. Ibid., pp. 16–17.
17. Ibid., p. 24.
18. Ibid., p. 19.
19. André Suarès, *Fiorenza* (1929), in *Le voyage du condottière* (Paris: Emile-Paul, 1964), p. 203.
20. Ibid., p. 204.

21. Ibid., p. 205.
22. Ibid., p. 206.
23. Ibid., p. 210.

CHAPTER 4

1. Henry James, "From Chambéry to Milan" (1872), in *Italian Hours* (1909), p. 88.
2. Jean-Louis Vaudoyer, *Italie retrouvée* (Paris: Hachette, 1950), pp. 53–57.
3. Ibid., p. 54.
4. André Suarès, *Vers Venise* (1910), in *Le voyage du condottière* (Paris: Emile-Paul, 1964), p. 32.
5. Ibid., p. 33.
6. Ibid., p. 34.
7. Ibid., p. 36.
8. Ibid.
9. John Ruskin, *Praeterita* (1885–89), in *Works* 35:115, 116.
10. John Ruskin, Entry of October 27, 1849, in *The Diaries of John Ruskin 1848–1873* (Oxford: Clarendon Press, 1958), p. 445.
11. D. H. Lawrence, Letter of October 23, 1913, to Lady Cynthia Asquith, in *The Letters of D. H. Lawrence*, ed. James T. Boulton (Cambridge: Cambridge University Press, 1979–), 2:88.
12. Herman Melville, Entry of April 6, 1857, in *Journal of a Visit to Europe and the Levant* (Princeton: Princeton University Press, 1955), p. 239.
13. Jean Giono, *Voyage en Italie* (Paris: Gallimard, 1953), p. 39.
14. James, "From Chambéry to Milan," p. 90.
15. Suarès, *Vers Venise*, p. 35.
16. Ibid.
17. Ibid.
18. Percy Bysshe Shelley, Letter of April 20, 1818, to Thomas Love Peacock, in *Letters of Percy Bysshe Shelley*, ed. Frederick L. Jones (Oxford: Clarendon Press, 1964), 2:8.
19. Cecil Headlam, *Venetia and Northern Italy* (London: J. M. Dent, 1908), pp. 62–63.
20. Adrian Stokes, *The Quattro Cento* (1932), in *Critical Writings* (1978) 1:165.
21. Ibid.
22. Ibid.
23. John Ruskin, *Modern Painters*, vol. 2 (1846), in *Works* 4:317–18.
24. Louis Simond, *A Tour of Italy and Sicily* [1817] (London: Longman, 1828), p. 12.
25. Charles de Rémusat, "Un voyage dans le nord de l'Italie," *RDM*, 2 pér., 11 (1 October 1857): 489.
26. Walter Pater, "Leonardo da Vinci" (1869), in *The Renaissance: Studies in Art and Poetry* [1873] (London: Macmillan, 1928), p. 125.
27. Ibid., p. 112.
28. James, "From Chambéry to Milan," p. 91.

29. Edith Wharton, "Picturesque Milan" [1903], in *Italian Backgrounds* (New York: Scribner's, 1905), pp. 164–65.
30. Ibid., pp. 165–66.
31. Evelyn Underhill, Entry of April 2, 1902, in *Shrines and Cities of France and Italy* (London: Longmans Green, 1949), p. 13.

CHAPTER 5

1. Edward Hutton, *The Cities of Lombardy* (London: Methuen, 1912), p. 186.
2. Cecil Headlam, *Venetia and Northern Italy* (London: Dent, 1908), pp. 328–29.
3. Edmond and Jules de Goncourt, *L'Italie d'hier: notes de voyages 1855–1856* (Paris: Conquet, 1894), pp. 13–14.
4. Charles de Rémusat, "Un voyage dans le nord de l'Italie," *RDM*, 2 pér., 11 (1 October 1857): 493.
5. Jean Giono, *Voyage en Italie* (Paris: Gallimard, 1953), p. 49.
6. Ibid., p. 70.
7. Walter Pater, "Art Notes in North Italy" (1890), in *Miscellaneous Studies: A Series of Essays* (London: Macmillan, 1895), p. 82.
8. Ibid., pp. 82–83.
9. Ibid., p. 83.
10. Arthur Symons, "Brescia and Romanino" (1903), in *Cities of Italy* (New York: Dutton, 1907), p. 258.
11. Pater, "Art Notes," p. 84.
12. Ibid., pp. 84–85.
13. Ibid., p. 85.
14. Ibid., p. 86.
15. Ibid.
16. Ibid., p. 83.
17. Ibid., pp. 83–84.
18. Ibid., p. 83.
19. Symons, "Brescia and Romanino," p. 259.
20. Headlam, *Venetia and Northern Italy*, p. 327; Edith Wharton, *Italian Backgrounds* (New York: Scribner's, 1905), p. 36.
21. Wharton, *Italian Backgrounds*, p. 37.
22. Gabriel Faure, "Brescia" (1909), in *Heures d'Italie* (Paris: Fasquelle, 1921), p. 48.
23. André Maurel, *Petites villes d'Italie* 1 (1906): 159.
24. Pater, "Art Notes," p. 86.
25. Edward Freeman, "Brescia," in *Historical and Architectural Sketches* (London: Macmillan, 1876), p. 285.
26. Ibid., p. 283.
27. J. Henry Dunant, *Un Souvenir de Solférino* (Geneva: Fick, 1862), p. 33.
28. Ibid., pp. 38–39.
29. Ibid., p. 40.
30. Ibid., p. 72.

CHAPTER 6

1. Israel Zangwill, *Italian Fantasies* (New York: Macmillan, 1910), pp. 238–39.
2. Edward Hutton, *The Cities of Lombardy* (London: Methuen, 1912), p. 207.
3. Ibid., pp. 217–18.
4. André Maurel, *Petites villes d'Italie* (Paris: Hachette, 1906) 1:248–49. The English translation appears in Maurel, *Little Cities of Italy*, vol. 1 (New York: Putnam's, 1911), pp. 240–41.
5. Maurel, *Petites villes* 1:249–50. English translation in *Little Cities* 1:241.
6. Maurel, *Petites villes* 1:252. English translation in *Little Cities* 1:243–44.
7. Charles de Rémusat, "Un voyage dans le nord de l'Italie," *RDM*, 2 pér., 11 (15 October 1857): 724–25.
8. André Suarès, *Vers Venise* (1910), in *Le voyage du condottière* (Paris: Emile-Paul, 1964), p. 83.
9. Ibid., p. 85.
10. Ibid.
11. Rémusat, "Un voyage," p. 723.
12. Edmond and Jules de Goncourt, *L'Italie d'hier: notes de voyages 1855–1856* (Paris: Conquet, 1894), pp. 55–56.
13. Charles Dickens, *Pictures from Italy* (1846) (London: Deutsch, 1973), pp. 135–36.
14. Vernon Lee, "The Lakes of Mantua," in *Genius Loci: Notes on Places* (London: Grant Richards, 1899), p. 165.
15. Ibid., p. 167.
16. Ibid., p. 165.
17. Ibid., p. 166.
18. Ibid., p. 168.
19. Ibid., pp. 168–69.
20. Ibid., p. 168.
21. Ibid.

CHAPTER 7

1. Charles de Rémusat, "Un voyage dans le nord de l'Italie," *RDM*, 2 pér., 11 (15 October 1857): 706.
2. Jean Giono, *Voyage en Italie* (Paris: Gallimard, 1953), p. 129.
3. Ibid., p. 119.
4. Ibid., p. 116.
5. Adrian Stokes, *Venice: An Aspect of Art* (1945), in *The Critical Writings of Adrian Stokes* (London: Thames and Hudson, 1978) 2:88.
6. Edmond and Jules de Goncourt, *L'Italie d'hier: notes de voyages 1855–1856* (Paris: Conquet, 1894), pp. 49–50.
7. Ibid., p. 50.
8. Henry James, "Venice" (1882), in *Italian Hours* (1909) (New York: Grove Press, 1959), p. 14.
9. Ibid., p. 23.
10. Maurice Hewlett, Letter of Easter 1898, in *The Letters of Maurice Hewlett* (London: Methuen, 1926), p. 40.

11. Ibid.
12. Antoine Valery, *Voyages en Italie* (Paris, 1831/1838) 1:299.
13. John Ruskin, *The Stones of Venice*, vol. 2 (1853), in *Works* 10:82.
14. Ibid., 10:83.
15. Ibid., 10:90.
16. Ibid., 10:92.
17. E. V. Lucas, *A Wanderer in Venice* (New York: Macmillan, 1914), p. 17.
18. James, "Venice," pp. 10–11.
19. André Suarès, *Vers Venise* (1910), in *Le voyage du condottière* (Paris: Emile-Paul, 1964), p. 132.
20. Ibid., p. 135.
21. Arthur Symons, "Venice" (1894/1903), in *Cities of Italy* (New York: Dutton, 1907), p. 79.
22. Ibid.
23. Herbert Spencer, *An Autobiography*, 2 vols. (New York: Appleton, 1904), 2:406.
24. Ibid., 2:407.
25. Goncourt, *L'Italie d'hier*, p. 20.
26. Ibid.
27. Osbert Sitwell, *Winters of Content* (1932) (London: Duckworth, 1950), p. 42.
28. Ibid., p. 43.
29. Jean-Louis Vaudoyer, *Italie retrouvée* (Paris: Hachette, 1950), pp. 87–88.
30. Suarès, *Vers Venise*, pp. 142–43.
31. Ruskin, *The Stones of Venice*, vol. 3 (1853), in *Works* 11:100.
32. Ibid., 11:103.
33. Ibid., 11:81.
34. John Ruskin, Diary entry of May 28, 1846, in *Works* 11:19, note 1.
35. Ibid.
36. James, "Venice," p. 25.
37. Ibid.
38. Ibid.
39. Jean-Louis Vaudoyer, "Venise d'après-guerre" (1920), in *Les délices d'Italie* (Paris: Plon, 1924), p. 93.
40. Ruskin, *The Stones of Venice*, vol. 3 (1853), in *Works* 11:379.
41. Ibid., 11:108–9.
42. Ibid., 11:109.
43. Ibid.
44. Adrian Stokes, *Venice: An Aspect of Art* 2:88.
45. Ibid., 2:89.
46. Ibid.
47. Ibid., 2:91.
48. Ibid., 2:89.
49. Ibid.
50. Ibid., 2:90.
51. Ibid.
52. Ibid.
53. Ibid.
54. Ibid.
55. Mary McCarthy, *Venice Observed* (New York: Raynal, 1956), p. 146.

56. Ruskin, *The Stones of Venice*, vol. 3 (1853), in *Works* 11:187.
57. Henry James, "Venice: An Early Impression" (1872), in *Italian Hours* (1909), p. 59.
58. Vaudoyer, "Venise d'après-guerre," p. 95.
59. Maurice Barrès, *Amori et dolori sacro* (1903), in *L'Oeuvre de Maurice Barrès* (Paris: Club de l'honnête homme, 1966) 7:19.
60. John Ruskin, Letter of September 24, 1845, in *Ruskin in Italy* (Oxford: Clarendon Press, 1972), p. 212.
61. John Ruskin, *Modern Painters*, vol. 2 (1846), in *Works* 4:270–71; *Stones of Venice*, vol. 3 (1853), in *Works* 11:403–28.
62. Ruskin, *Stones of Venice* 11:403.
63. Ibid., 11:428. See also Ruskin, *Modern Painters*, vol. 2 (1846), in *Works* 4:270.
64. James, "Venice: An Early Impression," p. 59.
65. Ibid., p. 58.
66. Ibid., p. 60.
67. James, "Venice" (1882), p. 22.
68. Ibid.
69. Ibid., pp. 21–22.
70. John Richard Green, "Venice and Tintoretto," in *Stray Studies from England and Italy* (London: Macmillan, 1904), p. 262.
71. Ibid., p. 263.
72. J. A. Symonds, "A Venetian Medley," in *Sketches and Studies in Italy and Greece* (London: Smith, Elder, 1898) 1:265.
73. Ibid., 1:266.
74. Richard Aldington, *Life for Life's Sake: A Book of Reminiscences* (New York: Viking, 1941), p. 351.
75. Sean O'Faolain, *A Summer in Italy* (New York: Devin-Adair, 1950), p. 179.
76. Paul Morand, *Venises* (Paris: Gallimard, 1971), pp. 133, 134, 136.
77. Vernon Lee, "The Lion of St. Mark's and Admiral Morosini," in *Genius Loci: Notes on Places* (London: Grant Richards, 1899), pp. 114–15.
78. Vernon Lee, "Out of Venice at Last" (1914), in *The Golden Keys, and Other Essays on the Genius Loci* (New York: Dodd, Mead, 1925), p. 74.
79. Ibid.
80. William Hazlitt, *Notes of a Journey Through France and Italy* (1826), in *Works* 10:267–68.
81. Ibid.
82. Suarès, *Vers Venise*, pp. 137–38.

CHAPTER 8

1. André Suarès, *Vers Venise* (1910), in *Le voyage du condottière* (Paris: Emile-Paul, 1964), p. 117.
2. Ibid.
3. Ibid., p. 118.
4. Vernon Lee, "Petrarch's House at Arquà," in *The Tower of the Mirrors* (London: John Lane, 1913), p. 181.

5. Maurice Hewlett, "Ippolita in the Hills," in *Little Novels of Italy* (1899) (New York: Scribner's, 1926), p. 68.
6. Antoine Valery, *Voyages en Italie* (Paris, 1831/1838) 1:412.
7. Ibid., 1:416.
8. Kenneth Clark, *Another Part of the Wood: A Self-Portrait* (London: John Murray, 1974), p. 162. See also Clark, "Donatello and the Tragic Sense in the Quattrocento" (1976), in *The Art of Humanism* (New York: Harper and Row, 1983), pp. 11–42, esp. 24–26.
9. Karl Scheffler, *Italien: Tagebuch einer Reise* (1913), 5th ed. (Leipzig: Insel, 1925), p. 72.
10. Suarès, *Vers Venise*, p. 122.
11. Ibid., pp. 121–22.
12. Ibid., p. 122.
13. Ibid.
14. Ibid., p. 123.
15. Ibid., p. 118.
16. Charles de Rémusat, "Un voyage dans le nord de l'Italie," *RDM*, 2 pér., 11 (1 October 1857): 508.
17. Jean-Louis Vaudoyer, *Compagnon d'Italie: lettres à Amicie* (Paris: Fayard, 1958), p. 65.
18. John Ruskin, *Giotto and His Works in Padua* (1853 and 1860), in *Works* 24:1–123.
19. Rémusat, "Un voyage," p. 510.
20. John Ruskin, *Modern Painters*, vol. 2 (1846), in *Works* 4:44.
21. Ruskin, *Giotto* 24:80.
22. Ibid., 24:78.
23. Ibid., 24:110.
24. Walter Starkie, *The Waveless Plain: An Italian Autobiography* (New York: Dutton, 1938), p. 112.
25. Ibid., p. 113.
26. Ibid., p. 114.
27. Scheffler, *Italien*, p. 73.
28. Ibid., p. 74.
29. Ibid., p. 65.
30. Evelyn Underhill, "Padua" (1903), in *Shrines and Cities of France and Italy* (London: Longmans Green, 1949), pp. 31–32.
31. Ibid., p. 32.

CHAPTER 9

1. Arthur Moeller van den Bruck, *Die italienische Schönheit* (Munich: Piper, 1913), p. 278.
2. Thomas Babington Macaulay, Letter of September 4, 1856, in *The Letters*, vol. 6 (Cambridge: Cambridge University Press, 1981), 58–59.
3. John Ruskin, Letter of September 7, 1845, in *Ruskin in Italy* (Oxford: Clarendon Press, 1972), p. 196.

4. John Ruskin, "Verona, and Its Rivers" (1870), in *Works* 19:433–34.
5. John Ruskin, " 'A Joy for Ever' " (1857), in *Works* 16:67.
6. Ibid., 16:66.
7. John Ruskin, *The Stones of Venice*, vol. 2 (1853), in *Works* 10:312.
8. Ibid.
9. Karl Scheffler, *Italien: Tagebuch einer Reise* (Leipzig: Insel, 1913), p. 44.
10. Ibid., p. 45.
11. Henry James, "Venice: An Early Impression" (1872), in *Italian Hours* (1909) (New York: Grove Press, 1959), p. 62.
12. Sean O'Faolain, *A Summer in Italy* (New York: Devin-Adair, 1950), p. 220.
13. Ibid., p. 239.
14. Ibid., p. 240.
15. Ibid.
16. Ibid., p. 230.
17. Ibid., p. 231.
18. Arthur Symons, "Verona" (1903), in *Cities of Italy* (New York: Dutton, 1907), p. 227.
19. J. A. Symonds, "Crema and the Crucifix" (1879), in *Sketches and Studies in Italy and Greece* (London: Smith, Elder, 1898) 1:212–13.
20. Adrian Stokes, *The Quattro Cento* (1932), in *The Critical Writings* (London: Thames and Hudson, 1978) 1:38.
21. Ibid., 1:39.
22. Ibid., 1:78.
23. Ibid., 1:79.
24. Ruskin, "Verona, and Its Rivers" 19:432.
25. James, "Venice: An Early Impression," p. 61.
26. John Hobhouse, *Italy* (London: John Murray, 1859) 1:67–68.
27. Edward Freeman, "Ancient Verona," in *Historical and Architectural Sketches: Chiefly Italian* (London: Macmillan, 1876), p. 32.
28. Ibid., p. 34.
29. Ibid.
30. Ibid.
31. Scheffler, *Italien*, p. 47.
32. Hobhouse, *Italy* 1:77.
33. James, "Venice: An Early Impression," p. 62.
34. Ruskin, *The Stones of Venice*, vol. 3 (1853), in *Works* 11:88.
35. Ibid.
36. Ibid., 11:90.
37. Ruskin, "Verona, and Its Rivers" 19:439.
38. Ibid., 19:441.
39. Ibid.
40. Israel Zangwill, *Italian Fantasies* (New York: Macmillan, 1910), p. 260.
41. Scheffler, *Italien*, p. 46.
42. André Maurel, *Petites villes d'Italie* (Paris: Hachette, 1906) 1:183.
43. Ibid., 1:179.
44. André Suarès, *Vers Venise* (1910), in *Le voyage du condottière* (Paris: Emile-Paul, 1964), p. 112.
45. Ibid.

46. Ibid.
47. Johann Wolfgang Goethe, Entry of September 17, 1786, in *Italienische Reise* (1816), in *Werke* (Hamburg: Christian Wegner, 1950) 11:51.
48. Gabriel Faure, "Vérone" (1913), in *Heures d'Italie* (Paris: Fasquelle, 1921), pp. 255–61.
49. Henri de Régnier, "L'Altana ou la vie vénitienne 1899–1924," *RDM*, 7 pér., 42 (15 November 1927): 396.
50. Ibid., p. 397.
51. Suarès, *Vers Venise*, p. 114.
52. Ibid.
53. Ibid.

CHAPTER 10

1. André Suarès, *Vers Venise* (1910), in *Le voyage du condottière* (Paris: Emile-Paul, 1964), p. 75.
2. Stendhal, Draft of October 17 to 28, 1840, for a letter to Honoré de Balzac, in *Correspondance. III. 1835–1842* (Paris: Gallimard, 1968). Jean-Louis Vaudoyer quotes a slightly different version in *Compagnon d'Italie: lettres à Amicie* (Paris: Fayard, 1958), p. 78.
3. Matthew Josephson, *Stendhal, or the Pursuit of Happiness* (Garden City: Doubleday, 1946), pp. 419–20.
4. Maurice Barrès, "L'automne à Parme" (1893), in *Du sang, de la volupté et de la mort* (1894), in *L'Oeuvre de Maurice Barrès* (Paris: Club de l'honnête homme, 1965) 2:137.
5. Ibid., 2:138.
6. Ibid., 2:139.
7. Ibid.
8. Osbert Sitwell, *Winters of Content* (1932), 2d ed. rev. (1950) (Westport, Conn.: Greenwood Press, 1978), p. 183.
9. Ibid.
10. Ibid., p. 182.
11. Ibid., pp. 190–91.
12. Ibid., p. 191.
13. Ibid., p. 192.
14. Ibid., p. 165.
15. Ibid., p. 164.
16. Edith Wharton, "Sub Umbra Liliorum: An Impression of Parma" (1902), in *Italian Backgrounds* (New York: Scribner's, 1905), p. 117.
17. Lady Sydney Owenson Morgan, *Italy* (1821), cited in Sitwell, *Winters of Content*, p. 164, note.
18. Charles de Rémusat, "Un voyage dans le nord de l'Italie," *RDM*, 2 pér., 11 (15 October 1857): 727.
19. Edward Freeman, "Romanesque Architecture in Lombardy," in *Historical and Architectural Sketches: Chiefly Italian* (London: Macmillan, 1876), pp. 251–52.

20. Ibid., p. 252.
21. Wharton, "Sub Umbra Liliorum," p. 118.
22. Bernard Berenson, *The North Italian Painters of the Renaissance* (New York: Putnam, 1907), pp. 133, 139.
23. Ibid., p. 137.
24. Wharton, "Sub Umbra Liliorum," pp. 113–14.
25. Ibid., p. 116.
26. J. A. Symonds, "Parma," in *Sketches and Studies in Italy and Greece* (London: Smith Elder, 1898) 2:152.
27. Ibid., 2:152–53.
28. Ibid., 2:152.
29. Ibid., 2:153.
30. Ibid., 2:154.
31. Ibid.
32. Ibid.
33. Ibid., 2:154–55.
34. Ibid., 2:157.
35. Ibid.
36. Suarès, *Vers Venise*, p. 77.
37. Ibid., p. 78.
38. Ibid., pp. 78–79.
39. Ibid., p. 79.
40. Stendhal, Entry of December 20, 1816, in *Voyages en Italie* (Paris: Gallimard, 1973), p. 390.
41. John Ruskin, Letter of July 13, 1845, in *Ruskin in Italy* (Oxford: Clarendon Press, 1972), pp. 145–46.
42. John Ruskin, *Modern Painters*, vol. 2 (1846), in *Works* 4:198.
43. John Ruskin, "The Relation Between Michael Angelo and Tintoret" (1872), in *Works* 22:97.
44. Sitwell, *Winters of Content*, p. 207.
45. Ibid., p. 206.
46. Ibid., p. 165.
47. Ibid., p. 205.
48. Ibid.
49. Ibid., p. 206.
50. Edwin and Evangeline Blashfield, "Parma," in *Italian Cities* (New York: Scribner's, 1900) 1:268.
51. Ibid., 1:276.
52. André Maurel, *Petites villes d'Italie* (Paris: Hachette, 1908) 2:49–50.

CHAPTER 11

1. William Hazlitt, *Notes of a Journey Through France and Italy* (1826), in *Complete Works* (London: Dent, 1932) 10:205.
2. Stendhal, Entry of December 28, 1816, in *Voyages en Italie* (Paris: Gallimard, 1973), p. 391.

3. Charles de Rémusat, "L'Italie: notes de voyage," *RDM*, 2 pér., 35 (1 September 1861): 336.

4. Percy Bysshe Shelley, Letter of November 9, 1818, to Thomas Love Peacock, in *The Letters of Percy Bysshe Shelley*, ed. Frederick L. Jones (Oxford: Clarendon Press, 1964), 2:53.

5. Vernon Lee, " 'Dusky, Many-Towered Bologna' " (1914), in *The Golden Keys and Other Essays on the Genius Loci* (New York: Dodd, Mead, 1925), p. 67.

6. Edmond and Jules de Goncourt, *L'Italie d'hier: notes de voyages 1855–1856* (Paris: Conquet, 1894), p. 64.

7. Osbert Sitwell, *Winters of Content* (1932), 2d ed. rev. (1950) (Westport, Conn.: Greenwood Press, 1978), p. 98.

8. Karl Scheffler, *Italien: Tagebuch einer Reise* (Leipzig: Insel, 1913), pp. 84–86.

9. Johann Wolfgang Goethe, Entry of October 18, 1786, in *Italienische Reise* (1816), in *Werke* (Hamburg: Wegner, 1950) 11:104.

10. J. A. Symonds, *Renaissance in Italy*, vol. 7 (1886) (New York: Modern Library, 1935), 2:886.

11. Ibid.

12. John Ruskin, *Modern Painters*, vol. 1 (1843), in *Works* 3:184, note.

13. John Ruskin, *Modern Painters*, vol. 2 (1846), in *Works* 4:203–4.

14. Johann Wolfgang Goethe, Entry of October 19, 1786, in *Italienische Reise* 11:105.

15. Ibid., 11:106.

16. Ibid., 11:107.

17. Shelley, Letter of November 9, 1818, in *Letters* 2:52.

18. Examples include Paul Bourget, *André Cornélis* (1887) and *Le Disciple* (1889).

19. Maurice Barrès, "L'Evolution de l'individu dans les musées de Toscane" (1894), in *Du sang, de la volupté et de la mort* (1894), in *L'Oeuvre de Maurice Barrès* (Paris: Club de l'honnête homme, 1965) 2:164.

20. Ibid., 2:165.

21. Ibid.

22. Ibid., 2:165–66.

23. André Suarès, *Sienne la bien aimée* (1932), in *Le voyage du condottière* (Paris: Emile-Paul, 1964), p. 415; and Kenneth Clark, *Another Part of the Wood: A Self-Portrait* (London: Murray, 1974), p. 124.

24. Freya Stark, *Traveller's Prelude* (London: Murray, 1950), p. 149.

25. Rémusat, "L'Italie: notes de voyage," p. 338.

26. Evelyn Underhill, Entry of April 3 to 7, 1902, in *Shrines and Cities of France and Italy* (London: Longmans Green, 1949), pp. 16–17.

27. Ibid., p. 17.

28. Ibid.

29. Ibid., p. 14.

30. Ibid., p. 16.

31. Lee, " 'Dusky, Many-Towered Bologna,' " p. 61.

32. Ibid., pp. 62–63.

33. Ibid., p. 64.

34. Ibid., p. 67.

35. Ibid., p. 64.

36. Ibid., p. 66.

CHAPTER 12

1. Edward Freeman, "Ravenna," in *Historical and Architectural Sketches Chiefly Italian* (London: Macmillan, 1876), pp. 44–45.
2. Ibid., p. 44.
3. Ibid., pp. 45–46.
4. Charles de Rémusat, "L'Italie: notes de voyage," *RDM*, 2 pér., 35 (1 September 1861): 349–50.
5. Ibid., p. 369.
6. Eugène-Melchior de Vogüé, "A Ravenne," *RDM*, 3 pér., 117 (15 June 1893): 926.
7. Ibid., p. 940.
8. Antoine Valery, *Voyages en Italie* (Paris, 1831–38) 2:395.
9. Maurice Barrès, "Dans le Sépulcre de Ravenne" (1894), in *Du sang, de la volupté et de la mort* (1894), in *L'Oeuvre de Maurice Barrès* (Paris: Club de l'honnête homme, 1965) 2:140.
10. Ibid.
11. Ibid., 2:141.
12. Ibid.
13. Ibid.
14. Ibid.
15. Ibid., 2:142.
16. Freeman, "Ravenna," p. 53.
17. Barrès, "Dans le Sépulcre de Ravenne" 2:144.
18. André Maurel, *Petites villes d'Italie* (Paris: Hachette, 1908) 2:122.
19. Henry James, "Ravenna" (1873), in *Italian Hours* (Boston: Houghton Mifflin, 1909), pp. 341, 342.
20. Evelyn Underhill, "Ravenna" (1903), in *Shrines and Cities of France and Italy* (London: Longmans Green, 1949), pp. 34–35.
21. Rémusat, "L'Italie: notes de voyage," pp. 366–67.
22. Freeman, "Ravenna," p. 50.
23. Vogüé, "A Ravenne," p. 932.
24. James, "Ravenna," p. 339.
25. Ibid.
26. André Suarès, *Vers Venise* (1910), in *Le voyage du condottière* (Paris: Emile-Paul, 1964), p. 176.
27. Rémusat, "L'Italie: notes de voyage," p. 360.
28. Freeman, "Ravenna," pp. 46–47.
29. Edwin and Evangeline Blashfield, "Ravenna," in *Italian Cities* (New York: Scribner's, 1900) 1:41.
30. Ibid., 1:40.
31. Underhill, "Ravenna," p. 34.
32. Ibid.
33. Ibid.
34. Vogüé, "A Ravenne," p. 928.
35. Blashfield, "Ravenna" 1:30.
36. Ibid., 1:32.
37. Ibid., 1:33.

38. Ibid., 1:34.
39. Ibid., 1:35.
40. Ibid., 1:37.
41. Arthur Symons, "Ravenna" (1903), in *Cities of Italy* (New York: Dutton, 1907), p. 175.
42. Ibid., p. 180.
43. Ibid., p. 181.
44. Underhill, "Ravenna," p. 35.
45. Vogué, "A Ravenne," p. 930.
46. Suarès, *Vers Venise*, p. 172.
47. Ibid., p. 173.
48. Karl Scheffler, *Italien: Tagebuch einer Reise* (Leipzig: Insel, 1913), p. 148.

CHAPTER 13

1. André Maurel, *Paysages d'Italie* (Paris: Hachette, 1913) 2:91–98.
2. André Suarès, *Vers Venise* (1910), in *Le voyage du condottière* (Paris: Emile-Paul, 1964), p. 151.
3. Ibid., p. 153.
4. Ibid., p. 154.
5. Adrian Stokes, *Stones of Rimini* (1934), in *The Critical Writings of Adrian Stokes* (London: Thames and Hudson, 1978) 1:260.
6. Ibid., 1:265.
7. Ibid., 1:266.
8. Ibid.
9. Ibid., 1:267.
10. Mary McCarthy, *The Stones of Florence* (New York: Harcourt Brace Jovanovich, 1959), p. 85.
11. Stokes, *Stones of Rimini* 1:253.
12. Ibid., 1:254.
13. Adrian Stokes, *The Quattro Cento* (1932), in *The Critical Writings* 1:179.
14. J. A. Symonds, "Rimini" (1874), in *Sketches and Studies in Italy and Greece* (London: Smith, Elder, 1898) 2:19–20.
15. Ibid., 2:29.
16. Ibid.
17. Ibid., 2:31.
18. Aldous Huxley, "Rimini and Alberti," in *Essays New and Old* (New York: George H. Doran, 1927), p. 99.
19. Ibid., p. 101.
20. Suarès, *Vers Venise*, p. 155.
21. Jean-Louis Vaudoyer, "A Rimini" (1909), in *Les délices d'Italie* (Paris: Plon, 1924), pp. 108–9.
22. Suarès, *Vers Venise*, pp. 186–89.
23. Vaudoyer, "A Rimini," p. 113.

Bio-Bibliography

This appendix sketches the careers and cites the writings about northern Italy of forty-five authors from five countries. Arranged alphabetically, the entries summarize judgments scattered throughout the book. Chapters that mention a writer are listed at the end of his or her entry. If no secondary works are cited, none could be found.

Three degrees of importance are signified. The fifteen writers on northern Italy whom I regard as the best have their last names capitalized, and the name is preceded by an asterisk (e.g., *LEE). Nineteen others, of slightly less importance, have their names in capitals but with no asterisk (e.g., WHARTON), while the remaining ones are neither capitalized nor starred. These rankings pertain to writing about northern Italy but not central Italy, where, for example, HEWLETT would deserve an asterisk.

Of the forty-five, almost half are English and almost a third French. There are twenty-one English, fourteen French, five Americans, four Germans, and one Swiss, four of the total being women. Of the premier fifteen, six are English (Freeman, Hutton, Lee, Ruskin, Stokes, and Symonds), seven are French (Barrès, Jules de Goncourt, Maurel, Rémusat, Suarès, Valery, and Vaudoyer), and two are American (Blashfield and James). Although only one is a woman (Lee), she may be the most perceptive of all.

*BARRÈS, Maurice (1862–1923), French novelist, politician, and essayist, born in Charmes-sur-Moselle (Lorraine), died in Neuilly (near Paris). The future French nationalist purported still to be a socialist when he revolutionized writing about Italy with eleven essays of 1893 and 1894 that were collected in *Du sang, de la volupté et de la mort* (Paris: G. Charpentier and E. Fasquelle, 1894; 2d ed., 1903). They are reprinted in *L'Oeuvre de Maurice Barrès* (Paris: Club de L'honnête homme, 1965) 2:121–67. Published alongside travel essays on Spain and Germany, his meditations on the Italian lakes, Parma, Ravenna, Bologna, Pisa, Siena, and Florence display egoism, bravado, and startling juxtapositions. His "cult of the self" *(culte du moi)* broke with the cautious positivism of Bourget and the lush impressionism of the Goncourt brothers in favor of a refined iconoclasm. A second group of essays, "La mort de Venise," in *Amori et dolori sacrum: la mort de Venise* (Paris: Félix Juven, 1902), reprinted in *L'Oeuvre de Maurice Barrès* (1967) 7:7–59, pursued the cult of the dead by celebrating previous visitors to the decaying city, which he had exalted in the climax of his second novel, *Un homme libre* (1889). There he hailed Tiepolo the Ingenious as the incarnation of Venice (*L'Oeuvre de Maurice Barrès* 1 [1965]: 237–46). A piece of wartime journalism, "Dix jours en Italie" (May 1916), in *L'Oeuvre de Maurice Barrès* 9 (1967): 57–121, described the front in Friuli and Venice.

On Barrès and Italy see Jules Bertaut, *L'Italie vue par les français* (Paris: Librairie des Annales, 1913), pp. 206–8; Enzo Caramaschi, "Maurice Barrès et Venise," in *Maurice Barrès: Actes du colloque organisé par la Faculté des Lettres et des Sciences Humaines de l'Université de Nancy* (Nancy: Annales de l'Est, No. 24, 1963), pp. 265–84; and Philip Ouston, *The Imagination of Maurice Barrès* (Toronto: University of Toronto Press, 1974), pp. 25–29.

See GENOA, MILAN, VENICE, PARMA, BOLOGNA, RAVENNA.

Berenson, Bernard (1865–1959), Russian-American art historian, diarist, and conversationalist, born near Vilna (Russian Poland), died in Settignano (near Florence). Superbly intelligent, thoroughly Europeanized, Berenson created a legend as a self-taught arbiter of Italian painting. Although a preference for conversation largely diverted him from writing, the diaries of his last two decades reflect the richness and suppleness of his mind, as in *Sunset and Twilight: From the Diaries 1947 to 1956* (New York: Harcourt, Brace, 1963). Fortunately, he kept a diary during trips he took while in his eighties to revisit old haunts. Entries in *The Passionate Sightseer: From the Diaries 1947 to 1956* (New York: Simon and Schuster, 1960), a book dedicated to Freya Stark, show him at his most observant, his memory supplying pungent comparisons about Venice, Romagna, and places in central and southern Italy. These travel notes make one wish that Berenson had started recording his impressions of Italy much earlier. Berenson's conversation, a tiny portion of which Umberto Morra recorded in *Conversations with Berenson* (Boston: Houghton Mifflin, 1965), is one of the lost treasures of the twentieth century.

See John Walker, *Self-Portrait with Donors: Confessions of an Art Collector* (Boston: Little, Brown, 1974), pp. 80–101; Kenneth Clark, *Another Part of*

the Wood: A Self-Portrait (London: John Murray, 1974), pp. 127–65; Ernest Samuels, *Bernard Berenson: The Making of a Connoisseur* (Cambridge: Harvard University Press, 1979); and Paul Barolsky, "Walter Pater and Bernard Berenson," *The New Criterion* 2 (April 1984): 47–57.
See PARMA.

*BLASHFIELD, Edwin (1848–1936), American painter and essayist, born in Brooklyn, New York, died in South Dennis, Massachusetts. After touring northern and central Italy during the 1890s, the mural painter and his wife, Evangeline, published one of the masterpieces of American travel literature, *Italian Cities*, 2 vols. (New York: Scribner's, 1900). The Blashfields' prose suits today's taste better than do the murals with which he adorned such shrines of culture as the Library of Congress, City College of New York, and the Massachusetts Institute of Technology. Trained in Paris during the 1870s under Léon Bonnat, Blashfield was a fine draftsman, who carried a gift for line into his prose.

Since his wife, Evangeline (who died in 1918), scarcely published separately (apart from a review of Eugene Schuyler's *Italian Influences* in *Book Buyer* 22 [March 1901]: 117–19), it is hard to disentangle what each contributed to their joint authorship. To judge from the review of Schuyler's book, Evangeline wrote in a style very like that of *Italian Cities*. It is just possible that she was the abler writer and he the keener observer. In any case, they collaborated in uniquely successful fashion.

See Edith Wharton, Review of Edwin and Evangeline Blashfield, *Italian Cities*, in *The Bookman* 13 (August 1901): 563–64 (laudatory in the extreme); and Leonard N. Amico, *The Mural Decorations of Edwin Howland Blashfield* (Williamstown, Mass.: Sterling and Francine Clark Art Institute, 1978).
See PARMA, RAVENNA.

Bryant, William Cullen (1794–1878), American poet and essayist, born in Cummington, Massachusetts, died in New York City. His *Letters of a Traveller*, First Series (New York: Putnam, 1850) and Second Series (New York: Appleton, 1859), concern mostly Tuscany and southern Italy, with two memorable letters dating from Venice in August 1835 and July 1858. Vivid phrasing and alertness to change made him a travel writer *manqué*, one far more perceptive than his contemporary Cooper.

See Charles Henry Brown, *William Cullen Bryant* (New York: Scribner's, 1971), esp. pp. 225–30.

Dickens, Charles (1811–1870), English novelist and essayist, born in Portsea (Kent), died in Gadshill (London). Dickens had just completed his *American Notes* (1844) and *Martin Chuzzlewit* (1844) when he undertook a sojourn in Italy from July 1844 to June 1845, spent largely in Genoa, from which he and his family ventured to Mantua, Verona, Venice, and cities of Emilia-Romagna. Letters to the *Daily News* were reworked to constitute *Pictures from Italy* (London: Bradbury and Evans, 1846; reprinted London: Andre Deutsch, 1973). While traveling on the Continent, Dickens played the naïf, alternately amazed, bewildered, and disappointed. Although he struck off memorable phrases, especially about places he disliked, he lacked training to analyze works of art, and, more surprisingly, he fell short of the Goncourt brothers at depicting street life. Dickens was too provincial to appreciate Italy as Hazlitt and Pater did.

See David Paroissien, "Introduction," in Dickens, *Pictures from Italy* (London: Andre Deutsch, 1973), pp. 9–34.

See GENOA, MANTUA, PARMA.

Dunant, Henry (1828–1910), Swiss philanthropist, born in Geneva, died in Heiden (Switzerland). In June 1859 the thirty-one-year-old Calvinist, who had served in French Algeria, happened to be visiting the vicinity of Brescia when French, Austrians, and Piedmontese fought the battle of Solferino. At his own expense, he published an account of the battle and its aftermath in *Un Souvenir de Solférino* (Geneva: Fick, 1862), which was distributed gratis. A painstaking narrative recounted the combatants' delays in caring for the wounded, while extolling the efforts of the Brescians. This travel essay sparked such outrage that Dunant summoned a conference to Geneva in 1864, at which the International Red Cross was born.

See Stefan Markus, *Henry Dunant: Schicksal und Bestimmung* (Affoltern: Aehren Verlag, 1946), pp. 50–91; and Jacques Pous, *Henry Dunant, l'Algérien ou le mirage colonial* (Geneva: Grounauer, 1979).

See BRESCIA.

FAURE, Gabriel (1877–1962), French novelist and essayist, born in Tournon (Ardèche), died in Paris. One of the most winsome of French writers on Italy, Faure lacked the learning of Valery, Rémusat, or Maurel, not to mention the brilliance of Barrès, Suarès, or Vaudoyer. His pieces on towns of northern Italy, first published in the *Revue des Deux Mondes* between 1907 and 1913, were collected in *Heures d'Italie* (Paris: Fasquelle, 1921). Essays in *Pèlerinages passionés. 2e série. Ames et décors romantiques* (Paris: Fasquelle, 1922) interpreted Musset, Lamartine, Sainte-Beuve, and Stendhal in Italy with fine insight, while *Au pays de Virgile* (Paris: Fasquelle, 1930) offered highly personal reminiscences. He commissioned from French authors a collection of travel pieces, *Le visage de l'Italie* (Paris: Horizons de France, 1929; reprinted Rome: Ente nazionale industrie turistiche, 1934), which is the finest anthology of its kind. Faure was the most lovable of French writers on Italy, comparable to Edward Hutton in humility and graciousness, while lacking his thoroughness and energy.

See A. Dujet, *Gabriel Faure* (Paris: Sansot, 1921); Charles Picard, "Gabriel

Faure," *Revue archéologique* 2 (October 1962): 222–23; and P. Hamon, "Faure (Gabriel-Auguste)," *Dictionnaire de biographie française* 13 (1972): 743.
   See MILAN, VERONA, BRESCIA, MANTUA.

*FREEMAN, Edward A. (1823–1892), English historian of Norman England and of church architecture, born in Harborne (Staffordshire), died of smallpox in Alicante (Spain). This prolific essayist first traveled to Italy in 1871 with his friend John Richard Green. A first collection of travel essays, *Historical and Architectural Sketches: Chiefly Italian,* covered all regions of the peninsula and was excerpted without permission by Augustus Hare in his *Cities of Central and Northern Italy* (1876). Freeman's sequel, *Sketches from the Subject and Neighbour Lands of Venice* (London: Macmillan, 1881), concentrated on Venetia, Apulia, and Dalmatia (especially Split). A posthumous collection, *Studies of Travel: Italy* (New York: G. P. Putnam's, 1893), covered Tuscany, Umbria, and the South. Unfailingly lucid and provocative, writing in a style modeled on Macaulay, Freeman commanded knowledge of every notable church in Europe, comparing buildings in England, France, Germany, and Italy with equal ease. A superb teacher who valued limpidity above advocacy, Freeman furnished an antidote to the moralizing of Ruskin, the attitudinizing of J. A. Symonds, and the poeticizing of Stokes.
   See James Bryce, "Edward A. Freeman" [ca. 1894], in *Studies in Contemporary Biography* (London: Macmillan, 1903), pp. 262–92; and William Richard Wood Stephens, *The Life and Letters of Edward A. Freeman,* 2 vols. (London: Macmillan, 1895).
   See INTRODUCTION, MILAN, BRESCIA, VENICE, VERONA, PARMA, RAVENNA.

GIONO, Jean (1895–1970), French novelist and essayist, born and died in Manosque (Basses-Alpes). Son of a Protestant shoemaker in the French Alps, Giono spent his entire life in his native village. Only in 1953 did he undertake a trip to Italy to visit sites dear to his Piedmontese grandfather, who had fought for Mazzini. His account of that trip, *Voyage en Italie* (Paris: Gallimard, 1953), is unlike any other. In recording mores more often than works of art, the novelist explored Italian ways of being happy.
   See Maxwell A. Smith, *Jean Giono* (New York: Twayne, 1966).
   See TURIN, MILAN, BRESCIA, PADUA, VERONA.

GOETHE, Johann Wolfgang (1749–1832), German poet, dramatist, novelist, and universal mind, born in Frankfurt am Main, died in Weimar. Goethe's trip to Italy from September 1786 to April 1788 marked a turning point both in his career and in German literature. Encounters with antiquities, artists, and sensuality in Rome opened the second half of his life.

His seminal book, *Die italienische Reise* [The Italian Trip], based on a diary, was published only in 1816, with the aim of championing classical art against romantic. The sections of *Die italienische Reise* on northern Italy are less profound than those on Rome, Naples, and Sicily, which constitute the heart of the book. As probably the single most influential travel book ever written about Italy, the work is somewhat overrated, at least as regards northern Italy. Even Goethe's father, who visited northern Italy in 1740, covered more ground. See J. Caspar Goethe, *Goethes Vater reist in Italien: "Reise durch Italien"* (Mainz: Kupferberg, 1972).

See Julius R. Haarhaus, *Auf Goethes Spuren in Ober-Italien* (Leipzig: C. G. Naumann, 1896); and René Michéa, *Le "Voyage en Italie" de Goethe* (Paris: Aubier, 1945).

See PADUA, VERONA, BOLOGNA.

*GONCOURT, Edmond de (1822–1896), French novelist, essayist, and diarist, born in Nancy, died in Paris.
*GONCOURT, Jules de (1830–1870), born in Paris, died in Auteuil. The Goncourt brothers pioneered impressionist travel writing in their journal of northern and central Italy, written mainly by Jules during 1855 and 1856 but published only in 1894, as *L'Italie d'hier: notes de voyages 1855–1856* (Paris: Conquet, 1894). It is embellished with lovely sketches by Jules. The fantasy "Venise la nuit: Rêve," ibid., pp. 257–85, published in *L'Artiste* (May 2 and 10, 1857), was part of a book, *L'Italie la nuit*, of which the brothers burned the manuscript because it seemed too "eccentric." (See *L'Italie d'hier*, p. 257, note.) A few letters in Jules de Goncourt, *Lettres* (Paris: Charpentier, 1885), pp. 97–128, shed a different light on the same trip. The Goncourts' *Journal: mémoires de la vie littéraire* [1887–96] is meager on Italy.

Apparently written mostly, if not exclusively, by Jules, the diary entries of *L'Italie d'hier* furnish a classical expression of impressionism in travel literature. Awareness of nuances of color, alertness to street scenes, and attraction to anything that changed from moment to moment constitute the kernel of this sensibility, which required the brothers to stretch French vocabulary and syntax. To behold something exotic jostling something familiar thrilled the brothers, who in "Venise la nuit" let their imaginations run riot in a phantasmagoria of images drawn from painting, carnivals, and street scenes. Had they published a book of such fantasies, it might have revolutionized writing about Italy.

Although the Goncourt brothers visited Rome in 1867 to prepare for their novel *Madame Gervaisis* (1869), their travel writing never again reached the intensity of 1855 and 1856. The death of the more talented Jules in 1870 left his brother a ghost of himself, who devoted too much time to commemorating his brother.

See André Billy, *Les Frères Goncourt: la vie littéraire à Paris pendant la seconde moitié du XIXe siècle* (Paris: Flammarion, 1954).
See BRESCIA, MANTUA, VENICE, PARMA, BOLOGNA.

Greville, Charles Cavendish Fulke (1794–1865), English diarist, died in London. Renowned for accounts of parliamentary intrigue, this master diarist spent March to July of 1830 in Italy, sojourning in Rome and Naples, with stops in Ferrara, Venice, Vicenza, Brescia, and Milan. The resulting narrative appears in Charles C. F. Greville, *The Greville Memoirs: A Journal of the Reigns of King George IV and King William IV,* ed. Henry Reeve, 3 vols. (London: Longmans Green, 1874), 1:288–417. A seasoned observer who noticed details missed by everyone else, Greville ranks with Hazlitt and Hobhouse as celebrant of the Grand Tour. His report of legal proceedings in Naples anticipated Gladstone's revelations a generation later (Ibid., 1:334–38).
See John Andrew Hamilton, "Greville, Charles Cavendish Fulke (1794–1865)," *DNB* 23 (1890): 158.

Hardy, Thomas (1840–1928), English novelist and poet, born in Dorset, died in Dorchester (Dorset). Having just published *The Mayor of Casterbridge* (1886), in spring 1887 Hardy visited Genoa, Lodi, Tuscany, and Rome, where he wrote eight poems, all but two about Tuscany and Rome. His poem "Genoa and the Mediterranean" expressed the incongruity of first viewing the sea of Homer and Virgil through a flutter of underwear in a street of Genoa. Italy, no less than England, brought out his gift for dramatizing contrasts between expectation and reality.
See Thomas Hardy, *The Complete Poems,* ed. James Gibbon (New York: Macmillan, 1976), pp. 100–109.
See GENOA.

HAZLITT, William (1778–1830), English essayist, born in Maidstone (Kent), died in London. Hazlitt was already a master of the familiar essay when he traveled through France and Italy from September 1824 to November 1825. The resulting *Notes of a Journey Through France and Italy* (London: Hunt and Clarke, 1826), reprinted in *Complete Works* (London: Dent, 1932) 10:85–339, written while abroad, covered Turin, Florence, Rome, Ferrara, Venice, Verona, and Milan in an unstudied style that breaks now and then into unforgettable passages. Not obsessed by any topic except the untidiness of inns, Hazlitt devoted equal attention to works of art, conditions of travel, and panoramas. Were he French or German, Hazlitt would be known as a feuilletonist, for he was one of England's leading practitioners of this half-playful, half-melancholy genre devised for the bourgeoisie. Neither ecstatic nor jaundiced, Hazlitt reacted to each city and each coach-lap on its merits, always turning a phrase to suit the occasion.

See Herschel Baker, *William Hazlitt* (Cambridge: Harvard University Press, 1962), pp. 442–48.

See TURIN, VENICE, PARMA, BOLOGNA.

Heine, Heinrich (1797–1856), German poet and feuilletonist, born in Düsseldorf, died in Paris. A master of the feuilleton, Heine wrote a number of travel books, mostly about Germany. *Reisebilder* (1826–31) contains two essays of 1830 on Lucca and the Baths of Lucca, as well as an essay on Genoa. Verbiage without substance mars these gossamer productions, which show that, regardless of his reputation as a writer on travel in Germany, Heine plays only a minor role in writing about Italy. Almost alone among Germans in Italy, he never visited Rome.

See Jeffrey Sammons, *Heinrich Heine: A Modern Biography* (Princeton: Princeton University Press, 1979); and Gabriel Faure, "Henri Heine à Gênes," in *Italiam* . . . (Paris: Arthaud, 1961), pp. 71–82.

See GENOA.

HEWLETT, Maurice (1861–1923), English poet, novelist, and essayist, born in Weybridge (Surrey), died in Broadchalke (near Salisbury). Hewlett's letters and novellas from northern Italy offer a foretaste of his masterpiece, *The Road in Tuscany: A Commentary* (New York: Macmillan, 1904), one of the most vigorous books about Italy. Although an archaic style mars his prose, Hewlett deserves to be rediscovered as surely as do Vernon Lee and André Suarès. The novella "Ippolita in the Hills," in *Little Novels of Italy* (London, 1899; reprinted New York: Scribner's, 1926), contains a cameo of Padua. As recounted in *The Letters of Maurice Hewlett*, ed. Laurence Binyon (London: Methuen, 1926), pp. 39–41, 49–51, 64–71, he visited Venice, Verona, Padua, and Ferrara in 1898 and Mantua in 1899 before undertaking the longer trip of March to May 1902 that produced *The Road in Tuscany*. Rivaling the Goncourt brothers in evoking shades of color, and Aldous Huxley in provoking Italians to talk, Hewlett could have written more masterpieces about Italy had he not retired to Wiltshire.

See Stephen Gwynn, "Maurice Hewlett," *Edinburgh Review* 239 (January 1924): 61–72; H.W. Graham, "Maurice Hewlett," *Fortnightly* 118 (July 1925): 47–63; and Bruce Sutherland, *Maurice Hewlett: Historical Romancer* (Philadelphia, 1938).

See VENICE, PADUA, VERONA.

HOBHOUSE, John Cam, later **Lord Broughton** (1786–1869), English politician and man of letters, born in Redland (near Bristol), died in London. Hobhouse owed his fame to a friendship with Lord Byron that began at Trinity College, Cambridge. He accompanied Byron to Greece and Sicily in 1809–10 and to Italy from autumn 1816 to January 1818, and later served as his literary executor. As a commentary on the Fourth Canto of Byron's *Childe Harold* he wrote *Historical Illustrations of the Fourth Canto of Childe Harold Containing Dissertations on the Ruins of Rome; and an Essay on Italian Literature* (London: John Murray, 1818), which offers detailed accounts of Ferrara, Clitumnus, and Rome. In 1859 Hobhouse, having become Baron Broughton in 1851, collected these and later writings in *Italy: Remarks Made in Several Visits from the Year 1816 to 1854*, 2 vols. (London: John Murray, 1859), which recounts not only the journey with Lord Byron but also a sojourn at the Congress of Verona in 1822. Except for Henri de Régnier in *L'Altana*, no one else summed up a lifetime of sojourning in Italy in a single volume.

See George Fisher Russell Barker, "Hobhouse, John Cam (1786–1869)," *DNB* 27 (1891): 47–50.

See MILAN, VENICE, VERONA, PARMA, BOLOGNA.

*HUTTON, Edward (1875–1969), English essayist and travel writer, born and died in London. This most prolific of English writers on Italy is also one of the most lovable. A prodigious output between 1898 and 1958 included ten volumes on northern and central Italy, which, having been published between 1905 and 1913, were revised during the 1920s and rewritten during the 1950s, a unique feat. Hutton's historical novel, *Sigismondo Pandolfo Malatesta, Lord of Rimini* (London: Dent, 1906), reprinted as *The Mastiff of Rimini* (London: Methuen, 1926), celebrated a figure whose ruthlessness contrasted with the Englishman's gentleness. A friend of most English writers on Italy, notably Arthur Symons, Janet Ross, and Norman Douglas, Hutton lobbied tirelessly on behalf of greater attention by England to Italy, helping to found the British Institute in Florence in 1917. Eleven years later he was received into the Roman Catholic Church in Assisi, consummating an inclination that was foreshadowed in his first major book, *Studies in the Lives of the Saints* (Westminster: Constable, 1902). Living on a private income in Boccaccio's former villa at Corbignano, not far from Berenson's villa of I Tatti, Hutton walked nearly every inch of Tuscany and Umbria, while tramping Lombardy, Emilia, and Venetia only slightly less thoroughly. Genoa he covered in *Florence and the Cities of Northern Tuscany* (1907). Above all, Hutton was a lovable companion, cheerful without being insipid, learned without being pompous. Thoroughly English in his ignorance of French writers and his contempt for nearly all Germans, Hutton combined sweetness of temper with rare powers of discrimination and phenomenal energy.

See Dennis E. Rhodes, *The Writings of Edward Hutton* (London: Hollis and Carter, 1955); and Rhodes, "Edward Hutton," *Burlington Magazine* 112 (January 1970): 51–52.

See MILAN, BRESCIA, MANTUA, PARMA.

*JAMES, Henry (1843–1916), American novelist, dramatist, and essayist, born in New York City, died in London. The most famous of American writers on Italy, James collected travel essays of 1872 to 1909 in *Italian Hours* (Boston: Houghton Mifflin, 1909; reprinted New York: Grove Press, 1959). His fiction owed something to the impressionism of the Goncourt brothers, the elder of whom he knew in Paris, for he shared their skill in depicting colors, street scenes, and resemblances between painting and life. No one except Ruskin, Lee, and Suarès matched his vivacity when he wrote at full throttle, as in the three essays that open *Italian Hours*. A novel about a young heiress dying in Venice, *The Wings of the Dove* (1902), climaxed James's thirty years of involvement with that city, which the novella *The Aspern Papers* (1888) evoked almost as wistfully. James infused American verve into European elegy to achieve a unique blend. In his travel essays no less than in his fiction, James proved himself the ultimate Europeanized American.

See Leon Edel, *Henry James*, 5 vols. (Philadelphia: Lippincott, 1953–72), esp. 2:81–180; and Nathalia Wright, *American Novelists in Italy: The Discoverers: Allston to James* (Philadelphia: University of Pennsylvania Press, 1965), pp. 198–248. For reminiscences of James as a travel companion see Mrs. Humphry Ward, *A Writer's Recollections*, 2 vols. (New York: Harper, 1918), 2:195–210.

See TURIN, GENOA, MILAN, VENICE, VERONA, RAVENNA.

Lawrence, David Herbert (1885–1930), English novelist, poet, and essayist, born in Eastwood (near Nottingham), died in Vence (near Nice). Although Lawrence wrote unremittingly about Italy, where he dwelt for a total of six years, his essays and poems concern Tuscany, Sardinia, or the South, except in *Twilight in Italy* (1916), which was written at Gargano on Lake Garda from September 1912 to April 1913. At that time Lawrence overflowed with a vitality that was all too palpably ebbing away fourteen years later when he wrote the elegiac *Etruscan Places* (1932). The affinity of a dying man with Etruscan tombs made that his best book on Italy. Engaging comments on certain cities pepper his letters, which are available in *The Collected Letters of D. H. Lawrence*, ed. Harry T. Moore, 2 vols. (New York: Viking Press, 1962), and *The Letters of D. H. Lawrence*, ed. James T. Boulton, planned in 7 vols. (Cambridge: Cambridge University Press, 1979–). Italy, the land of virility and "blood knowledge," disclosed more about Lawrence than he did about it.

See Paul Fussell, *Abroad: British Literary Traveling Between the Wars* (New York: Oxford University Press, 1980), pp. 141–64; and Jeffrey Meyers, *D. H. Lawrence and the Experience of Italy* (Philadelphia: University of Pennsylvania Press, 1982) [mentions only three or four other writers on Italy].

See INTRODUCTION, MILAN.

*LEE, Vernon, pseudonym of **Violet Paget** (1856–1935), English essayist, born in Boulogne (Pas-de-Calais), died in Florence. This born travel essayist grew up in Rome and near Pistoia, debuting as a woman of letters with a long book on Italian music, *Studies of the Eighteenth Century in Italy* (London: W. Satchell, 1880; 2d ed. London: Unwin, 1907). A year later appeared a collection of essays, *Belcaro, Being Essays on Sundry Aesthetical Questions* (London: W. Satchell, 1881), two of which anticipated the travel essays of two decades later. Although "In Umbria" (ibid., pp. 156–96) was her first travel essay, it took her another eighteen years to discover her vocation as a travel writer. Another early experiment in evoking places produced pieces on Pavia and Piacenza in "Lombard Colour Studies," in *Juvenilia, Being a Second Series of Essays on Sundry Aesthetical Questions*, 2 vols. (London: Unwin, 1887), 2:67–76.

According to Peter Gunn, Lee credited the mother of the painter John Singer Sargent with having introduced her to the cult of the Genius Loci as early as the 1860s. Five volumes of travel essays began with *Genius Loci: Notes on Places* (London: Grant Richards, 1899), which, like the ones that followed, covered France, Germany, and Italy in about equal measure. Essays of five to ten pages evoked a particular encounter with a place, detailing sensory minutia as a catalyst of memory in a manner reminiscent of Walter Pater. Lee grew more confident in *The Enchanted Woods and Other Essays on the Genius of Places* (London: John Lane, 1905), while *The Spirit of Rome: Leaves from a Diary* (London: John Lane, 1906) printed entries from a dozen visits to Rome between 1888 and 1905. The latter jottings are less vivid than her carefully composed essays, which resumed with *The Sentimental Traveller: Notes on Places* (London: John Lane, 1908). A fourth volume, notably rich on Italy, appeared as *The Tower of the Mirrors and Other Essays on the Spirit of Places* (London: John Lane, 1913). By then these had become Lee's most popular writings, abounding in historical lore, mythic fantasy, and personal insight.

Her final collection, *The Golden Keys, and Other Essays on the Genius Loci* (New York: Dodd, Mead, 1925), was written almost entirely before World War I. The most subtle of prolific travel essayists—she published more than 40 essays on Italy out of an *oeuvre* of 130 such pieces—has been all but forgotten.

A most beautiful tribute to Vernon Lee came from her friend Maurice Baring in the chapter entitled "Stimulants" in *Lost Lectures or the Fruits of Experience* (London: Peter Davies, 1932), pp. 83–90. See also Rudolf Borchardt, "Vernon Lee" [1935], in *Prosa*, 3 vols. (Stuttgart: Klett, 1960), 3:423–28; Peter Gunn, *Vernon Lee: Violet Paget 1856–1935* (London: Oxford University Press, 1964), esp. pp. 33–35, 180–84; and René Wellek, "Vernon Lee, Bernard Berenson and Aesthetics," in *Friendship's Garland: Essays Presented to Mario Praz on His Seventieth Birthday*, ed. Vittorio Gabrieli, 2 vols. (Rome: Edizione di Storia e Letteratura, 1966), 2:233–51.

See INTRODUCTION, MANTUA, VENICE, PADUA, BOLOGNA, RAVENNA.

*MAUREL, André (1863–1943), French essayist, born in Paris. This friend of Barrès undertook in 1898 to compose an *oeuvre* on Italian cities, which had grown by 1914 to comprise eleven volumes. The most sustained account of Italy to appear since Valery, this one covered every region except Piedmont-Liguria and included a volume each on Rome (1909), Naples (1912), Florence (1913), and Venice, as well as Sicily (1911). The first two volumes of *Petites villes d'Italie*, 4 vols. (Paris: Hachette, 1906–11) [translated as *Little Cities of Italy*, 2 vols. (New York: Putnam's, 1911–13)], covered Venetia, Tuscany, Lombardy, and Emilia-Romagna. *Paysages d'Italie*, 4 vols. (Paris: Hachette, 1913–23), treated Cremona, Sabbioneta, Imola, Faenza, and Forli in Volume 2 (1913) and South Tirol and Friuli in Volume 3. A close friend of Barrès until the Dreyfus affair separated them in 1897, and also of Bourget and Régnier, Maurel wrote essays on about a hundred cities, focusing each on a colorful period or salient personage. While shunning bibliography, Maurel assembled enough rare information to offer stunning interpretations. The essay "Les derniers pas: Crémone," in *Paysages d'Italie* 2 (1913): 1–4, surveys his Italian *oeuvre*, a topic that his memoirs, *Souvenirs d'un écrivain, 1883–1914* (Paris: Hachette, 1925), ignore. See also Maurel, "Quelques souvenirs sur la jeunesse de Maurice Barrès," *Revue de France* 4 (January 1, 1924): 202–10.

See BRESCIA, MANTUA, VERONA, PARMA, RAVENNA, RIMINI.

MICHELET, Jules (1798–1874), French historian and essayist, born in Paris, died in Hyères (near Nice). Best known for his *Histoire de France*, 17 vols. (1833–67), Michelet resembled Ruskin in combining moral passion, magnificent rhetoric, and wayward interests. An animus against the rich pervaded his essay on Genoa, "Le pays de la faim" [1854], in *Le banquet, papiers intimes* (Paris: Calmann-Lévy, 1879), pp. 3–142, which was written in Nervi just after he had completed the seven volumes of his *Histoire de la Révolution française* (1847–53). A rearranged version appears in *Oeuvres complètes* (Paris: Flammarion, 1980) 16:591–664, with a rich introduction by Paul Viallaneix, 16:571–90. Michelet's ability to coin metaphors, to visualize topography, and to summarize centuries is without peer. Unfortunately, his earlier writings on Italy do not live up to the intensity of this piece, written during convalescence on the Riviera. Travel jottings from Lombardy and Venice in 1838 appeared in *Sur les chemins de l'Europe: Angleterre, Flandre, Hollande, Suisse, Lombardie, Tirol* (Paris: Flammarion, 1893) but needed revising to impart coherence. They are reprinted in *Journal*, ed. Paul Viallaneix (Paris: Gallimard, 1959), 1:263–76. Although a stay in Rome in April 1830 exercised a pivotal influence, Italy never mesmerized Michelet the way it did Chateaubriand, Stendhal, or even Alfred de Musset.

Like Alphonse Karr, who visited Genoa a year or two after him, Michelet looms as a great travel writer *manqué*.

See Gabriel Monod, *La vie et la pensée de Jules Michelet, 1798–1852*, 2 vols. (Paris: Champion, 1923), esp. 1:173–80.

See GENOA, VERONA.

Nietzsche, Friedrich (1844–1900), German philosopher and cultural critic, born near Lützen, Saxony, died in Weimar, having succumbed to syphilitic paralysis in Turin in January 1889. Although letters of 1880 to 1883 from Genoa and of 1888–89 from Turin offer vivid phrases, Nietzsche wrote no travel essays. Besides those cities, Nietzsche frequented Rome and Sorrento and would have lingered in Venice if the climate had suited him. Endowed with mythic imagination and perpetual restlessness, Nietzsche possessed the ingredients to be a major travel writer, but his mission as a cultural critic led him in other directions. For letters about places, Nietzsche, *Briefe an Peter Gast* [1908], 3d ed. (Leipzig: Insel, 1924), will be indispensable as long as *Nietzsche Briefwechsel: Kritische Ausgabe* (Berlin: de Gruyter, 1975–) remains incomplete.

See Curt Paul Janz, *Nietzsche Biographie*, 3 vols. (Munich: Hanser Verlag, 1978–79); Ronald Hayman, *Nietzsche: A Critical Life* (New York: Oxford University Press, 1980); Wieland Schmied, "Turin als Metapher und Vision: Der Maler Giorgio de Chirico auf den Spuren Nietzsches," *Merian* 35 (June 1982): 31–34; and Anacleto Verrecchia, *Zarathustras Ende: Die Katastrophe Nietzsches in Turin* (Vienna: Böhlau, 1986).

See TURIN.

O'FAOLAIN, Sean, born **John Whelan** (1900–), Irish novelist and essayist, born in Cork. In numerous short stories and novels from 1932 on, O'Faolain expressed disillusionment with the Irish Republic, which he had helped to establish. To gain perspective on Ireland, he toured Turin, Genoa, Florence, Siena, Rome, Venice, and Verona in 1947, and in *A Summer in Italy* (New York: Devin-Adair, 1950) produced the sprightliest account of travel in northern Italy since Suarès. Although somewhat dated and overly preoccupied with Ireland, the book is more penetrating than its sequel on southern Italy, *An Autumn in Italy* (New York: Devin-Adair, 1953). As the last English-language novelist to take Italy seriously, O'Faolain expounded the country's tension between Then and Now as lucidly as anyone.

See G. T. Davenport, "Sean O'Faolain's Troubles: Revolution and Provincialism in Modern Ireland," *South Atlantic Quarterly* 75 (Summer 1976): 312–22.

See TURIN, GENOA, VENICE, VERONA.

*PAGET, Violet. See *LEE, Vernon.

PATER, Walter (1839–1894), English novelist and essayist, born in Shadwell (near London), died in Oxford. While a tutor at Brasenose College, Oxford, from 1864 to 1880, Pater drafted a manifesto of the impressionist mentality in the "Conclusion" (1868) of *The Renaissance: Studies in Art and Poetry* (London: Macmillan, 1873). Deleted from the second edition (1877) for fear of scandal, this credo of aestheticism urged making life a necklace of transcendent moments, each of which will justify the trouble of having lived. Emphasis on fleetingness, dissolution, and loneliness makes this a desperate cry against impending chaos. A historical fantasy, *Marius the Epicurean* (1885), grew out of Pater's stay in Rome during 1882 and 1883, evoking Rome and the coast of Tuscany under Marcus Aurelius. For all his potential gifts as a travel writer, Pater wrote only one essay on Italy, "Art Notes in North Italy" (1890), in *Miscellaneous Studies: A Series of Essays* (New York: Macmillan, 1895), which appraised paintings by Gaudenzio Ferrari in Varallo and Vercelli, as well as by Borgognone in Lodi, and by Moretto and Romanino in Brescia. Pater formulated a credo that can excite any traveler, for even if life is not a chain of eloquent moments, travel often is.

See Germain d'Hangest, *Walter Pater, l'homme et l'oeuvre*, 2 vols. (Paris: Didier, 1961); J. Hillis Miller, "Walter Pater: A Partial Portrait," *Daedalus* 105 (Winter 1976): 97–113; and Paul Barolsky, "Walter Pater and Bernard Berenson," *The New Criterion* 2 (April 1984): 47–57.

See MILAN, BRESCIA.

RÉGNIER, Henri de (1864–1936), French poet, novelist, and essayist, born in Honfleur (Normandy), died in Paris. This aristocratic aesthete wrote a novel about Italy, *La double maîtresse* (Paris: Mercure de France, 1900), before he ever went there. His first visit to Venice in September 1899 began a series of a dozen sojourns over twenty-five years, which are recalled in the memoir *L'Altana ou la vie vénitienne (1899–1924)* (Paris: Mercure de France, 1928), which was also published in the *Revue des Deux Mondes*, July to November 1927, and reprinted under the title *La vie vénitienne* (Paris: Mercure de France, 1963). *L'Altana*, which takes its title from a lookout platform atop Venetian houses, is a unique document, recalling twenty-five years of sojourning in its author's favorite city.

Régnier exercised a formative influence on Jean-Louis Vaudoyer, who developed in a more diverse way Régnier's gift for discerning affinities between art and places. Compared to *L'Altana*, which oozes with love of place, Régnier's novels of Italy are artificial and jejune. *Le passé vivant* (Paris: Mercure de France, 1905) and *L'Illusion héroïque de Tito Bassi* (Paris: Mercure de France, 1916) [on Vicenza] disclose the hollowness of love for the past that lacks roots in the present.

See Louis Bertrand, "L'Italie dans l'oeuvre de M. Henri de Régnier," *RDM*, 6 pér., 63 (June 1, 1921): 594–610; Jean-Louis Vaudoyer, "Henri

de Régnier—1864–1936" [1936], in *Dédié à l'amitié et au souvenir* (Paris: Plon, 1947), pp. 120–33; and Mario Maurin, *Henri de Régnier: le labyrinthe et la double* (Montréal: Presses de l'Université de Montréal, 1972).
See VENICE, VERONA.

*RÉMUSAT, Charles-François-Marie, Comte de** (1797–1875), French philosopher, politician, and essayist, born and died in Paris. His father was Napoleon's chamberlain, his mother Josephine's lady of honor. One of the best-educated men of his day, an expert on English and German philosophy, Rémusat traveled to Italy for the first time in 1857 while still proscribed from participation in politics under Napoleon III. His two articles, "Un voyage dans le nord de l'Italie," *RDM*, 2 pér., 11 (October 1, 1857): 465–510, and 2 pér., 11 (October 15, 1857): 705–46, which were never published as a book, offer the most discerning account of Italy by any writer whose first visit came after age fifty. A sequel recounting a trip of 1860 appeared as "L'Italie: notes de voyage," *RDM*, 2 pér., 34 (July 15, 1861): 289–311, and 2 pér., 35 (September 1, 1861): 289–311, but lacks the verve of the earlier articles. Drawing on a wide knowledge of Europe, especially England, Rémusat paralleled Gregorovius in pioneering the genre of historical strolls for the bourgeoisie. In perspicacity and rigor, Rémusat resembled a fellow liberal aristocrat, Alexis de Tocqueville, who had he ever written about Italy might have sounded like Rémusat. Both men brought the values of the French Enlightenment and English liberalism to bear on questions of the day.

See Prosper Duverger de Hauranne, "M. Charles de Rémusat," *RDM*, 3 pér., 12 (November 15, 1875): 315–69. Rémusat's *Mémoires*, 5 vols., ed. Charles Pouthas (Paris: Plon, 1958–67), contain unpublished notes, "Souvenirs politiques sur l'Italie 1860–1861," 5:117–46.

See INTRODUCTION, TURIN, GENOA, MILAN, BRESCIA, MANTUA, VENICE, PADUA, VERONA, PARMA, BOLOGNA, RAVENNA.

*RUSKIN, John** (1819–1900), English art critic, painter, educator, and essayist, born in London, died at Brantwood (near Coniston, Lancashire). Son of a Scottish sherry merchant, who transmitted Calvinist values through an encyclopedic education that owed much to the Scottish Enlightenment, Ruskin visited Italy no fewer than sixteen times between 1835 and 1888. He credited a gift of Samuel Rogers's poem *Italy* with first having aroused his interest in the peninsula. Two trips with his parents in 1835 and 1840–41 preceded a liberating visit by himself in 1845, impressions of which abound in *Ruskin in Italy: Letters to His Parents 1845*, ed. Harold I. Shapiro (Oxford: Clarendon Press, 1972). An adolescent unevenness in passages from 1840 and 1841 in *The Diaries of John Ruskin 1835–1847* (Oxford: Clarendon Press, 1950), pp. 97–195, had disappeared by 1845. Sojourns of that year in Lucca, Florence, and Venice induced the young author to change the tenor of *Modern Painters*, Volume 2 of which denounced the Bologna painters that he and nearly everyone else had previously admired. A visit with his parents in May and June 1846 to Bergamo, Verona, Venice, Bologna, and Florence got recorded all too briefly in *The Diaries of John Ruskin 1835–1847* (1950), pp. 328–44.

Of pivotal importance were two winters that Ruskin spent in Venice during 1849–50 and 1851–52. Volume 1 (1851) of *The Stones of Venice* followed the first visit, Volumes 2 and 3 (1853) the second, while firsthand impressions survive in *Ruskin's Letters from Venice 1851–1852*, ed. John Lewis Bradley (New Haven: Yale University Press, 1955). Letters by Ruskin are almost invariably more vivid than his diaries, which emphasize technical descriptions of paintings and buildings. A need to send almost daily letters to his father (who died in 1864) sheds light on why Ruskin never matured sexually, a fact that resulted in annulment of his seven-year-old marriage in 1855. Volumes 3 to 5 (1856–60) of *Modern Painters*, whose first volume had appeared in 1843, showed signs of a transition from Ruskin's being a writer on art to being a moralist who drew examples from art. A visit to Turin in July and August 1858 consummated years of growing disenchantment with evangelical Protestantism when a "squeaking" Waldensian preacher drove him to seek refuge with Veronese's painting of *Solomon and the Queen of Sheba*. (See *Praeterita*, vol. 3 (1889), in *Works* 35:495–96.)

Except for a sojourn in Milan during 1862 to study Luini, Ruskin did not return to Italy until he spent two months in Verona in the spring of 1869. His intention to write a book, *The Stones of Verona*, produced only a grandiose lecture, "Verona, and Its Rivers" [1870] (in *Works* 19:429–48). Renewed visits to old haunts followed in 1870, 1872, 1874, and 1876. With the exception of pieces on Florence and the lecture "The Relation between Michael Angelo and Tintoret" [1872] (in *Works* 22:77–108), Ruskin's writing of the 1870s tends to be preachy, relying too much on observations made two or three decades earlier. The decline shows in the gushing about Venice that mars *St. Mark's Rest* [1877–79] (in *Works* 24:201–424), the oracular tone of which recurs in letters from Venice published in *Fors Clavigera*, November 1876 to May 1877 (in *Works* 29:13–145). At his worst, Ruskin became a moral busybody, meddling in everyone's business while neglecting his appointed task of teaching people how to see.

A visit of 1882 to Florence, Pisa, and Lucca brought him into contact with an American, Francesca Alexander (1837–1917), whose writings he sponsored and with whom he engaged in a maudlin correspondence. By the 1880s severe depression alternated with days of extraordinary lucidity, during which he composed his autobiography, *Praeterita* [1885–89] (in *Works* 35:3–562). A final visit to Italy in 1888 included only Bassano, where he visited Francesca Alexander. Ruskin's lifelong ability to recall previous experiences untainted by earlier or later memories thrilled the young Proust, who exploited a similar ability to perfection in *A la recherche du temps perdu* (1913–27).

Ruskin looms over English writing about northern Italy like the Alps over the Padane Plain. Wherever one turns, one detects his influence, both for good and bad. Few writers have phrased outrageous opinions so magnificently or buttressed them with such a wealth of minute observations. Ruskin sketched, compared, and expounded architectural detail with greater devotion than anyone else. The drawings that stud the thirty-nine volumes of the Library Edition of his *Works*, ed. E. T. Cook and Alexander Wedderburn (London: George Allen, and New York: Longmans Green, 1903–12), attest to his eye for ornament in architecture and ensembles in landscape. Whatever his failings as a stuffed shirt, Ruskin was one of the greatest of travel writers because he knew how to look and how to make others think.

The chronology of Ruskin's life and work is detailed in a biography by his disciple W. G. Collingwood, *The Life and Work of John Ruskin*, 2 vols. (Boston: Houghton Mifflin, 1893). A superb interpretation of his genius appears in John D. Rosenberg, *The Darkening Glass: A Portrait of Ruskin's Genius* (New York: Columbia University Press, 1961). A succinct analysis of his views on landscape appears in Denis Cosgrove and John E. Thornes, "Of Truth of Clouds: John Ruskin and the Moral Order in Landscape," in *Humanistic Geography and Literature*, ed. Douglas C. D. Pocock (London: Croom Helm, 1981), pp. 20–46. See also John Unrau, *Ruskin and St. Mark's* (London: Thames and Hudson, 1984).

See TURIN, MILAN, BRESCIA, VENICE, PADUA, VERONA, PARMA, BOLOGNA, RIMINI.

SCHEFFLER, Karl (1869–1951), German art historian, born in Hamburg, died in Überlingen (Baden-Württemberg). This adept of German art visited Italy in 1911 to wrestle with the question "What is German in Italian art?" The resulting diary on Verona, Vicenza, Padua, Venice, Bologna, Ravenna, Florence, Siena, and Rome, while often cantankerous, offers deeper insights than the works of two contemporaries, Moeller van den Bruck's *Die italienische Schönheit* (1913) or Albert Zacher's *Italia Incognita* (1912). Published under the title *Italien: Tagebuch einer Reise* (Leipzig: Insel, 1913; 3d ed. 1925), this provocative statement of a völkisch point of view remains perhaps the most stimulating book to debunk the Renaissance.

See Karl Scheffler, *Eine Auswahl seiner Essays aus Kunst und Leben 1905–1950*, ed. Carl Georg Heise and Johannes Langner (Hamburg: E. Hauswedell, 1969).

See VENICE, PADUA, VERONA, PARMA, BOLOGNA, RAVENNA.

SHELLEY, Percy Bysshe (1792–1822), English poet, born near Horsham (Sussex), drowned off La Spezia. Shelley's sojourn in Italy, chiefly in Tuscany, from 1818 until his drowning on July 8, 1822, constitutes one of the most celebrated episodes in English literary history. In September and October 1818 he dwelt at a villa in the Euganean Hills that Byron loaned him. While there, he wrote "Lines Written Among the Euganean Hills," with its oft-quoted reference to "The waveless plain of Lombardy." Shelley's letters to Thomas Love Peacock from Milan and Bologna, like those to his wife from Naples, contain passages of incandescence that show the poet as a born travel writer. Had he lived beyond his thirtieth year, he might have rivaled Ruskin as an observer of Italian places. As it was, residence in Livorno, Pisa, and Lerici (near La Spezia) from 1819 to 1822 inspired some of the finest poetry ever written by a foreigner in Italy. He flashed across Italy like that skylark that he hymned outside of Pisa, one who "singing still dost soar, and soaring ever singest."

See *The Letters of Percy Bysshe Shelley. II. Shelley in Italy*, ed. Frederick L. Jones (Oxford: Clarendon Press, 1964); Paul Bourget, "Les derniers jours de Shelley" (1884), in *Etudes et portraits* (Paris: Lemerre, 1895) 2^2:299–316; Eugene Schuyler, "Shelley with Byron" (1888), in *Italian Influences* (New York: Scribner's, 1901), pp. 135-55; Anna Benneson McMahan, ed., *With Shelley in Italy: Being a Selection of the Poems and Letters of Percy Bysshe Shelley Which Have to Do with His Life in Italy from 1818 to 1822* (Chicago: A. C. McClurg, 1905); Montgomery Carmichael, "The Burning of Shelley's Body," in A. H. Hallam Murray, *Sketches on the Old Road through France to Tuscany* [1904] (New York: Dutton, 1927), pp. 183-202 [exceedingly well researched]; and John Lehmann, ed., *Shelley in Italy: An Anthology of Poems* (London: Lehmann, 1947), esp. "Introduction," pp. 7-40.

See MILAN, BOLOGNA.

Simond, Louis (1763 or 1767–1831), French essayist, born in Lyon, died in Geneva. A royalist émigré who settled in England and later in Switzerland, Simond published *Voyage d'un français en Angleterre* (1810–11) long before his journal of a trip to Italy in 1817 and 1818 appeared as *Voyage en Italie et en Sicile*, 2 vols. (Paris: Sautelet, 1828). One of the most antirevolutionary of all travelers, Simond seldom missed an opportunity to blacken Napoleon's reign in Italy or to praise Austria by contrast with it. Although this bias distorts his coverage of northern Italy, he included piquant details, especially on Venice, and grew more informative as he went further south. The English version, *A Tour of Italy and Sicily* (London: Longman, Rees et al., 1828), reads a bit stiffly, perhaps because it was translated by himself.

See MILAN.

SITWELL, Sir Osbert (1892–1969), English poet, autobiographer, and essayist, born in London, died in Florence. Osbert's five volumes of autobiography, running from *Left Hand, Right Hand!* to *Noble Essences* (1950), portray his father, Sir George Sitwell (1860–1943), and the latter's Tuscan villas unforgettably. Having "discovered" for English readers the baroque architecture of Apulia and Sicily, which he divulged in *Discursions on Travel, Art and Life* (London: Grant Richards, 1925), Osbert followed with travel essays about Venice, Parma, and Bologna in *Winters of Content and Other Discursions on Mediterranean Art and Travel* (London: Duckworth, 1932; 2d ed. revised 1950; reprinted Westport, Conn: Greenwood Press, 1975). In a town that pleased him, and he never wrote on any that did not, he could recreate how palaces must have looked in their heyday, peopling empty shells with merrymakers and charlatans. Compared to his brother Sacheverell Sitwell (1897–), whose Italian pieces concerned the South almost exclusively, Osbert waxed more ornate. His prose recalls the elaborateness of stage sets by the Bibbiena family, whose presence he felt pervading Bologna, no doubt because it already pervaded his sensibility.

See John Pearson, *The Sitwells: A Family's Biography* (New York: Harcourt, Brace, 1978); and John Lehmann, "Sitwell, Sir (Francis) Osbert (Sacheverell), fifth Baronet (1892–1969)," *DNB Supplement 1961–1970* (1981), pp. 951–53.

See INTRODUCTION, VENICE, PARMA, BOLOGNA.

Spencer, Herbert (1820–1903), English sociologist and essayist, born in Derby, died in Brighton. One of the luminaries of Victorian England, noted for an evolutionary view of society stated in terms of an overly cerebral positivism, Spencer described trips to Italy of 1868 and 1880 in *An Autobiography*, 2 vols. (New York: Appleton, 1904), 2:208–31 and 2:405–8. The latter passage denounced Venice for being all facade and Saint Mark's for betraying "the trait distinctive of semi-civilized art—excess of decoration" (2:407). While personifying a rationalist's intolerance for Venice, Spencer so delighted in the countryside that he pronounced Italy "a land of beautiful distances and ugly foregrounds" (2:229), a judgment that has come true in the industrial suburbs of the twentieth century.

See J. D. Y. Peel, *Herbert Spencer: The Evolution of a Sociologist* (New York: Basic Books, 1971).

See VENICE.

STARK, Freya (1893–), English travel writer, autobiographer, and essayist, born in Paris, has lived in Asolo since inheriting a friend's house there in 1926. Perhaps the most gifted travel writer who ever lived in Italy while writing so little about it, Freya Stark started traveling in Syria in 1927 and went on to publish half a dozen classics about the Near East. Eight volumes of *Letters* (Salisbury: Compton Russell, 1974–76; vols. 4–8, Wilton: Michael Russell, 1977–82), covering the period from 1914 to 1980, scarcely mention her home in Asolo. Fortunately, she depicted it, however briefly, in *Perseus in the Wind* (London: Murray, 1948; reprinted Boston: Beacon Press, 1956), pp. 3, 11–15, and 153–54, and in *The Journey's Echo: Selections* (New York:

Harcourt, Brace, 1964), pp. 59-60. An autobiography, *Traveller's Prelude* (London: Murray, 1950), evokes Dronero in Piedmont, where she grew up, and Bologna, where she worked as a nurse between 1914 and 1916, while recounting an odd upbringing that helps to explain her vocation as a travel writer. However skillfully she could make the exotic seem familiar, she lacked Vernon Lee's gift for making the familiar seem exotic.

See BOLOGNA.

STENDHAL, pseudonym of **Henri Beyle** (1783-1842), French novelist and essayist, born in Grenoble, died in Paris. Beyle showed love of Italy by choosing the birthplace of Johann Joachim Winckelmann as his pen name, for this aesthete from Stendahl near Magdeburg personified Italomania. In 1800 a first visit to Lombardy at age seventeen won Stendhal for life. Longer visits in 1811 and during every year from 1813 to 1821 and again in 1824, 1826, and 1827 resulted in four major books that are collected in *Voyages en Italie* (Paris: Gallimard, Editions de la Pléiade, 1973). Diary entries, whether in *Rome, Naples et Florence en 1817* or in an expanded version of 1826, expound northern Italy without always respecting facts. Stendhal preferred recording theater performances, local gossip, and other ephemera to characterizing a site or appraising art. Compared to the Goncourt brothers, Rémusat, or Maurel, he was a careless observer, relying more on local chatter than on books. A late work mostly about France, *Mémoires d'un touriste*, 2 vols. (Paris: Dupont, 1838; reprinted Paris: Pauvert, 1955), contains a memorable chapter on Genoa (pp. 637-46 in the edition of 1955).

Stendhal's passion for Italy culminated in the novel *La Chartreuse de Parme* (1839), which poured from his pen in just seven weeks in Paris. Barrès, Faure, Maurel, Suarès, and Vaudoyer could no more conceive Parma without Stendhal than they could imagine Versailles without Louis XIV.

On Stendhal's debt to Italy, Matthew Josephson, *Stendhal, or the Pursuit of Happiness* (Garden City: Doubleday, 1946), is highly readable, as is André Suarès in *Vers Venise* (1910), in *Le voyage du condottière* (Paris: Emile-Paul, 1964), pp. 94-102. Gabriel Faure exposed Stendhal's liberties with facts in *Stendhal, compagnon d'Italie* (Paris: Fasquelle, 1931), while Vaudoyer hymned his love of Lombardy and Emilia in *Quelques français en Italie* (Lisbon: Academy of Sciences, 1951), pp. 25-30.

See GENOA, MILAN, VENICE, PADUA, PARMA, BOLOGNA.

*****STOKES, Adrian** (1902-1972), English painter and essayist, born and died in London. The most original English writer on Italian places since Vernon Lee, and on Italian art since Ruskin, Stokes first visited Italy during the winter of 1921-22 before settling in Venice for several years during the late 1920s. An article on Rimini in T. S. Eliot's *The Criterion* 9 (October 1929): 44-60, laid the groundwork for two brilliant books, *The Quattro*

Cento: A Different Conception of the Italian Renaissance (London: Faber and Faber, 1932) and *Stones of Rimini* (London: Faber and Faber, 1934; reprinted New York: Schocken, 1969). These were reprinted together with numerous articles and *Venice, an Aspect of Art* (London: Faber and Faber, 1945) in *The Critical Writings of Adrian Stokes*, 3 vols. (London: Thames and Hudson, 1978). Stokes interpreted marble as a product of the sea and Italy as a land of carvers who knew how to elicit the flow of life deposited at the sea's bottom.

See John Russell, "Adrian Stokes's 70th Birthday," *Art News* 71 (October 1972): 92; John Golding, "Adrian Stokes," *Studio International* 185 (January 1973): 7–8; and Richard Wollheim, "Adrian Stokes," in *On Art and the Mind: Essays and Lectures* (London: Allen Lane, 1973), pp. 315–35. A tantalizing fragment of autobiography appears in Part One of *Inside Out: An Essay in the Psychology and Aesthetic Appeal of Space* (1947), in *The Critical Writings of Adrian Stokes* (1978) 2:142–69.

See GENOA, MILAN, VENICE, PADUA, VERONA, RIMINI.

*SUARÈS, André, pseudonym of Félix Scantrel (1868–1948), French poet, dramatist, and essayist, born near Marseille, died in Saint-Maur-des-Fossés (near Paris). Descended from a Portuguese Jewish family with some Tuscan ancestors, Suarès visited Italy five times between 1895 and 1928, favoring certain cities like Cremona, Venice, and Siena, while detesting others like Milan, Mantua, and Parma. His prose poems erected impudence into a method of extracting metaphor and unheard-of associations. *Le voyage du condottière* (Paris: Emile-Paul, 1964) collected *Vers Venise* (1910) on northern Italy, *Fiorenza* (1929) with an opening chapter on Genoa, and *Sienne la bien aimée* (1932). *Vers Venise* was first published in the *Grande Revue* of 1910 and appeared in German as *Die Fahrten des Condottiere: Eine italienische Reise*, trans. Franz Blei (Leipzig: Kurt Wolff, 1914). Read by only a small coterie, Suarès never achieved the fame he deserved. Barrès's greatest gift to Italy may have been to inspire this most original of prose poets.

See Mario Maurin, "André Suarès: esquisse de biographie," *Preuves* 2[18] (August-September 1952): 21–32; Marcel Dietschy, *Le Cas André Suarès* (Neuchâtel: La Baconnière, 1967), esp. pp. 281–83; and Yves-Alain Favre, *Le recherche de la grandeur dans l'oeuvre de Suarès* (Paris: Klincksieck, 1978), esp. pp. 154–60, 365–71.

See GENOA, MILAN, MANTUA, VENICE, PADUA, VERONA, PARMA, RAVENNA, RIMINI.

*SYMONDS, John Addington (1840–1893), English historian, poet, and essayist, born in Bristol, died in Rome. Best known for his seven-volume *Renaissance in Italy* (1875–86), Symonds popularized Burckhardt's conception of the Renaissance, presenting a wealth of information in florid prose.

His finest writing appeared in three volumes of travel essays, published as *Sketches in Italy and Greece* (London: Smith, Elder, 1874), *Sketches and Studies in Italy* (London: Smith, Elder, 1879), and *Italian Byways* (London: Smith, Elder, 1883), which his biographer, Horatio Brown, collected and rearranged in *Sketches and Studies in Italy and Greece*, 3 vols. (London: Smith, Elder, 1898). Sometimes grandiloquent to the point of bombast, more often Symonds wrote a majestic prose that approached that of Vogüé or Barrès in conveying ecstasy.

Together with Walter Pater, Symonds influenced a generation of English writers that ran from Vernon Lee through Edward Hutton. As the only one of these writers to prefer Lombardy, he stands as an exception to what may be called the Tuscan school of English travel writers. One of the least anecdotal of travelers, he differed from his contemporary Henry James in ignoring contemporary Italy. His daughter, Margaret Symonds (1869–1927), recounted one of his last trips in *Days Spent on a Doge's Farm* (London: Unwin, 1894), which evokes Vescovana between Monselice and Rovigo. Unfortunately, Symonds's *Letters*, 3 vols., ed. Herbert M. Schueller and Robert L. Peters (Detroit: Wayne State University Press, 1967–69), contain almost no passages about travel.

See Richard Garnett, "Symonds, John Addington (1840–1893)," *DNB* 55 (1898): 272–75; T. Herbert Warren, "John Addington Symonds," in *The Poets and the Poetry of the Nineteenth Century*, ed. Alfred Miles (London: Routledge, 1905), 6:477–84; John R. Hale, *England and the Italian Renaissance: The Growth of Interest in Its History and Art* (London: Faber, 1954), pp. 169–96; and Phyllis Grosskurth, *John Addington Symonds: A Biography* (London: Longmans, 1964).

See INTRODUCTION, MILAN, VERONA, PARMA, BOLOGNA, RIMINI.

SYMONS, Arthur (1865–1945), English poet and essayist, born in Wales, died in Wittersham (Kent). An early advocate of French symbolist poetry, this disciple of Walter Pater wrote a dozen essays on Italian cities between 1894 and 1904, which were collected in *Cities* (London: Dent, 1903) and again in *Cities of Italy* (New York: E. P. Dutton, 1907). This most wistful of impressionists gave up on Italy after suffering a nervous breakdown near Ferrara in 1908 and was never quite the same. He retold the story of his imprisonment in the Castello of Ferrara in *Confessions: A Study in Pathology* (New York: Jonathan Cape, 1930). His *Memoirs*, ed. Karl Beckson (University Park: Pennsylvania State University Press, 1977), depicts persons rather than places.

See Edward Hutton, Review of Symons, *Cities*, in *The Outlook* 12 (November 7, 1903): 396–97; Roger Lhombreaud, *Arthur Symons: A Critical Biography* (London: Unicorn Press, 1963), esp. pp. 239–51; John M. Munro, *Arthur Symons* (New York: Twayne, 1969); and David S. Thatcher, *Nietzsche*

in England 1890–1914 (Toronto: University of Toronto Press, 1970), pp. 126–32.
See BRESCIA, VENICE, RAVENNA.

UNDERHILL, Evelyn (1875–1941), English essayist and scholar of mysticism, born in Wolverhampton (Staffordshire), died in London. Prior to becoming an authority on Christian mysticism, Underhill kept a diary of annual trips to Italy between 1901 and her marriage in 1907. Published posthumously as *Shrines and Cities of France and Italy*, ed. Lucy Menzies (London: Longmans Green, 1949), these notes reveal Underhill as an ardent seeker of out-of-the-way places. Although by 1906 she was toying with the idea of converting to Roman Catholicism, she never did, joining the Church of England only in 1921. Her travel sketches showed the same ability to marshal masses of fact as her influential book *Mysticism* (1911).
See Marjorie Vernon, "Underhill, Evelyn, afterwards Mrs. Stuart Moore (1875–1941)," *DNB Supplement 1941–1950* (1959), pp. 897–98; and Christopher J. R. Armstrong, *Evelyn Underhill (1875–1941): An Introduction to Her Life and Writings* (Grand Rapids, Mich.: Eerdmans, 1975).
See MILAN, BRESCIA, PADUA, BOLOGNA, RAVENNA.

***VALERY, Antoine-Claude Pasquin** (1789–1847), French librarian and essayist, born in Paris. As librarian to the king at Versailles, Valery traveled in northern and central Italy during 1826, 1827, and 1828 before writing a fifteen-hundred-page account, *Voyages historiques, littéraires et artistiques en Italie pendant les années 1826, 1827 et 1828, ou l'indicateur italien*, 3 vols. (Paris: Lenormant, 1831–33). The second edition revised (Paris: Baudry, 1838) reposes in more libraries, while an authorized English translation appeared in one volume as *Historical, Literary and Artistical Travels in Italy: A Complete and Methodical Guide for Travellers and Artists*, trans. C. E. Clifford (Paris: Baudry, 1839). The best-informed travel book on Italy up to its time, Valery's *Voyages* has yet to be surpassed on such topics as Italian libraries, conditions during the 1820s, and French deeds in Italy. As administrator of the King's Library at Versailles, Valery consulted sources from the sixteenth, seventeenth, and eighteenth centuries that virtually no one else has used before or since. A witty, tireless writer who kept his royalist sympathies better in check than Louis Simond, Valery ranks with Rémusat as the ablest writer on Italy to have been totally forgotten.
See Charles Magnin, Review of Valery, *Voyages historiques et littéraires*, in *Revue des Deux Mondes*, 1 pér., 6 (June 1, 1832): 601–3; and George H. Calvert, *Scenes and Thoughts in Europe* [1846], 2d ed., 2 vols. (Boston: Little, Brown, 1863), 1:115, 122.
See INTRODUCTION, TURIN, GENOA, MILAN, MANTUA, VENICE, PADUA, VERONA, PARMA, BOLOGNA, RAVENNA, RIMINI.

VAUDOYER, Jean-Louis (1883–1963), French poet, novelist, and essayist, born in Plessis-Piquet (near Paris), died in Paris. Almost fifty years of writing about Italy began with *Suzanne et l'Italie: lettres familières* (Paris: Floury, 1909) and ended with *Compagnon d'Italie: lettres à Amicie* (Paris: Fayard, 1958). In between came four collections that contain some of the subtlest writing about northern Italy since Jules de Goncourt and Charles de Rémusat. *Les délices d'Italie: essais—impressions—souvenirs* (Paris: Plon, 1924) offers masterful essays on Rimini, Vicenza, Venice, Florence, and Rome, while *Italiennes: essais—impressions—souvenirs* (Paris: Plon, 1934; reprinted 1945) is a miscellany that includes a survey of Lombardy taken from Faure's *Visage de l'Italie* (1929) and memoirs of the Italian campaign during World War I. *Italie retrouvée* (Paris: Hachette, 1950), a diary of extended visits during 1947 and 1948, is the most poignant account of travel in the first years after World War II. A century and a half of romantic writing about Italy somehow end with this book. *Quelques français en Italie* (Lisbon: Academy of Sciences, 1951; reprinted 1955) sketches some of his favorite predecessors, including Chateaubriand, Stendhal, and Gérard de Nerval. *Compagnon d'Italie* (1958) is an old man's fond farewell to a land he has loved, while *La peinture vénitienne: ses débuts, son apogée, son déclin* (Paris: Somogy, 1958; English trans., London: Thames and Hudson, 1958) summarizes insights of a lifetime.

Elaborating poetic flashes akin to those of his mentor, Henri de Régnier, Vaudoyer dispensed intuitions about music and art that occurred to no one else. Like Rémusat and Stokes, he excelled at seeing similarities where others saw only differences.

See INTRODUCTION, TURIN, MILAN, BRESCIA, MANTUA, VENICE, VERONA, PARMA, BOLOGNA, RIMINI.

VOGÜÉ, Eugène-Melchior Vicomte de (1848–1910), French diplomat, historian, and essayist, born in Nice, died in Paris. Vogüé debuted with a travel book about the Near East, *Syrie, Palestine, Mont-Athos* (Paris: Plon, 1876), before introducing Russian fiction to France in *Le Roman russe* (1886). His elegy, "A Ravenne," *Revue des Deux Mondes*, 3 pér., 17 (June 15, 1893), was reprinted in *Histoire et poésie* (Paris: Colin, 1898). In a hypnotic style that recalled Chateaubriand, Vogüé celebrated the transience of all things with incomparable pathos. The supreme elegist among French travel writers, Vogüé leaves one regretting that he did not compose more essays to accompany the ones on Rome, Monte Cassino, and Ravenna.

See Edmund Gosse, "Eugene Melchior de Vogüé," in *Portraits and Sketches* (London: Heinemann, 1912), pp. 243–65.

See RAVENNA.

WHARTON, Edith (1862–1937), American novelist and essayist, born in New York City, died in Paris. Wharton launched her literary career with five years of publishing about Italy just after 1900. Her first novel, *The Valley of Decision* (New York: Scribner's, 1902), which she dedicated to Paul Bourget and his wife, evoked Turin, Venice, and a fictional duchy on the Po during the 1770s and 1780s. It remains one of the best historical novels about Italy. While doing research in four languages, she secured advice from Vernon Lee in order to prepare *Italian Villas and Their Gardens* (New York: Century, 1904), a work that has yet to be supplanted. Nine essays collected in *Italian Backgrounds* (New York: Scribner's, 1905) described Milan, Brescia, the Bergamasque Alps, Parma, and sanctuaries in Piedmont with rare poise. One of the most unruffled of travel writers, Wharton exuded bluff honesty, a quality that pervaded remarks about writers on Italy in her memoir *A Backward Glance* (New York: Appleton-Century, 1934), pp. 101–6, 129–42, 177–85. Among women writers on northern Italy, she is excelled only by Vernon Lee and Mary McCarthy. Although *The Valley of Decision* endures as one of the best novels by a foreigner about Italy, Wharton found her vocation writing about American society, starting with *The House of Mirth* (1905). In contrast to her friends Henry James, Paul Bourget, and Vernon Lee, she did not maintain a lifelong involvement with Italy.

See R. W. B. Lewis, *Edith Wharton: A Biography* (New York: Harper and Row, 1975), esp. pp. 102–7, 117, 121.

See INTRODUCTION, TURIN, GENOA, MILAN, BRESCIA, PARMA.

Index

Aachen, 135
Adige River, 92, 93
A. E. *See* Russell, George William
Agatha, Saint, 127
Agostino di Duccio, 145, 148, 149–50
Alaric, 133, 134
Alberti, Leone Battista, 145, 147, 149, 150
Alboin, 91, 134
Aldington, Richard, 78
Aldrovandi, Ulisse, 125
Alexander, Francesca, 184
Alexander VI, 125
Alexandria, 63, 80
Alfieri, Vittorio, 39
Algiers, 136
Alps, 31, 55
Altauf, 134
Ambrose, Saint, 29
America, 23, 89, 178
Angelico, Fra, 41, 74
Annecy, 13
Anthony, Saint, 84–85
Apennines, 123, 146, 153
Aquileia, 137
Argental, Count d', 107
Ariosto, 136
Aristotle, 118
Arquà, 84, 93
Asolo, 187
Assisi, 177
Athens, 80
Attila, 38
Augustine, Saint, 29
Augustus, 136, 145, 146, 150, 152

Austrians, 45
  in Brescia, 45, 46
  in Mantua, 48, 50
  in Padua, 87
  and Simond, 186
  in Venice, 80, 95, 136
  in Verona, 98
Avignon, 152

Bach, Johann Sebastian, 118
Balilla, 25
Balzac, Honoré de, 75, 108
Bandinelli, Bartolommeo, 51, 52
Barbarossa, Frederick, 29, 93
Barrès, Maurice, analyzed, 2, 169–70
  on Bologna, 122, 127–28
  on Bourget, 127–28
  and Jesuits, 128
  and Maurel, 180
  on Milan, 37
  and Padua, 85
  on Parma, 107, 110–12, 188
  on Ravenna, 133, 136–37
  and Stendhal, 111
  and Suarès, 69, 87, 189
  and Symonds, 190
  on Tintoretto, 75
  and Vaudoyer, 81
Bassano, 184
Bayard, 38
Bayreuth, 102
Beelzebub, 95
Beethoven, Ludwig van, 75, 120
Belisarius, 134
Bellini, Giovanni, 70, 74

INDEX

Bentinck, Lord William, 10
Berengar, 91
Berenson, Bernard, analyzed, 170–71
    on Correggio, 116
    and Hutton, 153, 177
    and James, 77
Bergamo, 40, 44
Berici Hills, 93
Bernardo, Pietro, 70
Bernhardt, Sarah, 139
Beyle, Henri. *See* Stendhal
Bibbiena family, 39
Bible, 78
Blake, William, 78
Blashfield, Edwin and Evangeline,
    analyzed, 5, 171
    on Correggio, 116, 120–21
    on Ravenna, 133, 134, 139, 140,
        141–42
Boccaccio, Giovanni, 89, 177
Bodoni, Giovanni-Battista, 108–9
Boethius, 134
Boiardo, Matteo Maria, 149
Bologna, described, 122–32
    Arcades, 122, 123, 124
    Asinelli Tower, 125
    Barrès on, 122, 127–28
    and Council of Trent, 52
    Gallery of, 128–29
    Goethe on, 125, 126–27
    Goncourts on, 123–24, 126, 132
    Hazlitt on, 122–23, 124
    Isis, Temple of, 130, 131
    Lee on, 123, 130–32
    and Padua, 83
    Painters of, 2–3, 125–29, 184
    Piazza Maggiore, 124
    Rémusat on, 122, 123, 129–30,
        132
    San Domenico, Church of, 130
    Santo Stefano, Church of, 130–32
    Scheffler on, 124
    Shelley on, 123, 127
    Sitwell on, 124, 132
    Stark on, 129, 188
    Stendhal on, 123, 126
    Suarès on, 128
    Symonds on, 125
    Underhill on, 130
    Valery on, 122, 132
Bonnat, Léon, 171
Bordeaux, Henry, 9
Borromeo, Saint Carlo, 32–33

Botticelli, 148, 149
Boucher, François, 116
Bourget, Paul, 127–28
    and Barrès, 127–28, 170, 180
    and Wharton, 193
Bramante, 30, 34
Brenner Pass, 92
Brescia, described, 38–47
    and Austria, 39, 45–47
    Cathedrals, 46
    Dunant on, 2, 45–47
    Faure on, 43
    Fortress, 40, 44
    Freeman on, 44
    Giono on, 39–40, 47
    Goncourts on, 39, 41
    Loggia of, 39
    Maurel on, 43
    Pater on, 40–44, 182
    Rémusat on, 39
    Symons on, 41, 42
    and Venice, 38, 43
    Vespasian, temple of, 39
    Wharton on, 42–43
Brosses, Charles de, 87
Broughton, Lord. *See* Hobhouse, John
Brown, Horatio, 79, 190
Browning, Robert, 2, 79, 108
Bryant, William Cullen, 171
Burckhardt, Jacob, 100, 121, 189
Burne-Jones, Edward, 148
Byron, Lord, 2
    on Bologna, 122, 126
    on Guercino, 126
    and Hobhouse, 176–77
    and Shelley, 186
    on Verona, 100
Byron, Robert, 3
Byzantium, 63
    in Ravenna, 134, 135, 138, 140,
        141–42
    in Venice, 63, 67

Caccini, Giulio, 56
Caesar, Julius, 145, 151
Cairo, 63
Caliban, 104
Calvinists, 12, 13, 52
Camargue, 136
Campi family, 43
Canova, Antonio, 69, 113
Carbonari, 110

INDEX

Carpaccio, Vittore, 74
Carracci, Agostino and Annibale, 3, 125–26
    Goethe on, 126–27
Carthage, 25–26
Cassano, 38
Castiglione, Baldassare, 136
Castiglione (town), 46
Cavour, Camillo, Count di, 10, 45
Cesena, 146
Charlemagne, 103, 135
Charles VIII, 44
Chartres, 30
Chateaubriand, René de, 136, 180, 192
Cherubino, 117, 119, 128
Chiaroscuro, 123, 124
China, 31, 114
Chioggia, 23
Cicero, 85
Cimarosa, Domenico, 119
Clark, Kenneth, 84, 90, 128
Colleoni, Bartolomeo, 69, 152
Columbus, Christopher, 23, 26
Como, Lake, 111
Como (city), 37
Condillac, Abbé de, 107, 108
Condottieri, 145
Constantine, 103
Constantinople, 63, 67, 104, 135
Constantius, 135
Cook, Thomas, 80
Cooper, James Fenimore, 171
Correggio, analyzed, 115–21
    and the Carracci, 126
    in Parma, 108, 109, 111, 112, 115–21
    Pater on, 42
    Ruskin on, 93, 119–20
    and Stendhal, 108, 111, 119, 121
    and Verdi, 109
Correggio (town), 119
Corsica, 18, 23, 25
Corvo, Baron, 79, 80
Cosenza, 134
Counter-Reformation, 52, 71, 134
Crassus, 86
Cremona, 43, 51, 93, 108, 109

Dante Alighieri, 3, 74
    on Giotto, 88
    in Ravenna, 135, 137
    and Rimini, 145
    in Verona, 93, 103

De Chirico, Giorgio, 16–17
Delacroix, Eugène, 68
Descartes, René, 13
Desiderius, 134
Dickens, Charles, analyzed, 5, 171–72
    on Correggio, 116
    on Genoa, 20
    on Mantua, 54
Domenichino, 126
Dominic, Saint, 130
Donatello, analyzed, 84–86
    and Agostino di Duccio, 150
    and Giotto, 85, 90
Douglas, Norman, 3, 4, 177
Dronero, 188
Dunant, Henri, analyzed, 172
    on Brescia, 2, 45–47

Edward I, 92
Eliot, George, 5
Eliot, T. S., 147, 188
Emmanuel Philibert, 14
Empson, William, 5
England, 88, 115
Epicurus, 104
Este family, 48
Etruscans, 178
Etty, William, 119
Ezzelino, 38, 84, 91, 93

Fabius, 86
Farnese family, 108, 109–10, 121
Farnese, Vanozze, 109
Fascists, 39, 49, 150
Faure, Gabriel, analyzed, 172–73
    on Brescia, 43
    on Parma, 107, 188
    on Verona, 103
Ferdinand of Savoy, 11
Ferrara, 48, 93, 176, 190
Ferrari, Gaudenzio, 182
Feuilleton, 102, 175, 176
Flaubert, Gustave, 5
Florence, 90
    and Bologna, 129
    and Cesena, 146
    and De Chirico, 16
    Hutton in, 177
    James in, 100
    and Milan, 33
    and Padua, 85, 90, 145
    and Pisa, 63, 92

and Rimini, 148, 149
    Ruskin in, 183, 184
Foix, Gaston de, 38, 44, 136, 137
Fontainebleau, 50
Foppa, Vincenzo, 37
Foscari, Francesco, 68
Fracastoro, Gerolamo, 51
Francesca da Rimini, 145
Franciscans, 69, 77
Francis I, 44
Francis, Saint, 130, 147, 150
Franz Joseph, 45
Frederick Barbarossa, 29, 93
Frederick II, 38
Freeman, Edward, analyzed, 5, 173
    on Brescia, 4
    on Parma, 115
    on Ravenna, 133, 134, 137, 138–39, 140, 141
    and Suarès, 74
    on Verona, 91, 98–99
Frye, Northrop, 5
Fuchs, Carl, 14
Fumiani, Zanantonio, 68
Fussell, Paul, 3–5

Galla Placidia, 133, 134–35, 137–38
Garda, Lake, 178
Gardens, 113–14
    in Genoa, 22
    in Verona, 103–4
Garibaldi, Giuseppe, 25, 137
Gast, Peter, 14, 181
Gattamelata, 83, 86
Gaul, 145, 151
Gavarni, 66
Geneva, 10, 47, 172
Genoa, described, 18–26
    Dickens on, 20
    Hardy on, 20–21
    Heine on, 3, 21, 24
    Hutton on, 177
    James on, 18–19
    Michelet on, 20, 22–24, 25, 180
    O'Faolain on, 19–20, 25
    Palazzo Peschiere, 20
    and Piedmont, 10
    Saint George, Bank of, 23
    Stendhal on, 188
    Stokes on, 19, 24
    Suarès on, 24–26
    Valery on, 18

and Venice, 19, 23, 67
    Wharton on, 21
Germans, 3, 177
    in Verona, 91–92, 102
Giono, Jean, analyzed, 173
    on Brescia, 39–40, 47
    on Milan, 32
    on Turin, 11–12
    on Venice, 59–60
Giorgione, 74
Giotto, analyzed, 87–90
    Clark on, 85
    Ruskin on, 71, 75–76, 88–89
Giulio Romano, analyzed, 51–54
    Maurel on, 121
    mentioned, 43, 48
    Suarès on, 51–52, 69, 71
Gladstone, William, 175
Goa, 150
Goethe, Johann Caspar, 174
Goethe, Johann Wolfgang, analyzed, 2, 3, 4, 173–74
    on Bologna, 125, 126–27
    and Verdi, 109
    on Verona, 92, 103
Goncourt, Edmond and Jules de, analyzed, 174–75
    and Barrès, 170
    on Bologna, 123–24, 126, 132
    on Brescia, 39
    and Dickens, 172
    on Giulio Romano, 53–54
    and Hewlett, 176
    and James, 41, 61, 178
    on Mantua, 53–54
    and Stendhal, 188
    and Vaudoyer, 192
    on Venice, 60–61, 66–67, 78, 81, 142
Gondolas, 59, 60, 73, 79
Gonzaga family, 48, 49, 53, 55, 56
Gounod, Charles, 118
Granet, François-Marius, 123–24
Green, John Henry, 77–78
Greene, Graham, 4
Gregorovius, Ferdinand, 3
    on Ravenna, 3, 134
    and Rémusat, 183
    and Valery, 2, 4
Gregory XIII, 125
Greville, Charles, analyzed, 175
Grey, Thomas, 122
Guarini, Guarino, 13

INDEX

Guercino, 123–24
  Barrès on, 127–28
  Goncourts on, 123–24
  Ruskin on, 126
  Shelley on, 127

Habsburgs, 53, 103
Hannibal, 26
Hardy, Thomas, analyzed, 175
  on Genoa, 20–21
Hare, Augustus, 173
Haynau, Julius, 39, 40
Hazlitt, William, analyzed, 5, 175–76
  on Bologna, 122–23, 124
  and Dickens, 172
  and Hobhouse, 175
  on Parma, 12
  on Turin, 10–11, 17
  on Venice, 81–82
Headlam, Cecil, 5, 33, 42
Heine, Heinrich, analyzed, 176
  on Genoa, 3, 21, 24
Henry VII, Emperor, 38
Hewlett, Maurice, analyzed, 4, 176
  on Padua, 84
  on Venice, 62
Hobhouse, John (later Lord Broughton), analyzed, 176–77
  and Hazlitt, 175
  on Verona, 98, 100
Honorius, 133, 135, 138
Hutton, Edward, analyzed, 5, 177
  and Berenson, 153
  on Brescia, 38
  and Faure, 172
  on Mantua, 49
  on Parma, 108
  on Rimini, 145, 149
  and Symonds, 190
Huxley, Aldous, 4, 150, 176

Impressionism, 60–61
  in the Goncourts, 60–61, 123, 170, 174
  in Pater, 36, 41, 182
  in Symons, 65, 142, 190
Ingres, Jean-Auguste-Dominique, 113
Inquisition, 37, 130
Ireland, 13
Isabella d'Este, 48, 50, 52
Isotta of Rimini, 147, 152

Istrian marble, 72
  in Rimini, 147, 151
  in Venice, 59, 72, 73
Italy, 1–2, 3
  James on, 12
  Lawrence on, 187
  as palimpsest, 110
  Régnier on, 104
  and renewal, 152–53
  Spencer on, 187
  Suarès on, 8

James, Henry, analyzed, 5, 178
  on Bellini, 70
  on Genoa, 18–19
  and the Goncourts, 41, 61, 178
  on Milan, 29, 32–33, 36
  and Padua, 85
  and Pater, 41, 42, 70
  on Ravenna, 138, 139
  and Ruskin, 41, 76, 78, 100, 152
  and Symons, 65
  on Tintoretto, 74, 76–77
  on Titian, 70
  on Venice, 61–62, 64, 70, 81
  and Wharton, 193
Jerome, Saint, 118
Jesuits, 13, 107, 128, 129
Josephson, Matthew, 109–10
Julius II, 136
Justinian, 133, 134, 139, 140, 141–42, 143

Karr, Alphonse, 181

Lamartine, Alphonse de, 172
Lamb, Charles, 4–5
Lawrence, D. H., analyzed, 3, 178
  on Milan, 31
Lee, Vernon, analyzed, 179–80
  on Bologna, 123, 130–32
  and James, 178
  on Mantua, 54–56
  mentioned, 2, 153, 169
  on Padua, 84
  on Shakespeare, 54–56
  and Stark, 188
  and Stokes, 188
  on Venice, 80–81, 82
  and Wharton, 193
Leonardo da Vinci, 34–36
Leopardi, Giacomo, 39
Leo X, 136

Livy, 83, 93
Lombardi brothers, 68
London, 31, 101–2
Lorrain, Claude, 11
Louis XIV, 13
Loyola, Ignatius, 128
Lucas, E. V., 64
Lucca, 176, 183, 184
Luini, Bernardino, 43, 184
Luther, Martin, 12

Macaulay, Thomas Babington, 92, 173
McCarthy, Mary, 74, 148, 193
Madrid, 15, 29, 74
Magdalene, Mary, 118, 119
Maggiore, Lago, 111
Malatesta, Sigismondo, 140, 145–47, 150, 152, 177
Manchester, 93, 94
Mann, Thomas, 79–80, 81
Mantegna, Andrea, 48
    in Mantua, 48, 55, 56
    in Padua, 86, 89, 93
Mantua, described, 48–56
    Dickens on, 54
    Ducal Palace, 2, 48–51, 54–56
    Goncourts on, 53–54
    Hewlett in, 176
    Hutton on, 49–50
    Lee on, 54–56
    Maurel on, 49, 50
    Monteverdi in, 2
    Rémusat on, 50–51
    and Shakespeare, 54–56
    Suarès on, 51–52
    Tè, Palazzo del, 48, 49–50, 52–54
    Valery on, 53
    and Venice, 62, 65
    and the Visconti, 33
    Zangwill on, 49
Marble, Stokes on, 72, 96–97, 148–49, 153
Marcus Aurelius, 182
Marecchia River, 151
Maria Theresa, 55
Marie-Louise, 111, 112, 113, 114
Masaccio, 85
Maurel, André, analyzed, 180
    on Brescia, 43
    on Correggio, 116, 117, 121
    on Mantua, 49, 50
    on Parma, 107, 108, 112, 188
    on Ravenna, 138
    on Rimini, 145–46
    and Stendhal, 188
    and Vaudoyer, 152
    on Verona, 91, 102
Maxentius, 103
Mazzini, Giuseppe, 25, 173
Medici family, 149
Mediterranean Sea, 20–21, 175
Melville, Herman, 32
Michelangelo, 71
    and Correggio, 116, 120, 125
    and Giulio Romano, 51, 53
    Ruskin on, 71, 74
    and Tintoretto, 74, 75, 120
Michelet, Jules, analyzed, 180–81
    on Genoa, 20, 22–24, 25, 122
    and Ruskin, 23, 97, 180
Michelozzo, 37, 146
Milan, described, 29–37
    Ambrosian Library, 30
    Barrès on, 37
    Brera Gallery, 126
    Cathedral, 31–34, 69, 87
    Giono on, 32
    James on, 29, 32–33, 36
    La Scala, 29
    The Last Supper, 30, 34–36
    Lawrence on, 32
    Melville on, 32
    Ospedale Maggiore, 31
    Pater on, 35–36
    Poldi-Pezzoli Museum, 30
    Portinari Chapel, 36–37, 130
    Railroad station, 30
    Rémusat on, 29, 32, 35
    Ruskin on, 31–32, 35, 36, 184
    San Lorenzo, Church of, 135
    Santa Maria della Passione, 37
    Santa Maria delle Grazie, 30, 34
    Shelley on, 33
    Simond on, 35
    Stendhal in, 29
    Stokes on, 34
    Suarès on, 29, 30–31, 33, 34, 143
    Underhill on, 37
    Valery on, 29
    Wharton on, 37
Millot, Claude-François, 107
Milton, John, 12–13, 56, 149
Mincio River, 33
Modena, 13, 15
    and Bologna, 123, 126, 129

INDEX

Cathedral, 115
   and Parma, 108, 113, 116
Moeller van den Bruck, Arthur, 91, 94, 185
Montaigne, Michel de, 29
Mont Cenis, 11
Monte Cassino, 192
Monteverdi, Claudio, 2
Monte Viso, 11
Morand, Paul, 79
Moretto, Alessandro, 40, 41–42, 43
Morgan, Lady, 113, 115
Moroni, Giovanni Battista, 44
Morosini, Francesco, 80
Morris, William, 95
Mosaics, 64
   in Ravenna, 138, 140, 141, 142–44
   in Venice, 64, 65, 66–67
Mozart, Wolfgang Amadeus, 117, 119, 128
Munich, 29
Musset, Alfred de, 172, 180
Mussolini, Benito, 39, 114, 146

Naples, 18, 21, 175, 186
   and Parma, 112, 113
Napoleon I, 87
   and Brescia, 44
   in Milan, 32, 35
   and Padua, 87
   and Parma, 107, 108, 111, 113
   and Piedmont, 10
   and Rémusat, 183
   and Simond, 186
   and Vogüé, 143
Napoleon III, 45
   and Michelet, 22
   and Rémusat, 183
Narses, 134
Nattier, Jean-Marc, 116
Neipperg, Adam, Count, 111
Nero, 145
Nerval, Gérard de, 192
Nervi, 22, 180
New York, 29
Nicholas V, 149
Nietzsche, Friedrich, analyzed, 181
   on Turin, 11, 14–17
Nile River, 135
Nîmes, 98
Normandy, 115
Novara, 11, 39, 40

O'Connell, Daniel, 19
Odoacer, 103, 134
O'Faolain, Sean, analyzed, 4, 181
   on Genoa, 19–20
   on Ruskin, 95–96, 102
   on Venice, 78–79
   on Verona, 95–96
Ostrogoths, 134
Otto I, 91

Padua, described, 83–90
   Arena Chapel, 75–76, 87–90
   Caffè Pedrocchi, 83
   and Florence, 85, 90, 145
   Gattamelata, statue of, 83, 86, 139
   Hewlett on, 84, 176
   Lee on, 84
   Prato della Valle, 92
   Rémusat on, 87, 88
   Ruskin on, 75–76, 87–88, 89
   Santa Giustina, Basilica of, 84, 87
   il Santo, 84–86, 90
   Scheffler on, 85, 89
   Scrovegni Chapel, 87–90
   and Shakespeare, 55
   Stendhal on, 83
   Suarès on, 83–84, 85–87
   Underhill on, 90
   Valery on, 84–85
   Vaudoyer on, 84–85
   and Venice, 83, 84
Paganini, Niccolò, 111–12
Paget, Violet. *See* Lee, Vernon
Palermo, 18, 112
Palladio, Andrea, 39, 73
Papal States, 89
Paris, 16
   and Mantua, 50
   and Milan, 29, 31
   and Parma, 107
   and Rimini, 152
   and Turin, 16
   and Venice, 62, 82
Parma, described, 107–21
   Baptistery, 115
   Barrès on, 107, 110–12, 188
   Berenson on, 116
   Blashfields on, 116, 120–21
   Botanic Garden, 113
   Cathedral, 109, 114, 115, 118, 120–21
   Correggio in, 108, 109, 111, 112, 115–21

Dickens on, 116
Faure on, 107
Freeman on, 115
Gallery of, 115–16
Hazlitt on, 108
Maurel on, 107, 108, 112, 116, 117, 121, 188
Morgan on, 113, 115
Pilotta Palace, 113
Public Garden, 113–14
Rémusat on, 110, 115, 116
Ruskin on, 116, 119–20
Saint Paul, Convent of, 115, 116, 120
San Giovanni, Church of, 117, 118
Sitwell on, 112–15, 116, 120
Stendhal on, 107–8, 109–10, 111, 112, 116, 119, 188
Suarès on, 107–8, 112, 116, 118–19, 188
Symonds on, 108, 116, 117–18, 119
Valery on, 110, 113
Vaudoyer on, 107, 108, 110, 112, 116
Wharton on, 115, 116–17
Parthenon, 80, 139
Pater, Walter, analyzed, 182
  on Alberti, 149
  on Brescia, 40–44
  and Dickens, 172
  and Hutton, 49
  and James, 40, 41, 70
  and Lee, 179, 190
  on Leonardo, 35–36
  on Moretto, 41–42, 43, 44
  and Symons, 41, 65, 190
Paul III, 110
Pavia, 33, 101, 179
Peacock, Thomas Love, 33, 127, 186
Pellico, Silvio, 110
Peloponnesus, 80
Pepin, 91
Perugino, Pietro, 42, 71
Peter Martyr, Saint, 37, 130
Petrarch, Francesco, 84, 93
Phoenicians, 25–26
Piacenza, 15, 101, 179
  and Bologna, 126
  and Via Emilia, 145, 151
Piedmont, 9–10, 18
Piranesi, Giovanni Battista, 87

Pisa, 23, 63, 91
  Campo Santo, 75
  and Shelley, 127, 186
Pisano, Niccolò, 130
Pliny the Elder, 92
Pollaiuolo, 86
Pompei, 138
Po River, 10, 125
Portugal, 23
Positivism, 66–67, 187
Préault, Auguste, 86
Pre-Raphaelites, 71
Primaticcio, Francesco, 53
Proust, Marcel, 184–85
Prud'hon, Pierre-Paul, 109, 116

Raphael, 74
  and Bologna, 126, 127
  and Correggio, 116, 118
  and Michelangelo, 51, 53, 120, 125
Ravenna, described, 133–44
  Barrès on, 133, 136–37
  Blashfields on, 133, 134, 139, 140, 141–42
  Freeman on, 133, 134, 137, 138–39, 140, 141
  Gregorovius on, 134
  James on, 138, 139
  Maurel on, 138
  pine forest, 135, 136, 137
  Rémusat on, 133, 134–35, 138, 140
  Sant'Apollinare in Classe, 136–37, 140, 149, 150
  Sant'Apollinare Nuovo, 138, 139, 141, 143
  San Vitale, Church of, 139, 141–44
  Scheffler on, 143–44
  Suarès on, 139–40, 143, 144
  Symons on, 140, 142
  Theodoric's Tomb, 136, 137
  Underhill on, 130, 138, 140–41, 142–43
  Valery, 133, 136
  and Venice, 121, 140, 142
  Vogüé on, 133, 134, 135–36, 139, 141, 143
Red Cross, 2, 45–47, 172
Régnier, Henri de, analyzed, 182
  and Hobhouse, 177
  and Maurel, 180
  and Padua, 85

INDEX

and Vaudoyer, 152, 192
on Venice, 68, 79, 81
on Verona, 103–4
Rembrandt, 65, 85, 117
Rémusat, Charles de, analyzed, 183
    and Barrès, 110, 111
    on Bologna, 122, 123, 129–30, 132
    on Brescia, 39
    on Correggio, 116
    on Mantua, 50–51, 53
    on Milan, 29, 32, 35
    on Padua, 87, 88
    on Parma, 110, 115
    on Ravenna, 133, 134–35, 138, 140
    and Ruskin, 97
    and Stendhal, 188
    on Turin, 11
    and Valery, 2, 4, 191
    and Vaudoyer, 192
    on Venice, 59, 60, 72, 81
    on Verona, 95, 98
Reni, Guido, 126, 127, 128
Reynolds, Sir Joshua, 125
Rimbaud, Arthur, 65
Rimini, described, 145–53
    Arch of Augustus, 145, 150, 152, 153
    Bridge of Tiberius, 145, 151, 153
    Hutton on, 145, 149
    Huxley on, 150
    Malatesta Temple, 101, 145, 147–51, 152
    Maurel on, 145–46
    Stokes on, 147–49, 150, 153, 188–89
    Suarès on, 146, 150, 151
    Symonds on, 145, 148, 149–50
    Vaudoyer on, 150–51, 151–52
Riviera, Italian, 18, 22
Rogers, Samuel, 183
Rolfe, Frederick, 79, 80
Romagna, 134, 146
Romanino, Girolamo, 40, 41, 42–43
Rome, 16, 100
    and Bologna, 122, 126
    and Goethe, 3, 173–74
    and the Goncourts, 174
    and Hardy, 175
    and Heine, 176
    and Hobhouse, 177
    and Lee, 130, 179
    and Michelet, 180

and Nietzsche, 181
Pantheon, 142
and Pater, 182
and Ravenna, 133–35, 138, 140, 141–42
and Rimini, 145, 149, 151–52
and Stendhal, 109–10
and Vaudoyer, 192
and Vogué, 192
Rosa, Monte, 40
Ross, Janet, 177
Rossini, Gioacchino, 117
Rousseau, Jean-Jacques, 13
Rubens, Peter Paul, 25, 42
Rubicon River, 145, 151
Ruffini brothers, 25
Ruskin, John, analyzed, 183–85
    and Barrès, 112
    on Correggio, 116, 119–20
    on Domenichino, 126
    and Freeman, 173
    on Guercino, 126, 127
    and James, 41, 76, 78, 100, 152, 178
    on Michelangelo, 71
    and Michelet, 23, 97, 180
    on Milan, 31–32
    O'Faolain on, 70
    on Padua, 85, 87–88, 89
    on Saint Mark's, 63–64
    and Scheffler, 89
    and Shelley, 186
    and Stokes, 153, 188
    and Suarès, 65, 68, 69, 71, 74
    on Tintoretto, 74, 75–76
    on Titian, 70–71
    on tombs, 68–69, 71, 100–101
    on Turin, 135
    on Venice, 63–64, 66, 68–69, 81
    on Verona, 69, 91, 92–94, 97, 98, 100–102, 103
Russell, George William, 95

Sade, Marquis de, 87
Sainte-Beuve, Charles Augustin de, 172
Sand, George, 5
Sanmichaeli, Michele, 95
Sardinia, 10, 95
Sartre, Jean-Paul, 80, 81
Savoy, Duchy of, 9–10, 11
Scaliger family, 69, 92, 93, 100–103
Scheffler, Karl, analyzed, 185
    on Bologna, 124

on Padua, 85, 89
  on Ravenna, 143–44
  on Verona, 91, 94–95, 99–100, 102, 103
Schiller, Friedrich, 89
Scutari, 104
Sforza, Duke Lodovico, 36, 86
Shakespeare, William, 39
  and Mantua, 54–56
  and Tintoretto, 74–75, 76, 78
  and Verona, 93, 94
Shelley, Percy Bysshe, analyzed, 185–86
  on Bologna, 123, 127
  and Byron, 2
  on Milan, 33
Siena, 129
Sigismund, Emperor, 53
Simond, Louis, analyzed, 186
  on Milan, 35
  and Valery, 191
Sitwell, Osbert, analyzed, 4, 186–87
  on Bologna, 124, 132
  on Correggio, 116, 120
  on gardens, 113–14
  on Parma, 112–15, 116, 120
  on Venice, 67
Sitwell, Sacheverell, 187
Sitwell, Sir George, 186
Solferino, Battle of, 2, 45–47, 103, 172
Sorrento, 181
Spain, 23, 113, 135
Spencer, analyzed, 187
  on Venice, 66, 67, 81
Split, 98, 99, 138, 173
Stark, Freya, analyzed, 187–88
  and Berenson, 170
  on Bologna, 129
Starkie, Walter, 88–89
Steinitzer, Alfred, 4
Stendhal, analyzed, 5, 188
  Barrès on, 111
  on Bologna, 123, 126
  and Correggio, 108, 109, 111, 119, 121
  and Faure, 172
  on Genoa, 188
  and Michelet, 180
  on Milan, 29
  on Padua, 83
  on Parma, 107–8, 109–10, 111, 112, 116, 119, 188
  and Prud'hon, 109

  Vaudoyer on, 108, 192
  and Verdi, 109
Stokes, Adrian, analyzed, 188–89
  and Freeman, 173
  on Genoa, 19, 24
  on Milan, 34
  on Rimini, 147–49, 150, 153
  on Venice, 60, 71–74, 81
  on Verona, 96–97
Suarès, Andre, analyzed, 189
  and Barrès, 112
  on Bologna, 128
  on Correggio, 116, 118–19
  on Genoa, 24–26
  and James, 178
  on Mantua, 51–52
  on Milan, 29, 30–31, 33, 122
  and O'Faolain, 181
  on Parma, 107–8, 112, 116, 118–19
  on Ravenna, 139–40, 143, 144
  on Rimini, 146, 150, 151
  and Ruskin, 65, 68, 69, 78, 81, 82
  on Venice, 64–65, 68, 78, 81, 82
  on Verona, 69, 102–3, 104
Svevo, Italo, 15
Symonds, John Addington, analyzed, 189–90
  on Bologna, 125
  on Correggio, 108, 116, 117–18, 119
  and Freeman, 44, 173
  and Padua, 85
  on Rimini, 145, 148, 149–50
  on Venice, 78
  on Verona, 96, 97
Symonds, Margaret, 190
Symons, Arthur, analyzed, 190–91
  on Brescia, 41, 42
  and Hutton, 177
  on Ravenna, 140, 142
  on Saint Mark's, 65
  on Verona, 96

Terence, 146
Terra-cotta, 31, 34, 96
Theodora, 137, 139, 143
Theodoric, 134
  in Ravenna, 135, 136, 138–39
  in Verona, 91, 93, 98, 103
Theodosius, 133
Tiberius, 145

INDEX 205

Tiepolo, Giambattista, 170
Tillot, Guillaumne Léon du, 107
Tintoretto, analyzed, 74–78
   and Correggio, 117
   Ruskin on, 74, 75–76, 95
Titian, 69, 74
   and the Carracci, 125, 126
   Pater on, 41
   Ruskin on, 70–71, 93
Tocqueville, Alexis de, 183
Tokyo, 29
Tombs, 68–69, 71
   in Ravenna, 133, 135–36, 136–37
   in Verona, 100–103
Travel writing, 1–6, 30
Trent, Council of, 52
Trier, 98, 99
Turin, described, 9–17
   Bordeaux on, 9
   Castello, 12
   and Genoa, 25
   Giono on, 11–12
   Hazlitt on, 10–11, 17
   Holy Shroud, Chapel of, 14
   James on, 12, 17
   Nietzsche on, 11, 14–17, 181
   Palazzo Carignano, 15, 16
   Palazzo Madama, 11
   Piazza Carlo Alberto, 15, 16
   Rémusat on, 11
   Ruskin on, 184
   San Lorenzo, Church of, 13–14
   Valery on, 14
   and Venice, 71–72
   Wharton on, 12–13, 17
Turks, 55, 80, 136
Turner, William, 60, 126

Underhill, Evelyn, analyzed, 5, 191
   on Bologna, 130
   and Lee, 132
   on Milan, 37
   on Padua, 90
   on Ravenna, 130, 138, 140–41, 142–43
Urbino, 149
Urias, 29

Valery, Antoine, analyzed, 4, 191
   and Barrès, 110, 111
   on Bologna, 122, 132
   on Genoa, 18
   on Mantua, 53
   and Maurel, 180
   on Milan, 29
   on Parma, 110, 113
   on Ravenna, 133, 136
   and Rémusat, 2, 4
   on Turin, 14
   on Venice, 62–63
Van Dyck, Anthony, 21, 25
Vasari, Giorgio, 88
Vaudoyer, Jean-Louis, analyzed, 192
   and Barrès, 110, 111, 112
   on galleries, 129
   on Milan, 30
   on Parma, 107, 108, 110, 112, 116
   and Régnier, 182
   on Rimini, 150–51, 151–52
   and Ruskin, 151
   and Stendhal, 108, 188, 192
   on Tintoretto, 74–75
   on Venice, 68, 70, 74
Velasquez, 112
Venice, described, 59–82
   Academy, 70, 74
   Arsenal, 80
   Barrès on, 75, 170
   and Brescia, 38, 43
   Brown on, 79
   Bryant on, 171
   Colleoni, statue of, 69
   Color in, 59–62, 72, 73
   Dogana, 60
   Doges' Palace, 59, 62, 70, 78
   Frari, Church of, 68, 69–71, 74, 77
   and Genoa, 19, 23, 67
   Giono on, 59–60
   Giudecca, 60
   Goncourts on, 60–61, 66–67, 78, 81
   Grand Canal, 71, 72–73, 82
   Green on, 77–78
   Hazlitt on, 81–82
   Hewlett on, 62
   James on, 61–62, 64, 70, 81, 178
   Lee on, 80–81, 82
   Lido, 62, 63, 80
   Lucas on, 64
   Mann on, 79–80, 81
   Morand on, 79
   and Nietzsche, 181
   O'Faolain on, 78–79
   and Padua, 83, 84
   Régnier on, 68, 79, 81, 182

Rémusat on, 59, 60, 72, 81
Ruskin on, 63–64, 66, 68–69, 81, 184
Saint Mark, School of, 69
Saint Mark's, Church of, 59, 62, 63–67, 72, 140, 142, 187
San Marco, Piazza, 62–63, 69
San Moïse, Campo, 63
San Pantaleone, Church of, 68
San Rocco, School of, 75–77, 78
Simond on, 186
Sitwell on, 67
Spencer on, 66, 67, 81, 187
Stokes on, 60, 71–74, 81, 188
Suarès on, 64–65, 68, 78, 81, 82
Symons on, 65
Tintoretto in, 74–78
Valery on, 62–63, 136
Vaudoyer on, 68, 70, 74
and Verona, 91, 92, 96, 97
Wharton on, 193
Zanipolo, Church of, 68–69
Vercelli, 40, 182
Verdi, Giuseppe, 53, 102, 109
Verlaine, Paul, 65
Verona, described, 91–104
　Arena, 91, 98, 99–100
　Brà, Piazza, 92
　Byron on, 100
　Congress of, 98, 177
　Erbe, Piazza dell', 92
　Faure on, 103
　Freeman on, 91, 98–99
　Giusti Gardens, 103–4
　Goethe on, 92, 103
　Hobhouse on, 98, 100
　James on, 95, 98, 100, 103
　Macaulay on, 92
　Marble of, 96–97, 149
　Maurel on, 91, 102
　Moeller van den Bruck on, 91, 94
　O'Faolain on, 95–96
　Palaces in, 94–95
　Porta dei Borsari, 91, 98
　Régnier on, 103–4
　Rémusat on, 95, 98
　Ruskin on, 69, 91, 92–94, 97, 98, 100–102, 103, 184
　Sant'Anastasia, Church of, 95
　San Zeno, Church of, 95
　Scaliger Tombs, 69, 92, 93, 100–103

Scheffler on, 91, 94–95, 99–100, 102, 103
Signori, Piazza dei, 100
Stokes on, 96–97
Suarès on, 69, 102–3, 104
Symonds on, 96, 97
Symons on, 96
and Venice, 91, 92, 94, 97
Zangwill on, 102
Veronese, Paolo, 74, 87, 126
　Ruskin on, 93, 184
Verrocchio, Andrea del, 69, 85
Versailles, 50, 188, 191
Vespasian, 86
Via Emilia, 145, 151
Via Flaminia, 145
Vicenza, 94, 101, 125, 182, 192
Victor Emmanuel II, 10
Villa d'Este, 104
Villiers de l'Isle-Adam, Comte de, 152
Virgil, 20, 93
Visconti, Gian Galeazzo, 33
Viterbo, 149
Vogüé, Eugène-Melchior, Vicomte de, analyzed, 192
　on Ravenna, 133, 134, 135–36, 139, 141, 143
　and Symonds, 190
Voltaire, 107

Wagner, Richard, 118, 131
Waldensians, 12–13, 184
Waldo, Peter, 12
Wall, Bernard, 9
Warens, Madame de, 13
Waugh, Evelyn, 3
Wharton, Edith, analyzed, 192–93
　on the Blashfields, 171
　on Brescia, 42–43
　on Correggio, 115, 116–17
　on Milan, 37
　on Turin, 12–13, 17
Winckelmann, Johann Joachim, 188
World War I, 45

Xavier, Saint Francis, 150

Zacher, Albert, 122, 185
Zangwill, Israel, 49, 102
Zola, Emile, 5